THE TRAINABLE
MENTALLY RETARDED
CHILD

THE TRAINABLE MENTALLY RETARDED CHILD

By

KATHLEEN BARNETTE WAITE

Extension Division
University of California
Davis, California

CHARLES C THOMAS • PUBLISHER
Springfield • Illinois • U.S.A.

Published and Distributed Throughout the World by

CHARLES C THOMAS • PUBLISHER

Bannerstone House

301-327 East Lawrence Avenue, Springfield, Illinois, U.S.A.

Natchez Plantation House

735 North Atlantic Boulevard, Fort Lauderdale, Florida, U.S.A.

©*1972, by* CHARLES C THOMAS • PUBLISHER

ISBN 0-398-02433-2

Library of Congress Catalog Card Number: 79-169889

*With THOMAS BOOKS careful attention is given to all details of
manufacturing and design. It is the Publisher's desire to present books that are
satisfactory as to their physical qualities and artistic possibilities and
appropriate for their particular use. THOMAS BOOKS will be true to those
laws of quality that assure a good name and good will.*

Printed in the United States of America

RN-1

FOREWORD

THE need for understanding is one shared by all mankind. The need to understand is matched by the need to be understood. To gain understanding one must undergo similar experiences. To gain understanding the trainable child must be exposed to daily living routines and problems similar to those which normal children experience.

Today most public schools make every possible effort to provide equal educational opportunities for all children and youth. However, these opportunities vary widely, for those directly responsible for providing them have been aware that individual differences in ability often determine what constitutes equality of opportunity. It is essential that each pupil be given the opportunity to profit to the full extent of his ability. But this becomes possible only when the educational program offered is sufficiently flexible to permit adaptations required to meet individual needs.

It is not enough to admit a child to class and treat him entirely from the lay point of view, for the child is as corporate a whole as any normal child. The inefficient functioning of any part of him affects every other part. Neither can we accept the child's limitations as they appear to the lay mind for they can be and are often misleading, or again in many cases they can be improved. Nor is it right to press the child too far, or cause him to feel that he can do more than he is, when it might well be the fact that he cannot.

Finally, it is not enough to have a child eager to participate and striving to learn. First the foundation work must be carefully prepared, that is, the child must have inner harmony as well as a certain amount of self-control. To attempt to impose learning on a child without this readiness is comparable to allowing the flesh to grow over a wound before it has completely healed from the inside. This is called "proud" flesh. Undoing the damage caused to the flesh and to the wound is a serious matter. This writer considers the imposition of learning on a child who is not ready "proud" in the same way, and with the same amount of danger involved.

It is absolutely essential to have some knowledge of the cause and the extent of the child's mental deficiency, the behavioral patterns and personality characteristics associated with the disorder, and to understand the basic concepts involved in child growth and development. To do one's best in "training and teaching" the retarded we must understand the basic factors involved in learning and the principles that govern the learning process. Furthermore, effective methods of discipline and classroom management must be considered as a necessary part of a good guidance program for these children.

It is never a quick job to help the retarded if one does it fully. They must take their own time getting there, and we must be patient with them.

PREFACE

TEACHERS who work with trainable retarded children inevitably face a variety of classroom problems. Being able to meet and solve such problems in a professional manner not only affords much satisfaction and assists individual learning, but is of vital importance to the general welfare and mental health of both the children and teacher.

With these facts in mind, the author has prepared this volume as a guide for teachers and others who work with TMR children to assist them with planning a classroom program which emphasizes dynamically designed curriculum.

This book offers practical information on
  1. The clinical types found among trainable children;
  2. The physical, mental, and emotional growth of children;
  3. Learning in retarded and normal children;
  4. Discipline and classroom management;
  5. Physical and motor development;
  6. Daily living routines for teaching the TMR.

Success in teaching is dependent on forming a plan of approach. We must plan our efforts in and out of the classroom with the thought of putting into practice, from the very first day of school, what is learned from experience, consultation with colleagues and readings.

The Author humbly submits this book to you "teachers of our less endowed" with the sincere hope that it will assist you in the evolvement of your plan of approach to teach.

KATHLEEN BARNETTE WAITE

HEAVEN'S SPECIAL CHILD

A meeting was held far from earth,
'It's time again for another birth,
Said the angels to the Lord above
This special child will need much love.
His progress may seem very slow,
Accomplishment he may not show;
And he'll require extra care
From folks he meets down there.
He may not run or laugh or play;
His thoughts may seem quite far away.
In many ways he won't adapt
and he'll be known as 'handicapped.'
So let's be careful where he's sent,
We want his life to be content.
Please, Lord, find the parents who
will do a special job for You.
They will not realize right away
The leading role they're asked to play.
Comes stronger faith and richer love
And soon they'll know the privilege given
In caring for this gift from Heaven.
Their precious charge so meek and mild
Is heaven's very special child.'
            Author — unknown 204

ACKNOWLEDGMENTS

THE author is greatly indebted to many persons: to the authors of published books and articles, listed in the bibliographies, from which many facts and points of view included in this text were obtained; to her students who have contributed suggestions for curriculum and management of the TMR, to teachers who have contributed points of view and illustrations from their first-hand experience in working with the TMR, especially Joseph Garcia, to Miss Amy Matsumoto, who has assisted with research and editing, to the Fifteen County Curriculum Project Committee for providing ideas on planning specific day to day activities for the TMR, and my special thanks go to Mrs. Elizabeth Day, Sacramento County Consultant, Special Education programs for Mentally Retarded, Mrs. Marguerite Coffey, Sacramento County Department of Special Schools and Services Secretary, and Mr. Walter O. Olsen, Folsom-Cordova School District for their time and effort spent to refine the TMR Curriculum Project.

K.B.W.

CONTENTS

Section One

THE TMR CHILD

Section Two
TEACHING THE TMR CHILD

Contents

THE TRAINABLE
MENTALLY RETARDED
CHILD

Section One

THE TMR CHILD

THE first four chapters of this book are concerned with the definition of TMR, the factors involved in severe retardation, behavioral patterns associated with etiologies, the physical, mental, emotional, and social development of children, the basic factors in learning, kinds of learning and acquiring skills, and the discipline and classroom management of the TMR.

I

THE TRAINABLE RETARDED CHILD

S INCE 1950 a concerted effort has been made to establish programs for trainable mentally retarded pupils in the public schools of the United States. Prior to 1950 most of these children were kept in the seclusion of their own homes without planned training by educators, or they were placed in state institutions where training specially designed to meet their need was not always provided. The movement to open the public schools to trainable retarded pupils is part of a larger plan to enrich the lives of all mentally retarded persons by bringing them into fuller participation in the activities and services of their local communities.

The changing attitude of the public toward mentally retarded persons is one of the most significant social trends of the second half of the twentieth century. Indifference and rejection are giving way to collective concern and positive action. This changing attitude is due largely to the parents of the mentally retarded, acting first as loosely organized groups at local levels and since 1950 acting as well-planned units of the National Association for Retarded Children. Many of these parents made it clear that they wished to keep their trainable children at home and that they wanted these children enrolled in the tax-supported public schools of the nation.

Historically, public schools have enrolled deviant children only when (a) the children were educable and could profit from a modified type of academic program; (b) the children had potentialities for becoming economically independent; (c) the children had the ability to achieve a high degree of social competence and to function independently. These conditions do not prevail in the case of the trainable retarded pupils.

WHO ARE THE TRAINABLE?

The trainable retarded individuals are those with an IQ of 25 to 50. They are also termed as the moderately and severely retarded by some sources, and severely retarded by other sources. A former classification for this group was imbecile. As adults they range from 3.5 to 7.5 years old in mental age. The following portion from the chart, "Learning Capacity with Degrees of Retardation" (15) will give a general description of the trainable mentally retarded:

Moderate – IQ 35-52
Preschool: (0-5) Maturation and Development

5

Noticeable delays in motor development, especially in speech; responds to training in various self-help activities.

School Age (6-21) Training and Education

Can learn simple communication, elementary health and safety habits, and simple manual skills; does not progress in functional reading or arithmetic.

Adult (21 and over) Social and Vocational Adequacy

Can perform simple tasks under sheltered conditions; participates in simple recreation; travels alone in familiar places; usually incapable of self maintenance.

Severe – IQ 20-35

Preschool: Marked delay in motor development; little or no communication skill; may respond to training in elementary self-help, e.g., self-feeding.

School Age: Usually walks barring special disability; has some understanding of speech and some response; can profit from systematic habit training.

Adult: Can conform to daily routine and repetitive activities; needs continuing direction and supervision in protective environment.

Their mental development is between one-quarter and one-half that of an average child. The trainable mentally retarded may also have multiple handicaps to consider. One or more of the following disabilities may be present: epilepsy, deafness, blindness, hemplegia, cerebral palsy, congenital heart disease, anomalies, and emotional disorders.

Basically one can summarize by saying that the trainable mental retardate is one who is capable of caring for his own personal needs, doing household tasks, learning common dangers, traveling within the community he is familiar with, developing social skills, and doing simple one-step tasks and following directions in a sheltered workshop setting. He is not capable of employment in the competitive job fields, of academic functioning, or of living on his own.

They cannot be expected to do general classwork because they are incapable of learning academic skills, such as reading and arithmetic, beyond the learning of some simple words and numbers.

Incidence of Severe Retardation

It has been estimated that one out of every 250 persons in the United States, or more than 600,000 persons is in the mentally retarded group (212). Approximately 0.3 percent of the population falls in the trainable mentally retarded range of intelligence. Among school-age children, about 0.12 percent (40% of the trainable retarded) will have been institutionalized (public or private) and 0.18 percent (60% of the trainable) will still be residing at home (50).

Factors in Retardation

The majority of the trainable mentally retarded are retarded because of pathological causes — brain injury, metabolic disorders, genetic aberrations — and their height and weight tend to be below average. Motor coordination is usually poor, and there is present a much higher incidence of visual, auditory, and other sensory and physical problems than is true for the general population.

The complex nature of mental retardation defies simple definition and classification. It is generally agreed that the combination of symptoms commonly associated with mental retardation is, in most cases, a result of multiple factors. Presently, only a few types of retardation are subject to accurate diagnosis and treatment; the majority of cases remain un-differentiated as to nature and cause. Since this volume deals with the training of the severely retarded child, some clinical aspects of the causal factors will be mentioned here.

Clinical Types Found Among Trainable Children

The various etiological factors may operate singly or in various combinations; and they may operate before, during, or after birth. Among the most common disorders are (40):

  I. Prenatal factors
    A. Mongolism: One in every five hundred births is a mongoloid. This means that about twenty-three mongoloid babies are born daily into American families. The exact number of mongoloids is not known although it is estimated to be over one hundred thousand. Chromosomal anomaly is the cause of mongolism although the reason for the failure to separate is not clear.
    B. Cretinism: In this condition the thyroid has either failed to develop properly or has undergone degeneration or injury, and the infant suffers from a deficiency in the thyroid secretion.
    C. Microcephaly: This is a specific type of mental retardation originating from a failure of the cranium to attain normal size with consequent faulty development of cerebral tissue. The chief characteristic of the microcephalic is the small head, which rarely exceeds a circumference of seventeen inches as compared with the normal of around twenty-two inches. The skull is usually rather cone-shaped, with a marked recession of the chin and forehead.
    D. Hydrocephalus: This results from the accumulation of an abnormal amount of cerebrospinal fluid within the cranium causing damage to the brain tissue and enlargement of the cranium.
    E. Phenylketonuria (PKU): Phenylketonuria is a rare metabolic disorder occurring once in ten thousand to twenty-five thousand births. This condition is caused by the lack of an enzyme in the

body which is needed to break down phenylalanine, a substance which builds up in the blood and damages the brain.

   F. Prenatal infections: Maternal diseases, such as syphilis, encephalitis, and German measles, during pregnancy often cause brain damage to the unborn child.

  II. Types of mental retardation resulting from birth trauma

   A. Brain injuries: Difficulties during labor may cause bleeding within the brain, thus damaging the brain tissues.

   B. Anoxia: This stems from delayed breathing of the new-born infant. The lack of oxygen damages the brain.

  III. Mental retardation from trauma or disease in infancy and early childhood.

   A. Postnatal head injuries: Serious postnatal head injuries may result in permanent brain damage, although these injuries are not so frequent as is often assumed by parents.

   B. Diseases: Some common diseases of childhood — measles, mumps, chicken pox, influenza, and others — may produce a structural alteration in the brain tissue with consequent arrested mental development or other disorders. More serious childhood diseases, such as encephalitis and cerebrospinal meningitis, may leave lasting damage to the brain.

  IV. Pseudo retardation at the trainable level

Occasionally a child functioning at the trainable level responds favorably to the classroom situation and is found to be, in reality, educable. Sometimes it is discovered that the pupil is not truly mentally retarded after all. Among the possible factors responsible for the original underachievement are the following:

   1. Personality disturbance: Children suffering from severe personality maladjustments commonly function at a less effective level.

   2. Environmental deprivation: When the subject has had an impoverished experimental background, the intelligence test results are sometimes spuriously low.

For purpose of instruction, it is important that the personnel working with the child understand the most common causes of retardation and realize the educational implications involved. An understanding of the learning and behavior problems associated with severe retardation enables the worker to anticipate the problems and formulate an appropriate educational program at the earliest possible time.

Characteristics and Behavioral Patterns Associated with Specific Disorders

Endocrine disturbances during the prenatal period and during early childhood are responsible for some types of retardation.

MONGOLISM. The definite cause of mongolism is still unanswered even though scientific investigation has unraveled many clues which hopefully will establish its etiology in the near future.

Various theories have been offered to explain the pathology of mongolism. One relates this condition to the age of the mother at the time of birth of the child (exhaustion theory). This theory proposes that any cause which may disturb metabolic function may account for the condition. Another theory suggests that the cause of mongolism is a disturbance in the glandular system (9).

Most mongoloid children rank at the imbecile level, though some have intellectual capacities at higher and lower levels. Goldstein has pointed out two distinct kinds of mongols (89). The first is the predominantly thyroid-deficient mongol, who is short in stature, has wide facial features, short pudgy hands, walks more awkwardly, and has a comparatively higher IQ. The second type is taller and thinner, more restless, shows more emotional disturbance, and has a lower IQ.

According to Clarke (39) one type of mongolism results from non-disjunction. (The chromosomes fail to separate, and both pass into the same gamete, with the other gamete being left without the chromosome of that pair.) The chromosome involved is known as the "small arocentric chromosome pair No. 21." The mongol is called *trisomic* and has a total of forty-seven chromosomes rather than the usual forty-six. The majority of cases are due to nondisjunction.

Another type of mongolism may result from translocation. In this case, there is no additional chromosome present, but a condition of extra chromation exists because two chromosomes lose pieces which then are exchanged from one chromosome to another.

The mongoloid has a reputation for being much happier, more friendly, and more easily managed than other retarded children. However, this "charming personality" characterization occasionally is challenged. One of the more recent studies by Menolascino (151) has described some of these children who have been diagnosed chronic brain syndrome with behavioral reaction, chronic brain syndrome with adjustment reaction, and chronic brain syndrome with psychotic reaction.

Wunch has also pointed out hostile-aggressive behavior in mongoloids (219). But in summary of the various studies, there seems to be an agreement that the greater percent of mongoloid children are affectionate, content, relaxed individuals with a cheerful and friendly disposition.

CRETINISM. The cause of cretinism has been well established and is attributed to an insufficient secretion of the thyroid glands. It is recognized within the first four months of the infant's life, unless the condition is very mild. The child may be born with hypothyroidism, and sometimes the gland may be completely missing. Cretinism tends to occur in certain areas of the world where there is an inadequate amount of natural iodine in the water and soil. Two types of cretinism have been identified as sporadic and endemic.

Cretinism is recognized by the presence of many physical symptoms such as: small dwarfish body; short thick legs; large head; short, wide hands with fingers that have square ends; dry, coarse and "scaly" skin; large protruding tongue; peg-shaped teeth; everted lower lip; thick eyelids which appear swollen; short thick neck, and a hoarse voice.

Cretins, as a group, are somewhat stubborn and resistive in their relationships with other children and adults. They seem to lack spontaneity in their behavior reactions. They tend to be more placid and taciturn rather than quarrelsome and aggressive.

In intelligence, they show a wide range of capabilities. They may range from the idiot through the moron level, and some attain a "borderline" classification.

MICROCEPHALY. The brain of a microcephalic child is small and simple in its physical structure. It often has many deformities. The head is seldom over sixteen inches in circumference. This is a developmental condition, one in which the brain did not grow or some parts may even be missing.

These children have an alert vivacious temperment. They are usually the happy type, but their interest changes rapidly from one thing to another. They imitate the actions of others, and their speech is very repetitive. Their intelligence is usually in the high range of idiocy or the low range of imbecility; a few cases may reach the moron level.

HYDROCEPHALY. This condition may occur at birth (congenitally), or it may be acquired later. It is characterized by an unusually large head due to the accumulation of cerebrospinal fluid within the skull.

The physical and mental attributes of a hydrocephalic child depend upon the amount of the brain damage involved. Some may participate in normal activities if their intellectual handicap is only mild. In cases which can be arrested before permanent damage occurs there may be no intellectual deficit. However, the usual intellectual level of hydrocephalic children is in the range of severe mental retardation.

PHENYLKETONURIA. Phenylketonuria (PKU) is probably the best-known metabolic disorder which produces lowered intellectual functioning. There is some evidence to indicate that this is possibly a hereditary condition, transmitted by inheritance of an autosomal recessive gene.

PKU consists of a block in the metabolic transformation into tyrosine of the protein substance phenylalanine, which is present in most foods. Because of this block, incomplete metabolites, including phenylpyruvic acid, are released into the body. Consequently the level of phenylalanine rises in various tissues of the body, including the brain.

About 90 percent of affected children are blond and blue-eyed with fair skin. The teeth are broad and widely spaced. The child bends his head and trunk in a peculiar posture while slightly flexing his arms and legs. This produces an awkward walk with short steps.

The degree of retardation may vary. A few have been reported to have no retardation, and some, only moderate retardation, but most of the affected individuals without treatment show severe retardation.

In addition to retardation, other behavioral symptoms of brain damage may be evident. Neurological development of persons in this group compares with others who have similar degrees of retardation.

According to Leland (144), autistic and other psychotic type behavioral symptoms have been noted in many severely affected children.

Allen (2) has reported neurological and behavioral problems in PKU persons with normal intelligence.

Many children suffering from PKU show severe maladaptive behavior. Bjornson (22) states that schizophrenic-like symptoms may be expected in some, but that there is no general pattern of behavioral reactions that differentiates this child from other retarded children, nor does any specific categorizable physhological defect exist. However, he noted that children who show dull, expressionless faces, negativistic behavior, unreal emotional outbursts, and speech disturbances have often been diagnosed as phenylketonuria cases.

Other Causative Factors

PRENATAL INFECTIONS. There is a great deal of evidence to support the fact that diseases of the mother during pregnancy may affect the physical and mental development of the unborn fetus.

CONGENITAL SYPHILIS. This has been recognized as a cause of retardation for a long time. The child may be infected through placental circulation before birth or in passage through the birth canal during delivery.

RUBELLA (GERMAN MEASLES). This may cause blindness, deafness, and mental retardation in a child if the mother is affected with this disease during the first three months of pregnancy.

ENCEPHALITIS. Encephalitis is a form of brain inflamation which is often caused by one of several viruses. The mother who suffers from this viral infection during pregnancy may give birth to a child whose degree of brain damage could range from slight mental deficiency to complete idiocy.

Prenatal brain damaged children may exhibit personality and behavioral patterns similar to those found in other brain-damaged retardates whose degree of injury is comparable.

BRAIN INJURY. Most teachers will encounter children with some degree of brain damage sometime during the years they spend in the classroom, but the teacher of severely retarded children faces this situation daily.

Understanding the causes of brain damage and the behaviors usually associated with the damage will enable the teacher to better meet the needs of the children.

Brain damage may occur at any stage of development. It may be the result or genetic factors, toxic agents, infectious disease, injury of physical deprivations. If retardation is due to damage of the central nervous system, the educational goals should consider the maximum development of the intact areas to compensate for the faulty functioning in the damaged areas.

Behavior Patterns Associated with Brain Damage

No constellation of behavioral patterns can be identified to a particular group of retarded individuals, but there are characteristics found more consistently among some groups. Those commonly associated with brain damage are the following:

PERCEPTUAL DISTURBANCES. The child has difficulty in comprehending wholeness. He is inclined to focus on minor details, but fails to see the relation to the whole. The separation of foreground and background is confusing. He tends to respond to everything with the same degree of intensity. Images of environmental objects are not clearly received; drawings show distortion and disorganization.

THINKING DISORDERS. Children with thinking disorders see unusual relationships. They may classify objects according to some minor detail rather than the significant features. The brain-damaged child tends to base his responses upon hypothetical or imaginary situations and has difficulty in seeing his world in its true perspective.

BEHAVIOR DISORDERS. The child who suffers from organic damage may display behavior completely different from that usually associated with organicity. Some behavior disorders which frequently accompany brain damage are hyperactivity, distractability, perseveration, emotional instability, unpredictable conduct, and general erratic responses. Inconsistent behavior is revealed by sudden changes from withdrawal and resistance to hyperactivity and anxiety. The child may become severely emotionally disturbed if these symptoms are not recognized as problems and treated accordingly.

MOTOR DISTURBANCES. Posture and movement reveal lack of precision and control; the child may be clumsy and unable to participate in the physical activities of children of his age group.

Rhythm and laterality disturbances are apparent if the child is unable to skip, to hop on one foot, to balance, or to throw and catch a ball. Motor problems may range from minor disorders to the gross disabilities associated with cerebral palsy.

Pseudo Retardation

PERSONALITY DISTURBANCES. This factor may often cause children to function as though they were severely retarded.

Psychological retardation may be caused by psychiatric illnesses such as autism and severe neuroses. It should be differentiated from intellectual handicap. It is also caused by sensory, cultural, emotional, or educational deprivation. Since we place so much reliability upon school performance as an index of intelligence, we should give more attention to this entire complex of environmental deprivation.

Children in this category have acquired habits of behavior sufficiently different from other children reared in similar circumstances so that their behavior is considered to be personally and socially deviant. Their behavior may range from aggressive to complete withdrawal. They cannot do what is expected of their normal peers. These children may come from lower, middle, or upper class families. Their personal and social learning is inappropriate, but the reasons for this are not clear.

Environmental Factors

The number of mentally retarded children with no obvious organic defect exceeds the number with organic defect. Considerable research has been conducted to determine the effects of heredity and environment upon the mental functioning of these children. Those who subscribe to the theory that heredity is the determining factor believe that large groups of subnormal individuals locate in the low socioeconomic areas because they are biologically defective and cannot meet the social and economic demands outside these areas.

The intellectual and educational level of the homes is rather low. Many of the parents have not more than a partial elementary education, while others have finished high school. If tested, it is doubtful that the majority of these parents would achieve IQ's which exceed the borderline range. Numerous parents are mildly retarded persons who have met circumstances which permitted them to make full use of their abilities.

The retarded offspring from this group of families are usually seen as natural variants of the ability levels represented by their parents. They are seldom exposed to circumstances which are especially advantageous to their growth and development; however, they cannot generally be labeled the most unfortunate in our society.

Nowhere is the nature-nurture controversy so alive as with respect to the etiology of cultural-familial mental retardation.

Behavior Patterns Associated with Environmental Factors

Fortunately all students from low-economic areas are not equally affected by their cultural environment. The conditions which prove detrimental to one person may serve as a stimulant to another. Disadvantaged areas have produced top ranking students and highly successful adults; however, the generally low achievement and concomitant problems of adjustment tend to stereotype the population. It is unwise to attempt to generalize concerning the total intellectual level, behavior, or aspirations of the population, but it is possible to recognize some persistent social patterns among the low achievers. These patterns include:

LACK OF MOTIVATION. Some factors which contribute to the apathy and indifference found among many students and adults may be the lack of home motivation, the absence of books in the home, the limited opportunities for travel, and other social experiences.

FAULTY SELF-CONCEPT. Living with indifferent and negative attitudes influences the child to accept failure and defeat. His level of aspiration will continue to be low, without some intervention to help him realize his worth.

POOR HEALTH AND NUTRITION. Many children from the low socioeconomic group do not receive corrective treatment for dental, visual, auditory, and other health problems. Poverty and poor management may contribute to malnutrition for some children.

FAMILY DISORDER. Many families are insecure and instable because of broken homes, unemployment, inadequate housing, and frequent changes of address, crime, and delinquency, and the overall conditions which generally exist among the low socioeconomic groups. These factors tend to have a negative effect upon the child's adjustment.

INADEQUATE THINKING AND PERCEIVING. During infancy the development of concepts and thinking processes begin. If the young child is not provided with opportunities for communication, experimentation, exploration, and social interaction, he may fail to develop the basic concepts and thinking processes upon which his later learning depends.

The conditions that affect the students' school and social adjustment also determine the relationship between school and home. The teachers usually are of a higher socioeconomic status, and may understand and respect only middle-class standards. Parents from the lower socioeconomic group generally do not feel close to the school. Their lower educational status, lack of family stability, and high mobility contribute to the poor relationship.

The child whose low level of functioning is due to cultural impoverishment may actually be normal, but appears subnormal because he has failed to develop the acuity, skills, and attitudes needed to meet the standards of the society in which he lives. A comprehensive program for improvement must involve social action to upgrade general living conditions.

In order to give the teacher a clearer picture of the trainable retarded child, this chapter has described the child, stated some causative factors, and explained behavior patterns which may accompany particular etiologies.

II

THE BEHAVIORAL CHARACTERISTICS
OF CHILDREN

TEACHERS often wonder just what they should expect of the children assigned to their classes. As each star differs in brightness, so do the children of man, even those found in the trainable programs. Therefore, it is essential that she concern herself with individual appraisals and to recognize and understand the heterogeneous groupings we have in respect to chronological age, mental age, emotional stability, and degree of organic impairment. We cannot overlook the fact that mental age is the key to learning ability.

Furthermore, the teacher must understand what a normal child is expected to accomplish at a given age. We assume that a normal child of a given age has a like mental age, for example, the child whose C.A. is six years also has a M.A. of at least six years. But we assume that the M.A. of a trainable six-year-old is somewhere between 1.5-2 years.

We need a reliable guide to assist us in setting up realistic behavioral objectives for trainable children. The writer has found the following descriptions of normal three, four, five, six, and seven-year-olds to be of valuable assistance when planning for the trainable whose C.A.'s range from six to twenty-one years of age.

THE NORMAL THREE-YEAR-OLD

Of all the preschool years, the third year is one of the most fascinating in the growth of the child. The three-year-old can do things. He can run and jump and climb; he can ride a tricycle. He bustles back and forth, up and down stairs, and can even turn corners and stop abruptly. He can do things with his arms and hands and with his legs and feet. He delights in playing with modeling clay and in his sand box. He can make a train or a tower out of blocks or cubes. He can fold a piece of paper crosswise or lengthwise and can draw crosses on paper with crayons. He can put away his toys when playtime is over. He will help with dressing as well as with undressing himself. Sometime between three and four he learns to unbutton buttons — much to his delight.

The three-year-old is in equilibrium with people and things around him, perhaps because he is in better equilibrium with himself. He no longer seems to need the protection of rituals of always doing everything the same way. Greater maturity has led him to feel much more secure — secure with himself and secure in his relations with others.

At three years of age there is a great adjustment from the two-year-old. His attention span has increased considerably, so much so that he can concentrate on one activity much longer than he ever did before. Better coordination is permitting better results and better results in turn create greater interest and amazement in self-accomplishment. No longer is his goal only to build a tower of blocks to knock down; he builds with a definite purpose in mind, i.e. builds a bridge of blocks and attempts to push cars underneath and through in a repeated manner.

Above all, his increased ability with an interest in language helps him to be a delightful companion. His own vocabulary and ability to use language have increased tremendously in most cases.

There are certain types of behavior evident in the three-year-old. While it is true that what we say is common behavior in the three-year-old it usually does not apply to your child at this level. In answer to this we must keep in mind that no child is raised in the same way and by the same people. But if your child gets plenty of restful sleep, eats the right foods, is healthy and happy, and is basically interested in many things, then we can be safe in saying this is —

Common Behavior

These are some of the common behaviors of the three-year-old.

Speaking

At this age he becomes a chatterbox. He is using a great many verbs also pronouns, though he still gets them mixed up (as when he says "help my" for "help me").

The child speaks in short sentences and usually with animation. He likes to listen to simple stories and nursery rhymes, and he loves being a bear or a doggie or a horse. He is very curious about people and things around him and asks many simple questions. Girls tend to talk a little earlier than boys and tend to be slightly superior in language ability throughout the early years.

Twins, being so closely associated with each other that they do not have good speech to copy, are likely to be somewhat slower in language development and cling to their poor pronunciation longer than other children. They catch up in the early school years however. Parents can help very much by speaking clearly and carefully so that their children have good speech models to copy.

By the time many children are three and one-half years old they begin to stutter even though they have not stuttered before. There is nothing alarming about this. It is because they are making enormous strides as conversationalists, and the result is a mixing up of pronouns.

Dressing and Cleaning

Many three-year-olds love to try to comb their own hair, brush their teeth, and wash their own faces. If a low-hung mirror is provided, they can see how successful or not their efforts are.

The three-year-old can do a good part of his dressing, although he still sometimes gets pants or a sweater on hind side front and makes a hit-or-miss job of lacing his shoes. This phase depends a great deal on the parents' part as to how well the child will or will not dress himself. Mama may always do it for them, thereby never giving him a chance, while on the other hand he may be put on his own entirely and become an accomplished dresser by the time he is four.

Toilet

This is one phase that makes the three-year-old so much more pleasant to be with and have around. Most of them can sleep through the night without wetting the bed and, if given a hand with buttons, when necessary, can go to the toilet by themselves during the day.

Accidents may happen though, but they should not be made an issue of or reason for punishment. Take him to the toilet and change him without comment.

If bed-wetting persists you may have to get him up at intervals throughout the night or you may awaken him when you go to bed to make a trip to the bathroom. Continue this until your mission is accomplished.

Eating

The three-year-old is in feeding, as in all his behavior, much easier to handle than the child just younger. His eating is definitely better. His appetite fluctuates less. He has become a good chewer. He handles a cup and glass with ease and sureness. He feeds himself more efficiently, and even demands a fork to spear his meat. This might incite parents to have him at the dinner table with them. This might prove to be too much of a burden on him thereby having him resort to other activities not associated with good eating.

Above all do not let eating become an issue between you; mealtime should be treated as a pleasant moment in the day when everyone eats as a matter of course and not because he is forced to eat.

Fears

Since the child of three speaks the language and understands many times more the amount said about him, and since his imagination is zooming, anything said in his presence must be carefully considered.

However, many fears are perfectly natural — necessary for survival in a primitive society — withdrawing from that which may harm him.

Some of the most outstanding fears likely to develop in the three year old for no reason at all are:
1. Wrinkled people (visual)
2. Masks, bogeyman
3. The dark
4. Animals
5. Policeman
6. Burglars
7. Mother or father going out at night.

A fair proportion of the children develop occasional nightmares or mild phobias at this age, which last for a few weeks or months, and they gradually disappear. If a child with a temporary symptom of this slight degree has a good relationship with his parents, is not tied to their apron strings, is not too difficult for them to manage, if he seeks the company of other children and is able to hold his own with them, then there will be no cause to worry.

Sex Play

The child's interest in sex may be embarrassing, but it usually is not particularly devastating to you so long as it remains in the realm of pure theory. His questions about babies and about the relations of the two sexes to each other may be embarrassing, but they usually do not really disturb you.

The three-year-old verbally expresses interest in physical differences between sexes and in different postures of urinating. Girls attempt to urinate standing up.

Play

As in language, the three-year-old is much more sure of himself in play. Apparatus for climbing, swings, and teeter-totters are not too advanced for him. Although he can play very well without any difficulty, he is likely to leave his play yard to explore and roam about the alley, the yard next door, the sidewalk out in front, or wherever his interest may carry him.

Precautions must be taken to prevent this without any supervision. By this I mean take him around the neighborhood occasionally so that he may become familiar with it and no longer be curious about it.

The following are some of the things designed to promote motor control and all-around physical development:

Large hollow blocks
Packing boxes arranged for safe climbing (if you can find them)
Slide
Ladder that must be fastened securely to a sawhorse, fence or bars
Tricycle
Hammer, shovel, saw, and workbench (watch out!)
Dump trucks, trains, airplanes (favorites)
Wagon
The following are materials needed for a child's creative self-expression:
Clay
Crayons
Plenty of newsprint
Blocks of many sizes

THE NORMAL FOUR-YEAR-OLD

The child at four presents to the eye of the casual observer a simple and rather delightful picture. A bright, busy, sure, out-going youngster, his physical appearance seems to belie his age. He appears rather mature compared to three, and the quick look on his face often leads adults astray in dealing with him. "Four" is very much a little child with a tremendous eagerness to test and try the world around him and himself.

The undeniable and inevitable eagerness following closely the relative calm and naivite of three proves a challenge to himself, his family, and his teacher. He must know how it feels, how it goes, and if he can do it with no interference (he hopes). The world is his oyster, and he practically dares everyone to prove the situation otherwise. Dr. Gesell (83) calls four the out-of-bounds age. Laymen frequently refer to four as "spoiled brats." People who are interested in the four-year-old recognize that his out-of-bounds behavior is not necessarily the result of poor upbringing, but more probably a manifestation of his increasing intellectual and physical growth. The firm hand of understanding parents is a real necessity to the four-year-old to help him to reestablish his boundaries which have broadened, but must still remain limited. As he approaches five, the out-of-bounds behavior seems to diminish. The child shows that he knows the limits of his confines and is now prepared to explore them more explicitly.

Motor Development

Early "four" experimentally climbs, skips, hops, jumps, and becomes more sure-footed every minute. At 4.5 he climbs to heights that terrify most adults. He is a master handler of tricycles and wagons and can weave intricate maneuvers at bewildering speeds with remarkably few casualties. In hopping, skipping, and galloping, he is no way concerned with perfection for these motor skills are no longer important in themselves, as they were at three, but serve as acompaniment to his dramatic play. Now he is a policeman, mother, pilot, duck, cowboy, monkey, baby, etc. He finds climbing, hanging from bars, and jumping from stacked boxes good muscular activities in themselves. His growing muscular development and control foster self-confidence. He glows with accomplishment at the top of the "jungle gym." He needs little help in being lifted, pushed, and put, and resents having his joy of doing spoiled by oversolicitous aid. Occasionally too much help from grown-ups can result in a tantrum. Though the muscles of the hands are far from capacity growth and utility, four is busy buttoning, hair combing, clay modeling, wiping, hammering, etc., in more accurate and complex ways. As four becomes 4.5 these rudimentary motor abilities evolve toward skills. He cuts on the line with his scissors and laces his shoes. His gestures are more precise and defined. His dancing and hand movements exhibit a kind of natural grace. This is, of course, the result of a combination of muscular and mental growth. The body moves less as a single simple thought and more as a complicated idea of many parts. This makes his joints seem more mobile. At three and two he tossed a ball in a propulsive manner with much torso participation. He now swings back a more independent arm and executes a strong overhand throw.

Four seems perpetual motion – but watch closely for a period of time, and he will demonstrate the balance of activity and rest which is common to young children. This "balance" of activity and rest is an important but little understood phase of development. The constant activity we observe is not so constant. The "rest" we observe is very sudden and informal. In the midst of great activity the child may squat quietly and contemplate the shape and color of a stone, or he may stop pedaling the trike and stare at the scene before him literally without moving a muscle. The rest seems restorative no matter how momentary, but rests of longer duration are really still needed before and after the noon meal even though the child cannot nap.

Language and Communication

Four-year-olds exhibit wide differences in their ability to use language. At one extreme we find short incomplete sentences with poor enunciation, and at the other extreme we find a well-developed complete sentence with perfect enunciation and occasionally the rudiments of secondary languages (if the opportunity is presented). Generally, four makes himself understood in a clear fashion. How he loves to repeat himself — and how maddeningly persistent he can be. He delights in the music of his own voice, making the same noises again and again. This repetition is not utterly wasted for it results in a perfect command of the word even when the meaning of the word escapes him. He loves to play with words, invent new words. He uses many words he does not understand, and frequently the explanation is beyond his understanding as well, but the child may enjoy the word for itself. Questionable words are exciting too. "You old pooh-pooh," etc. and "toilet talk" are always fun for their possible shock value. He loves simple singing-acting games and delights in silly words and nonsense rhymes.

When asked, the four-year-old literally cannot "tell us about what happened this morning." He may not remember that far back or possibly cannot put his thoughts into words at will. Frequently an incident will remind him of "what happened this morning," and out it will pour spontaneously — sometimes on the same day, sometimes much later. When pressed, the child says the first thing that pops into his head or gives us the answer we want. Of course, the child is not lying — this concept is still beyond him — nor is he even shading the truth as adults often do. He simply does not know or cannot put it into language. The four-year-old confounds adults because they can only rarely be certain that his report is accurate. For example, he may say, "Tomorrow is my birthday." Since the child may not know when "tomorrow" really is, his statement bears further inquiry. Adults, at a loss in conversation with children, often ask questions to cover up silences, but children are quite comfortable in periods of silence. Approaching 4.5, he becomes somewhat more reliable because he understands more of what he is saying.

Young "Four" indulges in the "collective monologue" which is a verbal version of parallel play. He derives great satisfaction from this "conversation," although it is not a true exchange. One child is talking about "his new baby" while the other is telling how he feels about playing in the sandbox. They do not talk directly to one another except for an occasional "no!" or "stop," or "mine!" They talk at or about one another to themselves or to mother or teacher. There is much clutter and irrelevance in four conversation. As he gets older, he is almost able to address the group directly and to shape his thoughts without so many tangent references.

Comprehension: Time, Numbers

"Fours" understand small amounts such as one, two, three and "a lot." He knows about the "other one," but may not understand the word "pair."

"Dozen," "twenty," and "fifty" have little or no meaning for him. He begins to understand taking "turns," but do not ask him to count them because he is not ready for such accuracy. Numbers are used very infrequently. His time sense is rudimentary. He understands "before" and "after" and things like "when you wake up." However, "next week" and "last week" remain vague.

Self

Somewhere around the age of three or four, the sense of "I" achieves some degree of organization. The child knows who he is. His intelligence is strained by new sets of problems. Everything has a "because" — he wants to know the "because" of everything. He believes in pictures. Books for him are truth. Reality and imagery are very closely interwoven. A vulnerability that comes with self-awareness is expressed in new fears at four. The child who pretends he is a tiger can well start a shrieking frightened panic among his contemporaries. To the four-year-old dreams are real events taking place in real space. He may not want to sleep in certain rooms. He says things like, "There are too many dreams in that room." Magicians do not impress four because he lives magic and cannot see what is so unusual about taking a rabbit out of a seemingly empty hat.

Imaginary companions appear for about 20 percent of four-year-olds. They serve many different functions. Sometimes it is just a true friend. For other children it may serve as a scapegoat, conscience, model, escape, or even an unwelcome invading hallucination. At about 4.5 we see signs of internal government in the personality of the child. Parents and teachers now have an agent working for them in the form of conscience. There seems to be a value in a child having some guilt feelings. His own moral repudiation will eventually serve to inhibit his impulse to repeat asocial acts on the next occasion. He knows, somehow, that we cannot forever separate the doer from the deed.

The child of four is very interested in the bathroom. He likes to see other children use the bathroom, though he may place a premium on his own privacy. He likes to watch people undress. He is interested in genital differences, although he does not always realize that these differences determine sex. He is more certain it is a girl when she wears a dress, a boy because of his close cropped hair. One remarked about a nude infant creeping across a lawn, "It's so hard to tell if it's a boy or a girl, especially with their clothes off."

Play

The bathroom is not only interesting because it provides opportunity to see and sometimes to show, but also because of soap and water, powder, lotion, nail polish, etc. He takes prolonged and delicious delight in handling water and suds. Splashing and dripping are great fun. Soap play is only rarely used in connection with cleanliness. Sand and water are good for long periods of all absorbing pleasure. Although "Four" can now be rather creative with crayon, clay, and paint, he is more fascinated and concerned with the qualities of the medium than with its use as a means of description. He enjoys big splashes of color and will unrestrainedly bang, flatten, and squeeze clay. He may start painting a horse but the long drips will soon suggest new patterns which he may want to follow. The completed product is a combination of many superimposed inspirations. "What is it?" can often be a tactless embarrassing question. Toward 4.5 his interest in the end result of his efforts with clay, paint, etc., becomes more and more apparent. Often the child of four cannot resist playing chemist with his food, and if he is not stopped, a fine mess results. Blocks are used to make things. Great loose sprawling structures are dominant. The meaning and shape of the con-struction are always changing, and this provides great sport for a short period. Toward five, his block structures start with a definite idea and retain it. At four a single prop can represent the whole idea. Thus, a cowboy hat stands for cowboy, gun, lasso, horse, etc., and high-heels can cover playing grown-ups.

Social Life and Attitudes Toward Children and Adults

Dramatic play is well-developed at four and can proceed at a fairly cooperative pace up to fifteen minutes. There is much, "You be" and "I'll be" talk. However, getting along well, is still a complicated process, and "Four" is busy experimenting. There is yet much to be desired in his understanding of the social amenities. Much experimental hostility is expressed in pushing, spitting, biting, making faces, hurling insults and objects, etc. Big and little wrongs call forth similar aggression and condemnation. His attitude toward other children is generally negligent and carefree with a regal expectancy that they will conform to his desires. Regardless of the source, the child's passions run high, but come and go quickly. Yet, in a flash of anger, if his strength were equal to the job, there is little doubt that "Four" would kill without compunction. Boys tend to exhibit more and more aggressiveness through four while girls become more amenable. Enmities are as unstable as friendship and endearments may follow attempts at annihilation in a period of minutes. Four is not without sympathy which he expresses by staring at a child in distress or consoling him or scolding the offender.

Although very attached to mommy, daddy, or teacher, etc., the four-year-old casually expects that they will obey him. He freely attempts to bribe them, "If you let me do so and so, I'll be your best friend." He can effectively ignore grown-ups unless he needs them for his own purposes and then can become imperious or wrangling. He is definitely resistant to adult pressures and has no enthusiasm for their concept of order. He will pick up after himself only when he has exhausted the possibility of avoiding the task. Adult sympathy and affection are a soothing balm, and he thoroughly enjoys basking in hugs, kisses, and approval.

Four is utterly contrary, paradoxical, out-of-bounds, at odds with himself, his contemporaries, and adults. All the possible seeds of human emotion and motivation seem to be sprouting within him at once. He is showing and telling how he feels and what he thinks all the time.

Honest, very firm, and tactful guidance are truly a necessity of his life. As he approaches five, he begins to realize what is "in-bounds" and derives great pleasure from his understanding of the "rules" which he actively bucked a few months before. His trying four behavior evolves toward an easier and happier time for himself.

THE NORMAL FIVE-YEAR-OLD

Five years marks the time of an extreme and delightful equilibrium. The child is reliable, well-adjusted, stable, and feels secure inside himself. "Mother" is the center of the five-year-old's world, and he likes to do things with her and for her. He likes to obey commands, enjoys instructions, and likes to get permission before doing things. This year between five and six marks the end of the baby period, and the child begins to take a more mature role in life.

Physical Development

Physical Growth

Girls may be about a year ahead of boys in physiological development. Girls and boys are about the same in height, which ranges from thirty-eight to forty-six inches. Their weight is from thirty-six to fifty pounds, which is thirty percent of their mature weight. The first four permanent teeth may appear, and the development of girls is advanced over that of boys. The head is almost as large as it is ever going to be. Many children of the five-year-old age are far-sighted. Eye-hand coordination are not yet complete.

Motor Characteristics

The large muscles are better developed than the small muscles that control the fingers. The child is very active, has good coordination, and a good sense of balance. His postural attitude shows more grace; he can skip smoothly and jump well and is therefore less cautious on the playground. The child can care for himself by washing his face, combing his hair, brushing his teeth, and dressing and undressing himself. There is less dawdling because of the greater motor maturity. He has a better sense of rhythm.

Eating

There is a distinct rise in appetite at this age. Since television has such a far-reaching effect on the child, his choice of foods is increasing, perhaps because of this. He cannot yet cut with his knife, but uses all other utensils well; he enjoys participating in the meal time conversation.

Sleep

The five-year-old tires easily, but will not willingly give up and rest. He is frequently disturbed by dreams and nightmares, but can usually be calmed by his parents. He needs a rest period or nap each day, and must get ten to twelve hours sleep at night.

Health

At five years the child has very good health. He may have only one or two colds in winter. At five and one-half he has complaints about his feet, head, neck region being hypersensitive, and has frequent colds, headaches, and earaches.

Emotional Development

Tension Outlets

The five-year-old does not have much overflow. Thumb sucking may occur before sleep, or he may sniffle or twitch his nose. Various little exhibitions occur, usually at the end of the day. The five and one-half-year-old exhibits more devices at one time and shows more signs of tension.

Fear

This is not a fearful age. Many fears can be eliminated by showing their cause. More fears are visual or concrete, such as falling. They may fear the dark or having their mothers taken away from them.

Responsibility

The five-year-old is usually dependable and obedient at home and has little trouble with his everyday activities. He has much interest in household activities, such as sweeping or dishes. He likes rules and likes to be told what to do. He can be trusted to go to the store and make small purchases, and he is gaining respect of others. He has a great deal of pride in his own accomplishments and possessions.

Sex Interests

There are fewer "show" games played as the child is more modest now. He is not so interested in the bathroom and bathroom play as he was, but has a great deal of interest in babies and where they come from. He is usually satisfied with a simple answer but would like a baby of his own.

Mental Development

Language

The child can usually speak clearly by this age and has a vocabulary of approximately 2200 words. His questions are more for information than practice in speaking, and he can give definitions himself in terms of usage. He uses words accurately and elaborately and uses all types of sentences.

Adaptive Behavior

He is realistic and perceives order, form, and detail fairly well. He can solve problems involving spatial relationships. He is paying attention to detail as shown in his drawings, and he can count to ten and add simple combinations. He enjoys more realistic stories rather than imaginative ones. He now has an increased attention span and recognizes many of the letters of the alphabet.

Reasoning Ability

He still has trouble understanding the viewpoint of others and still has some difficulty exchanging ideas with others. He is very conscious of social organization and is trying to understand it. He still lacks the power to reason synthetically and displays an intellectual innocence which is profoundly primitive in spite of his speech ability.

Moral Development

The five-year-old can usually distinguish between truth and falsehood. He is interested in things that are pretty. He is also beginning to form understanding about God and asks many questions about Him.

Social Development

Parent-Child Relationships

This child is very loving, obedient to his mother, friendly, and willing and anxious to do as mother asks. He may frequently try to put mother's welfare above his own. The five and one-half-year-old is tending toward his father and may thrust out against his mother. He is very proud and fond of father and may obey father more promptly than mother. He has a smooth relationship with his father.

Sibling-Child Relationships

He is often protective toward his siblings, especially if someone else is there. He likes to play with older brothers and sisters and likes to help with baby.

Child-Child Relationships

He may still play best with just one child at a time, yet he does play in groups of two to five with sociability. He prefers associative play to solitary and parallel types. He definitely desires companions and enjoys group projects and is quite sensitive to social situations. He has become more conscious of the differences of sexes and displays social conformity.

THE NORMAL SIX-YEAR-OLD

Behavior Profile

The six-year-old is at the threshold of what many psychologists call "middle childhood" — that period sometimes also called the "dark ages" of childhood. This term indicates how little we really know about this period. Despite some studies on the behavior of school-age children, notably those by Dr. Arnold Gesell and Dr. Frances Ilg (84), there is no one general statement that can be made about the psychological changes that take place during these years.

In the preschool years the child grows rapidly both physically and in his awareness of people. He must learn to control his own body impulses, to become accustomed to regular eating, sleeping, and elimination. For the young child, then, part of learning to be sociable is a matter of inhibiting impulses of his body, or giving up some of his infantile behavior.

A child well along in the "middle years," however, grows slowly, without too many sudden internal changes that call for major readjustments. The control of bodily functions (which by and large he has mastered) is not so important now as the control of muscles, the physical coordination that helps him work and play in school.

Parents may wonder, then, why the child of five or five and one-half, a most placid creature, perhaps, begins at six to show behavior that is very disturbing to adults. He begins to question rules and regulations at home, whereas at five parental authority seemed good to him. His worries about what happened at school may come out at home in bursts of temper, crankiness, defiance, or back-talk.

"He is a changed child!" Many a mother has said ruefully, when her former five-year-old begins to lose his angelic five-year-oldness. "He is a changed child, and I do not know what has gotten into him!" There is some mystification about this change. But as early as five and one-half he began to be brash and combative in his behavior, as though at war with himself and the world. At other times, of course, he was quite delightful and companionable. "But I can't understand him. What has gotten into him?"

Perhaps nothing more than six-year-oldness!

The sixth year (or thereabouts) brings fundamental changes, somatic and psychological. It is an age of transition. The milk teeth are shedding the first permanent molars are emerging. Even the child's body chemistry undergoes subtle changes, reflected in increased susceptibility to infectious diseases. "Six," as we shall call him, is not as robust nor staunch as he was at five. There are other important developmental changes which affect the mechanisms of vision, and indeed the whole neuromotor system.

We have said that during the middle years there are few sudden internal changes. This is true, except at the transitional edges. The child of six is on the borderline between early childhood, with its many changes. So he continues to develop with some radical changes, until he gets into the more steady years of middle childhood. In passing, we might mention that more turbulence is to be seen again as the transitional period of preadolescence comes into view in middle childhood.

Yes, "Six" is passing through a transitional stage. He is a different child because he is a changing child. In describing his traits, we might point out again that at no stage does the child suddenly become something radically different from what he was yesterday, last week, or last month. The colors of the developmental spectrum shade into each other by imperceptible graduations. But to paint a vivid and useable maturity portrait, we must dip our brush where the pigment is strong. With this much apology to the six-year-old, we shall now try to do him developmental justice, remembering that such justice bridges the chasm between angels and demons.

At no time are children ever typical five, six, or seven-year-olds in all phases of their growth. At all times they represent what they were, what they are, and what they will be.

The action system of the child is now undergoing growth changes, comparable in their way to the eruption of the sixth year molars. New propensities are erupting, new impulses, new feelings, are literally coming to the surface, because of profound developments in the underlying nervous system. From fetus to the preschool child we have seen that in the child a fast evolution of mankind has taken place. "Five" has already come into a large share of the racial inheritance. "Six" is coming into a later portion. This is "What has gotten into him."

Psychological inheritance, however, does not come in neat packages. It comes in the form of behavior trends and dynamic forces that must be reconciled and organized within a total action-system. Some conflict is a normal accompaniment of developmental progress. So we should take a constructive and optimistic view of the difficulties that "Six" encounters. The adult is all too often inclined to take the "dim view" or short-sighted view of the six-year-old's activities, especially when they frustrate or inconvenience the adults — be they parents or teachers.

The child also experiences frustration when he enters the new field of action as "Six" at home and at school. Diametric opposites have almost equal sway. But he also finds it hard to "buckle down" to do the thing that will bring the happy result. The child of six is still something of a baby in that he still has the urge to play when he knows that he should be at work. And so, he dawdles the mornings away from his paper. This tendency to oscillate between two alternatives is called "bipolarity" — a see-saw awareness of both ends of a dilemma.

The six-year-old manifests his bipolarities in many different ways. He may cry easily, but is easily diverted to laughter. He may turn on his best friend in an instant of rage. We do not encourage "Six" in his irresponsibilities, but we can recognize and deal patiently with these warring intensities.

His difficulties in situations which are emotional or social, carry over into educational problems of learning. Any primary teacher is familiar with reversals in writing and reading. The small "b" and "d" are confused in writing. The same numerals may be reversed and done correctly interchangeably on the same paper. "Saw" and "was" are often confused in reading. This also might be considered forms of bipolarity.

Life is charged with double alternatives, even for you and me. Is it any wonder that "Six" in our complex culture finds these alternatives crowding in upon him rather thickly? When he does the wrong thing he is called bad, but there is no use asking him why he is bad. He is not clear on these things. At the age of five, awareness and capabilities were in better balance. Six is aware of more than he can well manage. He often goes to extremes — he is over-enthusiastic, or he dawdles. He wants to win, but he cannot or will not pay the price. He has great energy, but he may tire easily, and often.

One approach to the problem of growth and development has been evolved by Dr. Robert Havighurst (99). At each life period, he points out, people are confronted by certain developmental tasks, skills, attitudes, understands, that they need to achieve, and are expected to achieve. He gives the following tasks for middle childhood (6 to 12 years):

1. Learning physical skills necessary for ordinary games.
2. Building wholesome attitudes toward oneself as a growing organism.
3. Learning to get along with age-mates.
4. Learning an appropriate masculine or feminine role.
5. Developing fundamental skills in reading, writing, and calculating.
6. Developing concepts necessary for everyday living.
7. Developing conscience, morality, and a scale of values.
8. Achieving personal independence.
9. Developing attitudes toward social groups and institutions.

Developmental Tasks and the School

To the school has been entrusted the tasks involving the mental skills — the three R's. But today the school becomes a place where boys and girls can learn many other skills — social, moral, and economic. There is no task which has been mentioned that the school can completely ignore. They are all interrelated. Failure in one may lead to failure in another task.

Transition from Home to School

It is easy to forget that "Six" has to adjust to two worlds — the world of home and the world of school. His emotional anchorage remains in the home, but he has to acquire a modified set of emotional moorings in school. Ordinarily this adjustment is not too difficult to make, though many children suffer gastrointestinal symptoms and severe emotional reactions at first. If the parents have wisely prepared the child for his entrance into school, and the teacher is an understanding, likeable person, the child of six soon comes to enjoy this new world. Pleasant and cheerful school atmosphere also helps to relieve the first-days-of-school tensions.

In general, the child who is well-developed physically, who has had good care and nutrition, and who has been given books and kindergarten materials to work with, comes to school prepared to do first grade work. If he is well past six, we find that he has a great advantage over those who have not even turned six until the deadline at the end of the calendar year.

The school room represents the tool and the technique by which our culture attempts to pattern these abounding energies of "Six." He feels the interrelationship of home and school. He brings many things to school: stuffed animals, bugs, shells, rocks, flowers, apples for the teacher. These are brought to show his classmates, or more especially his teacher. He also takes things home as well, such as his drawings, papers, and other school work. The thrill of the year comes which he takes home his first preprimer that he has mastered. It is to be hoped that his parents will not criticize any errors in his moment of triumph.

The wise teacher can create an atomosphere of tolerance and security which is hospitable to a certain dramatic quality in the six-year-old. What do we mean by this dramatic quality? Healthy "Six" is supple, sensitive, and alert. He reacts with his whole action-system. He uses his body to express emotions and ideas that are taking shape within him. Through an all-round program of music and creative rhythmic activities the child expresses himself.

The Role of the School in Developmental Progress of "Six"

Learning Activities

Often the six-year-old is referred to as being in the "I" period, an age in which the child thinks that he is the center of the universe. It is the egotistical period, exemplified by such outbursts as "I did this," "Look at me," etc. It is the age of constant chatter and self-expression and a stage where the star performer is himself. The program in first grade should capitalize on this, giving the child the opportunity to learn through his natural desire to express himself.

Healthy children of six are in constant motion and find it next to impossible to stand or sit still. They bounce when they sit, or scuffle their feet; run instead of walk. They jump puddles, pull, push, climb over everything. They love to move because it is fun. The activities best suited to this age are free and unorganized (as opposed to the more complicated "organized" games). When adults take the clue from the child there is little danger of his overdoing. Rhythms and spontaneous dances, directed by the child's activity needs, provide the opportunity for self-regulation. Not all can take the same amount.

Doing-learning

"Six" needs to use the large muscles which are better developed than the small muscles. In general, muscle development is uneven and incomplete, and the large muscles cry for action.

This need of the child for activity and expression can very well be an avenue for the building of concepts and vocabulary. When the six-year-old enters school he has a limited vocabulary, which increases with constant conversation about happenings of the moment, day, or week. Concepts of time, space, largeness, smallness, highness, lightness, and heaviness develop out of the child's own experiences. Such concepts cannot be acquired through mere verbal learning. Creative rhythmic movement is used as a medium of expression to help develop them.

Because children have vivid imaginations, they dramatize life around them. At times they may confuse imagination and memory, which to the adult seems to be falsehood. Six-year-olds like to dramatize, as evidenced in their own spontaneous play. A well-conceived, creative rhythms program can provide for all kinds of emotional outlets and dramatic interests. Transposing themselves into the heaviest, the biggest, the bumpiest things they can think of not only enhances their imaginations, but also expresses concepts.

The ordinary child of six is not immediately ready for purely formal instruction in reading, writing, and arithmetic. These subjects can be approached through "readiness" work, various activities which help prepare the child for the next step in education. Also, the subjects themselves can be vitalized only through association with creative activity and motorized life experiences.

The Arts

The creative activities touched upon above constitute a part of an all-round arts program. Closely allied and useful in these activities would be a varied music program. All the arts should be related at various points to the other arts. All the arts should be related to and integrated with all other subject matter. In a social studies unit on the farm, a mural as a class project can be done to give concrete ideas about the farm.

The graphic arts are a very useful technique for the development of many ideas. The child of six will draw his world as he sees it — not as the adult sees it. The sky is overhead. Do not argue if it is not connected to the earth. The ground is down below. Children know that the sky is up over the world with space between where birds fly. Consequently, he will invariably paint the sky in a blue band across the top edge of the paper. Children know, too, that the sun is in the sky, and they are fascinated by its warmth and brilliance. So we find a sun in nearly every child's drawing. The child can be encouraged to express his own feelings through art. This and the pure enjoyment of making something beautiful to look at may be the beginning, in the first grade, of a lifetime of pleasant activities.

Developing Fundamental Skills in Reading, Writing and Calculating

Biological Basis

The nervous system becomes mature enough and complex enough to permit the learning of reading, writing, and arithmetic during the early years of middle childhood. There is some evidence that the body is not biologically ready for handwriting before the sixth year. Many educators feel that the child should be at least six and one-half before attempting to teach him reading or writing. We know that the small muscles are as yet partially undeveloped. Writing at first should be large and at the blackboard, then on one-inch ruled paper so that the undeveloped finger muscles will not be required to do too fine work.

The eyes are not ready for reading until about six and one-half years also. That is, the fine coordination required of the eye muscles for moving rapidly over the page of print is achieved partly as a result of nerve and muscle growth. Furthermore, most children are naturally far-sighted in early childhood. They become normal-sighted and best adapted to reading at about eight years of age.

The findings concerned with biological maturation in the process of learning to read and write indicate that children are sometimes taught these skills before they are ready for them. We are still putting pressure on the child of six to learn these complex skills, however. It has been found that children learn rapidly and easily if allowed to wait until seven or even eight before starting.

Readiness

This is a term used in relation to all forms of school learning. In reading readiness a great many things are tied together. Physical readiness means that the eye can focus on the printed page. Mental readiness means that the child begins to understand that words mean something and are not just squiggles on paper. Emotional readiness means that the child has no fear of tackling the job. Readiness also involves a child's experience with things around him. Does he hear sounds around him? Does he see differences in shapes of things? Does he have a good vocabulary of words that he understands and uses? Has he been read to? Parents are usually advised not to try to teach reading at home, but there is a wealth of experience that the thoughtful parent can provide in this readiness.

In the field of arithmetic "Six" should be given endless experiences in handling and counting objects before he should be expected to understand what purely quantitative thinking means.

Achievements

The first grade teacher may sigh as she hands out the last report or letter to parents for the year, as she wonders just what has been accomplished for Johnnie or Mary. But she will take heart if she can turn back to those first drawing or writing papers. She should remember that even the slowest learner has probably picked up a great deal that will be a good foundation for the next year. The most alert children have learned to read a great many books and have acquired a great many skills over the year. Probably in no other school year will a child make such measurable strides as he will in his first year in school.

THE NORMAL SEVEN-YEAR-OLD

Profile

The seventh year is one of many changes. Understanding him is a challenge.

The child is quieter than at six; he has periods of calmness and self-absorption, and a tendency to sit and dream. He may sit and think, then have a sudden flash of understanding. He relates new experiences to old.

At seven, the child is more withdrawn and easier to live with than he was at six. He likes to be alone and have his own room and a place for his things. He is beginning to be aware of self and others and likes to please and do things for others at home.

"Seven" likes radio and television, almost as if he builds up his sense of self by watching and listening. He tends to stay on the edge of the scene.

The seven-year-old is a good listener; he likes to be read to and resents intrusions when he is reading or listening. He likes to bring things to a conclusion.

He is becoming aware of time, but needs and expects to be warned in advance.

At seven, the child's interest in the community is expanding. He tends to report behavior which is satisfying. He may draw something over and over with slight variations. He likes pencils; the sharp, defined stroke of lead is preferable to the loose stroke of crayon.

The seven-year-old often demands too much of himself and may be aware of a task, but unable to complete it. He needs to have stopping points defined, as he may go too long and become exhausted. He shows evidence of reasonableness and the ability to be critical. He takes time to think and is interested in conclusions.

Tantrums are vanishing. His mood changes from sweet-and-good to cross and tearful. He is more apt to complain about things than to rejoice. When playing, he may leave the scene muttering instead of staying and demanding his rights. His facial expression may mirror his dissatisfaction with life.

The seven-year-old has good and bad days and the wise mother keeps him in bed if his day starts badly. He has times when he feels everything is against him; people do not like him; they pick on him; other kids cheat; parents are unfair. He may threaten to run away, not wanting to be a member of the family. He thinks everybody mistreats him and typifies a "nobody loves me" attitude.

Parents should steer a delicate course between being sympathetic to his complaints and still not taking them too seriously. The teacher probably is not quite so bad, and the children do not cheat so much. Good days increase as he gets older. By the time he is eight he will be ready for almost anything.

It is important for all children of this age to have personal relationships with teacher. The wise teacher moves about the room quietly talking individually with each one.

A child of seven has an expanding interest in the community. He asks more questions now and wants proof; his skepticisms and questioning may be a sign that he is expressing a more realistic interest in religious matters. At six he was content to know God was in Heaven; now he wants to know how He got there.

Motor Characteristics

The seventh year is marked by slow, steady growth. The child grows two to three inches annually. He loses teeth; most "Sevens" have their six-year-old molars. Small muscles are better controlled. The eyes are not developed enough for much close work, but there is better eye-hand coordination.

The seven-year-old shows sudden spurts of active behavior. He exhibits extremes in indoor and outdoor play, sometimes tearing about, other times being content to sit and play cards or just stand around. He is more cautious in his approach to new performances, and has a new awareness of heights and is more cautious when he climbs a tree.

Carpentry is his favorite occupation. He favors sawing over hammering, liking the tug and pull of saw. His favorite posture is to lie prone on the floor, resting on one elbow while reading, etc. Frequently he drops his head on one arm as he writes or listens. He grasps the pencil tight when he works, but is apt to drop it often while working.

A child of seven is interested in comparative size, and his letters are becoming more uniform when he writes. In drawing, human figures are represented in a more accurate comparison than formerly.

He is still apt to touch and manipulate anything he sees.

Personal Hygiene

At seven, a child is less apt to finger feed himself but he still has difficulty getting some food on a fork or spoon without using his fingers. Some use a pusher or piece of toast, but most would rather use fingers. May express likes and dislikes of food, but not as strongly now. The seven-year-old conscientiously eats disliked foods, perhaps eating those first to make things easier. He does not dawdle as much while he eats. A friend waiting in the yard motivates him more strongly than anything else.

At this age, a child usually goes to bed between 7 P.M. and 8 P.M. Some go to bed by themselves, while others still need help with bathing. Some still hate baths, but the biggest problem is getting started. Once in a tub the child does not mind, although he needs to have someone check on his progress. He is usually good washing his face and hands before meals if reminded by mother.

The "Seven" might have difficulty going to sleep, he sings or talks to himself as though carrying on conversation between two people and may still want to take something to bed (gun or old panda). Usually he does not have to use the bathroom at night, but if he does he does not wake his parents.

There are fewer tensional outlets now; most of the old ones are overcome. Those who still suck their thumbs, bite their nails, or stutter are trying to control it. It is better for parents to set up a goal for successful control than to argue. Some blink their eyes or rub them, and some have a tendency to scowl. They show extreme fatigue, yawning, and stretching.

A seven-year-old has fewer illnesses than he had at six, but colds last longer. German measles and mumps are frequent; chicken pox and measles may occur. One hears complaints of knees or legs aching.

Dressing and Care of Clothes

The seven-year-old can dress without help if clothes are selected for him. He does not care if his shoelaces remain untied, although he can tie them. He may dawdle until he gets ready to dress, then dresses quickly.

Appearance varies. Some girls like to look neat and may be neater than they will be when they are eight. Some boys like to look sloppy. In general, the child is careless about tears in clothing; he drops them wherever he removes them. He is easily distracted while he is dressing.

Emotional Expression

A child of seven has a tendency to withdraw from situations. He is protective of self and puts his hands over his ears to keep out loud noises.

He lacks confidence to point of not wanting to try. When asked questions, he may reply, "I don't know," or "We haven't had that yet." When asked to do something, he may reply, "I'm too tired," or "I don't feel like it."

He may sulk or attack his mother, saying, "You're mean" when he gets into difficulty with her. He is more likely to rush off to his room and slam the door, and may threaten to run away and even go so far as to pack his bag. However, he usually does not go beyond the front door or a little way up the street.

If things do not go right when he is playing, the child of seven may prefer to play alone. He cries less than at six, but screeches more. He seems to shout his criticisms of life in general with his, "That's not fair!"

He sets goals which are too high for himself and brings home only his 100 papers. He does not take correction well and may say, "I was just going to," or "That's what I meant." He has trouble starting things, but does not know when to stop. He is conscientious and takes his responsibilities seriously. He feels a need to talk to someone and talks all day long. He persists in innumerable questions to support his thinking.

Fears and Dreams

At seven, the child's fears focalize upon himself and are somewhat protective. He hesitates before acting and does not like to experience new situations by himself. He may have worried all summer about starting second grade.

The seven-year-old may still want his parents to stay home at night, but can resign himself to their leaving. He is not so afraid of the dentist because he knows what he does and that he can lift his hand if something hurts.

Space and time take on new meaning. Cellars have strange creatures in them and attics are inhabited by ghosts. He thinks shadows are ghosts and witches. He is afraid of war, spies, and people hiding in closets or under beds. He is afraid of being late for school and not being liked. His fears are stimulated by reading, radio, television, and movies. Parents should respect his fears and should not make him afraid of them. The child who fears being late for school may never actually have been late.

The dreams of "Seven" are mostly about himself. He really enjoys himself as he swims along and flies through the air. He carries on long conversations showing he is involved. He needs to have movies and television supervised because some of them give him bad dreams.

Self and Sex

At seven, the child is aware of his body and sensitive about exposing it. He may refuse to go to the rest room at school if it does not have a door. Girls are sensitive about their hair and afraid they might not be recognized if braids were cut off. Boys begin to break away from mother's domination in refusing to wear raincoat, rubbers, and hats.

Pets help the seven-year-old to understand about sex. He is less likely now to be involved in sex play and may not want to undress or go to the bathroom if a younger sibling of opposite sex is near.

At seven, the child experiences an intense longing for a new baby in the family, and he knows older women do not have babies. He is satisfied to know that a baby comes from two seeds; one from mother and one from father. He associates the size of pregnant women with the presence of a baby and is interested in his mother's pregnancy and books about babies. He wants to know how baby is fed, and how big it is.

Boy-girl pairs are fairly common at school. The child may become involved in an elementary love affair, and boys able to write may write love notes.

Interpersonal Relations

A child of seven is becoming a real member of the family group. He is ready to assume some household responsibilities and may do such routine chores as making his bed, and emptying wastebaskets or garbage pails. Help is sometimes spotty because he tires of one task and wants to change to another.

He behaves better than he did at six; his chief trouble occurs when he is interrupted at something he is doing.

The seven-year-old gets along well with his mother and also with his father. Girls may be jealous of attention their father shows their mother. Some "Sevens" have difficulty adjusting to the home situation and may even feel they are adopted.

The child is inclined to be jealous of a sibling and feels that he may have more privileges. Much bickering occurs. Gesell (84) says to let one child divide the play items; then let the other child choose which he wants.

At seven, the child does not demand companionship as he did at six. He spends lots of time by himself writing lists of things or other solitary play. As a rule he plays well with playmates his own age. Sex lines are not clearly drawn, but some discrimination against the opposite sex is beginning to appear. Boys cannot be bothered with girls, and girls do not think boys are very well-behaved. Both are becoming more adept at meeting strangers, and they like to go visiting.

Play and Pastimes

The seven-year-old is inclined to be obsessive in his play interests. He seems to have a mania for guns, funny books, and coloring. He goes as far as he can in buying, reading, and collecting and bartering comics. His favorites are generally adventures of superman or daily adventures of ordinary people. Some prefer more violent type of comics. It is best for parents to regulate purchases instead of prohibiting them.

Many are fair readers, they can get the sense of a story without knowing all the words.

Magic and tricks are favorites.

Some want to take music lessons. They enjoy playing simple tunes on the piano. It is best to wait for violin lessons, as wrist muscles and bones are not fully developed.

School Life

The child who enters first grade too young may have difficulties in second grade. Parents may feel the teacher is at fault when actually the tasks are too difficult for him. His unreadiness and immaturity show up. More is demanded of him at this level than last year. Many spend the previous summer worrying that the second grade will be too hard.

When school starts, he is constantly afraid of being late. Mother can make all preparations, give warnings, and time signals; then she should leave things up to him. Usually he dawdles until the last three minutes, then dresses like a "blitz." There are two extremes: those who worry excessively and those who dawdle about school.

At seven, the student is not as belligerently uncooperative as he was at six, but he does not respond promptly. It may be that there are some sounds he does not hear. His hearing acuity is not fully developed. He may hear directions, but forget what you told him, or he may start to obey, then become detoured along the way.

The seven-year-old likes school and his teacher, but still has to see how far her authority extends at times. He is more dependent on her now. He needs her moral support and questions her constantly, "Shall I start now?" "How far do we go?" "Am I supposed to begin on the top line?"

The teacher is the most important aspect of school. Her appearance is important to the child. Many boys fall in love with her and may act silly and embarassed toward her. The experienced teacher should be aware of the reason. He likes to take gifts and have her notice him.

The personal relationship with the teacher is important. She should be a person who really likes children. This is the age of strong emotional response to a teacher. At six school was a big wonderful experience. This year the important part is the child's relationship with his teacher. Many girls are antagonistic and might get along better with a man teacher.

Nervous habits, such as nail-biting, tongue-sucking, scratching, and pulling at his ears, are common when he works. He still uses large pencils and crayons when working and seems to feel a constant need to erase. He may appropriate pencils and erasers, minor pilferings are common, especially in second grade. Prevention is better than scolding.

There may be marked differences in individual reading differences. The student enjoys looking up familiar words in a child's dictionary. He grips pencils tightly close to the point. Pressure varies, but is apt to be heavy.

The seven-year-old needs to have classroom routine varied. It is difficult for him to sit still for long. He also needs adult approval and is very sensitive to the feelings and attitudes of his peers.

At seven years, the child is interested in what subject follows what in school. He can tell what time it is, also how many minutes past, or of, the hour it is. If asked, "What is time?" he answers, "Time is to be ready for school."

He is not good about taking blame for things he does. Characteristic alibis are, "He did it," and "It was his fault." He exaggerates; he may fight with words rather than blows. Learning is best when he can move around. He is anxious to do well and is self-critical. He likes to do things with his hands.

Special Needs

The seven-year-old needs to be independent and yet have adult support. He does not trust himself yet, but may be rebellious at over-control. The learning situation should include concrete objects. He needs an adult to help him adjust to the playground routine, as he is apt to become too rough. We need to be aware of his tempo and give him time to finish his task.

The seventh year is a transition stage for a child. It is easier for him to make up his mind now. He can make simple choices and decisions, especially if both alternatives are appealing to him. It is still hard to change his mind. Occasionally he will listen to reason and change his mind without displaying his temper.

TYPICAL BEHAVIOR PATTERNS OF MENTALLY RETARDED CHILDREN

Teachers searching for a general understanding of the personality and behavior of mentally retarded children are continually watching for specific behavior patterns or ways of adjusting which are typical to them as a group. However, it is unwise to make generalizations about people, because each person, whether mentally retarded or not, has unique characteristics and is essentially different from every other person.

Effect of Low Intelligence

The low intelligence of the retarded provides a basis for some conclusions about the general behavior of this group. For example, they have difficulty in understanding how their present behavior may affect the future, i.e. they lack the ability to forsee the consequences of present behavior. Limited capacity to evaluate and accept their own limitations is another characteristic which seems to be typical of the retarded. They experience difficulty in understanding themselves, in solving problems, in perception of their environment, and in their awareness of why and how things happen. This is in contrast to the normal child's ability to accept what happens because he has some idea of why it happens, and often he can even predict that it will happen.

Emotional Immaturity

Retarded children often express emotions outwardly, dramatically, and very suddenly. They seem to establish emotional attachments quickly, but they are often rather superficial. Their response to social situations may be very similar to that of a child much younger than their own chronological age because of immature personality development. They are direct, forceful, and somewhat demanding in forming emotional attachments. Their demands are often self-centered. Even though emotional responses are quickly aroused in retarded children, usually they are just as quickly resolved. It is essential, therefore, that the teacher use good judgment and not be too hasty to take disciplinary action. She should be very careful not to misinterpret the emotional outbursts of retarded children. She must establish a good working relationship with them by building feelings of confidence and trust.

Dependency

Retarded children as a group are usually described as over-dependent. They depend greatly upon the judgment of the teacher or other adults or the peers in their environment. Often they rely completely upon the decision-making of the teacher and feel very insecure if they are asked to make a decision on their own. It is easy for the teacher to fall into the habit of making all the decisions. She may tend to foster the over-dependence which has developed, and this interferes with the mental health and social development of the child. The retarded child, like the normal child, must acquire the general ability to cope with problems and social situations. To accomplish this he should learn to face, to some extent, the consequences of competition and stress and accept the fact that the world is not always just as he would like it.

Fixed Behavior

The retarded are prone to stereotyped, or rigid, ways of behaving. They seem to be less capable of adjusting to a variation of daily needs or to changes in the environment. They tend to rely on habitual modes of behavior even though the behavior is not appropriate to the situation. Retarded children have a strong need to compensate for their own inability to cope with stressful or problem situations. Usually they can see no way of resolving or solving their problems and this creates feelings of insecurity.

Friendliness

Mentally retarded children as a group are very friendly and trusting. It is very important for them to feel loved, accepted, and trusted, and to feel that people care for them. They have an almost continuous need for reassurance because they are not very sure of themselves. Through reassurance they are able to maintain confidence in their own behavior since it is consistently checked by the reaction of people around them.

It is not unusual for the teacher to be over-protective of the child, to provide a safe, secure environment for him. However, the teacher must help the child to become as self-sustaining as possible, in terms of psychological and social needs, and help him to learn to accept failures as a part of every day life.

In summary, we must remember that the trainable child comes to the classroom with his own capacity for growth in an education program. Just like any other child, he is an integration of biology and culture shaped by people and events. He is what he is because of developmental factors determined by a combination of genes, prenatal and postnatal environment, and learning factors — the ability to use his limited intellectual capacities to learn from experiences.

This child has the same need to be loved and wanted that the normal child has. He needs to relate to others. He needs to feel secure. He needs to be creative and active. The teacher must be aware of the innate needs in order to plan meaningful experiences for the individual child.

Children who are classified as trainable retarded develop so slowly that they cannot profit from curriculum designed to meet the needs of the educable retarded. However, their potentialities indicate that they should not be confined to a custodial situation. In varying degrees these children are capable of learning the following: to communicate; to get along in the family and community; to share and respect the property of others; to become independent of their parents in self-care, health habits, and safety; to help with simple household tasks; to participate in routine work of sheltered environment. We must realize that they will require supervision, care, and economic support throughout their lives.

Like the normal child, they will also develop behavior patterns. They will grow physically if given the proper diet; become aggressive, hostile, or withdrawn when they are unable or not allowed to express themselves; react to people in varying ways; attach odd and unrealistic meanings to experiences that are beyond their comprehension. Usually their physical and emotional development is much faster than their intellectual development.

Teachers of the trainable retarded have pointed out that physical movement and sound production are the personal mannerisms that characterized the behavior of the children they have taught. Their need for movement indicates an effort to release both physical and emotional tensions. Two kinds of vocal production mentioned by teachers were self-produced sounds (screaming and guttural noises) and verbal activities. This is their endeavor to communicate, the sounds being the earlier stage and later followed by verbal activity.

These children will be considered socially adjusted when they can do the following: get along with other people, practice good work habits; follow simple directions; properly groom themselves; practice some degree of self-control; be trusted; attain personal adequacy in self-care; follow safety rules. To achieve these goals they must be able to communicate. This is the immense task — *teachers* — you assume when the trainable retarded enter school.

III

LEARNING PHENOMENA IN CHILDREN

THE LEARNING PROCESS

I T is the contention of many authorities that principles governing the learning process in the normal child apply to the retarded. Conceived of in its broadest aspect, learning may be thought of as a dynamic process whereby the continuous interaction between the organism and environment produces growth and development of the total personality. Further, learning may also be thought of as a continuous process of adjustment on the part of the individual in his environment. It takes place, in all persons, in the same way, regardless of differing rates of learning ability. To many of us, learning means that the person is finding and establishing new or better ways of responding or behaving in situations. In any situation there is present the individual and his need as a learner and the environment which provides the means for learning. Learning may be incidental, as for example, when the young child babbles, without consciously defining his need, or it may be planned; as the child grows older, the adults at home and at school are constantly guiding him in situations where his need is consciously formulated, thus directing the course that his learning takes.

For the present purpose, the learning process for the child of school age may be as follows: First, he realizes a need for adjustment to his present environment; the condition of awareness in the learner is a vital part of the learning process. This need directs him as he responds. Second, as he progresses, consciousness of success makes him more aware of his objective, guiding his progress toward it. Third, there must be a sufficient recurrence of situations for the new behavior to become a part of him.

The slower the child, the less he learns incidentally on his own, and the more teaching and direction he needs. Systematic step-by-step instruction is necessary for him. He learns to perceive and to acquire communication through directed experiences with the concrete. He needs specific instruction in transfer of training. He learns to generalize from many concrete specific experiences where the same concepts and skills are needed over and over. He needs recognition for his achievements so that he may develop a feeling of success.

LEARNING CHARACTERISTICS OF THE RETARDED

Some personality theorists maintain that learning is important, but they also disagree as to its relation to other determinants of behavior. For example, Freud, tended to place little significance on learning and greater significance on biologic factors. Gestalt psychologists have emphasized innate structures of the central nervous system; learning and experience are of major importance in the physiological theory of D. O. Hebb (101). Even the theorists who emphasize the role of learning in personality development seem to overlook the essentials of the actual learning process.

In contrast, many psychologists have devoted themselves mainly to exploring the characteristics of the learning process. They have evolved comprehensive theories of learning. There is both agreement and disagreement among the psychologists who have proposed theories to explain the manner in which organisms learn. Even the agreed-upon aspects of learning have been recognized only recently to have implications necessary for an understanding of mental retardation. The inclusion of retarded children in laboratory learning studies is a relatively late development.

We are now aware that there is no simple relationship between learning ability and age — chronological age or mental age, which is calculated by the results of a standardized intelligence test. However, we do admit that mental age is probably the single best clue to a child's ability to master cognitive learning tasks, but there are significant differences in learning ability among individuals whose mental ages are the same but whose chronological ages are not.

In the past few years, clinical psychologists who are interested in learning theory have conducted many studies of the learning process; some involved retarded children. Through these studies advances have been made toward understanding their learning behavior, but no clear-cut picture of their learning capacities and learning deficits has emerged.

Perhaps the reason for this is that the psychologists may have been more interested in the learning process than in the nature of the individual who was learning. But the evidence accumulated about the learning behavior of retarded children indicates that the general laws of learning apply to them as well as to other organisms.

At this time, it would seem appropriate to point out that there are still relatively few studies which deal specifically with how retarded children learn. Any report on how they learn must depend in part upon what is known about how children learn generally.

Perhaps, we should consider some of the very early studies of the learning of the retarded which continue to influence teaching theories and procedures. For example, on the basis of her own work, Hollingsworth (109) concluded that the rate of learning of retarded children is most nearly like the rate of learning of normal children of the same mental age, and this has had great affect on experimentation and practice. But we must remember that the rate of mental growth of normal children is faster than that of dull or retarded children. Even if a borderline retarded (dull normal) child started regular class in the beginning of the school term with a group of normal children, whose average mental age matched his, he would have fallen behind by the end of the term because his mental age would then be lower than the average mental age of the group that he started with. On the other hand, if he was placed in special class, his rate of mental growth would more nearly match that of the others in his group. This has been one of the principal reasons for special classes. This observation is even more significant for the trainable retarded. Most of the studies seem to conclude that, at any given moment and over a very brief timespan, retarded children learn about as well as other children of the same mental age. The greater part of the educational problem with the severely retarded, therefore, is the very low mental ages they show.

Mental Maturation

McPherson (150) pointed out an aspect of learning often overlooked, namely, that a minimum age may be necessary for successful learning of a given task. Both teachers and parents should consider this before presenting some tasks to children. Pascal (158) suggests that at lower mental ages, delay between assignment and performance of the task by the child makes for inefficient learning.

Variability

McPherson (150) also found evidence to indicate that there is a greater variability and inconsistency in the learning process of the retarded than in that of the normal. The teacher of the trainable retarded may expect to find a great deal of variability of this type in performance of these children.

Transfer

The ability to transfer the results of learning from one situation to another has often been considered to require a high level mental age. Therefore, it has sometimes been assumed that the retarded would show little or no transfer and they should be taught everything quite specifically. Hollingsworth (109) was among the first to report evidence of transfer of training in the retarded, but her findings have been confirmed by others.

Barnett and Canter (8) have demonstrated transfer in a simple discrimination task in a group whose mean Stanford Binet IQ was 42. Transfer occurred at levels both above and below an M.A. of six years three months. Cruickshank and Blake (49) have also studied the problem of transfer with positive results.

It would appear, therefore, that the existence of transfer, at simple levels, has been demonstrated in the learning of the retarded. Our major concern at this time seems to be the mental ages and level of complexity at which transfer is possible.

The teacher may assume transfer at simple levels, but must watch carefully for the possible breakdown at more complex levels. When transfer breakdown occurs, the teacher must supplement the learning situation with more specific teaching.

Attention

Woodrow (216) early presented evidence of deficiency in the power of sustained attention in the retarded. Others have also concluded that the retarded were inferior to normal children in this respect. However, it is very possible that the power of attention is not a simple ability, but is dependent to a considerable extent on contributing factors, such as motivation and interest of the materials, distractions in the environment, etc. The studies of the severely retarded by Gordon, O'Connor, and Tizard (90) suggest that, under favorable circumstances, the severely retarded can sustain attention for limited lengthy periods of time.

Self-Criticism

The inability to judge the quality of one's own product has been considered a characteristic of the retarded, since the time of Binet. Several experimental studies have supported this view. According to Herrick (102), it appears that the inability may be a deterrent to learning in this group. The teacher of the retarded should be aware of this and assist her students in evaluating their accomplishments.

Reasoning

Since the time of Binet, lowered reasoning ability also has been frequently mentioned as a special defect of the retarded. Data to support this view has been presented by Fox (74). This is not a simple problem because much may depend on the complexity and abstractness of the reasoning required.

Some of the more recent studies tend to agree with the findings of some earlier studies.

For example, Cowley (42) found that there is no significant difference between the productive thinking abilities of retarded and nonretarded children of equal mental age. According to Jones and Benton (127), the simple reaction times to both auditory and visual stimuli were measured for normal and educable retarded children. The results of groups of subjects matched for C.A. showed that the normals responded more quickly than the retardates under all conditions. When the results of groups differing in C.A. but matched for M.A. were compared, there were no significant differences between the normals and retardates.

Lunzer and Hulme (147) studied discrimination learning and discrimination learning sets in subnormal children and concluded that their ability to learn visual discrimination and to form a discrimination set was not significantly different from that of normal preschool children when matched for M.A.

Milgram and Furth (153) conducted a study involving 180 normal children who were evenly divided into two age groups with a mean C.A. of 6.3 and 9.4 years, respectively, and 112 retarded children with M.A. of either 6 or 9 years. The concept to be attained was part-whole, the notion that "A is part of B." Their findings indicate that age level (C.A. for normal and M.A. for retardates) is the most important single factor in enhancing conceptual control.

According to Richard and Rosenburg (171) the effects of exposure time and matrix size upon the errors and the search time was evaluated with sixty-four high level retarded subjects (C.A. 12-24 years). Two exposure times, four and twelve seconds, and two matrix sizes, sixteen and thirty-six items, were used. The subjects spent more time and made more errors when searching the thirty-six-item matrix. An increase in exposure time from four to twelve seconds brought about an increase in search time, although no effect on errors was noted. No interactions were found, and there was a significant negative correlation ($-.347$) between C.A. and errors.

Stinnett and Prehm (192) studied the rote learning and retention performance of sixty retarded and sixty nonretarded children who were randomly assigned to one of three treatment groups in order to learn a paired-associate task. Retention was assessed by immediate recall scores and twenty-four-hour recall and relearning scores. Data analysis indicated (a) inferior learning performance for retarded subjects, and (b) a twenty-four-hour retention deficit for retarded subjects. The analysis further indicated that learning method strongly influences the results of comparisons of rote learning and retention in retarded and nonretarded subjects.

Berkson and Baumeister (17) found that in addition to being slower than normal in reaction time tasks, a mentally deficient group was more variable. Apparently many deficient individuals do not work close to their limit of speed.

Ellis (64) and others conducted a study in which three ability level (IQ) groups of retardates were compared on a probe-type short-term memory task using high-meaningful (pictures of common objects) and low-meaningful (nonsense shapes) stimuli. In group I, the IQ's (Wechsler and Binet) ranged from 28 to 37, and C.A.'s from seventeen to twenty-five years. In group II,

IQ's ranged from 51-61, and C.A.'s, from eighteen to twenty-three years. For Group III, the IQ range was 66 to 78, and C.A.'s ranged from seventeen to twenty-five years. Both sexes were included, and subjects were selected without regard for clinical type, though mongoloids were excluded. They concluded that the retarded do not process information in an adequate manner, but the more intelligent subjects stored more information in secondary memory than did the less intelligent.

Research in learning and retention by Vergason (206) indicates that the memory of the mentally retarded child can be improved by pretraining, motivation, mediation (word-association), teacher usage of attention-holding audiovisual equipment, and clear frequent repetition of instructions. When materials are meaningful and overlearned, the mentally retarded demonstrate long-term memory equal to that of normal children.

Both early and present day teachers of the trainable retarded also stress the following:

Motivation (Drive)

It is generally agreed that back of all learning we find motivation. When the trainable retarded child comes to school there are certain primary motives that can be appealed to: the need for security, the desire to be accepted and to belong, the desire for self-direction, the urge for activity, etc. The skillful teacher encourages growth toward more complex motives, to behave like others, to be neat and orderly, and to identify with the group.

Objectives

Effective learning is objective-oriented. A child learns better when he has some objective (purpose or goal) which is clearly identified, understood, and accepted by him. The objective may be very simple: learning how to tie a shoe by himself or put away toys. The important thing for the teacher to keep in mind is that the child must have some idea of the objective to be accomplished and have the desire to reach it, as well as the means by which the objective may be realized. Objectives will tend to be rather immediate, as far as these children are concerned. The long-range objectives will be primarily in the mind of the teacher. Always keeping long-range objectives in mind, the teacher may be able to bring each child from an immediate objective to another related one which will, in turn, present a new challenge to him. "Now, you have learned to button your shirt so well; wouldn't you like to learn how to tie your shoes, too?"

Comprehension

Effective learning requires some understanding on the part of the child.

One common cause of failure to learn is the fact that the child had no real comprehension of what he was trying to do. The teacher must check comprehension, in addition to motivation and objectives.

Extinction

Some undesirable behaviors will need to be eliminated. In educational psychology, this is called *extinction.* Generally the stronger the old drives and habits, the slower the extinction process. For example, the child who has long been dependent will take longer to learn independence. Praise and reward hasten the process, and practice without reinforcement will lead to extinction of the old undesirable habits. In other words, if the child has been too dependent, ties his shoe alone several times without someone instantly going to aid him a step has been taken toward extinction of his habit of dependency.

Practice

Practice is necessary for retention. It must be active; the child should actually do what he is learning. Practice periods must be not too long, but the intervals between practice periods should also be short. The longer the interval between practices, the less efficient the learning is.

With the trainable retarded, it is usually helpful to break down complex skills into simpler units for effective learning. The teacher should not attempt complex learnings with these children. It leads only to frustration on the part of teacher and child. Generally, the MA and IQ are useful guides to the level of difficulty for which the child is ready.

Home Training

The severely retarded child usually enters school later than the average child and may be more fixed in particular ways of doing things that he has been taught in his own home. Some children have been trained firmly in matters of discipline and conduct, while others have recieved little or no training. This creates the need for the teacher to know and understand the family's attitude toward and methods of dealing with the child. The teacher must watch for emotional blocks to learning resulting from such practices.

Readiness

The children in the trainable group may also have different stages of readiness. Some will be young, without previous school experience; others will be older in chronological age, with previous school experiences. Some will be in the adolescent age range, nearing the end of the school-age period. Another aspect of readiness to be considered is the fact that, as a group, they will probably not have experienced community contacts that average children have. The teacher must consider this in planning curriculum and in introducing the children to group experiences.

Evaluation

There are many factors which make continuous study of each child desirable. Often inaccuracies appear in the first test, so later testing is desirable. Intellectual evaluation alone is not sufficient; the children must be evaluated on other criteria, such as social adjustment, motor development, and so on. There will be many gradations on each criterion of development. Some children may fail to adjust to their initial placement or their growth rate may be faster than that which was predicted. If the child's major complicating factor is instability, his general efficiency level may change as he becomes more stable.

Many school systems anticipate these changes and provide for them through a regular trial placement period for each child, followed by reevaluation and placement after his school adjustment in the school situation has been observed for a period of time.

At present if we should make any generalization regarding the learning of the trainable retarded, it would be that they differ from other children more in the level of difficulty or complexity of the tasks which are possible for them to learn. This also seems to correspond somewhat to their mental age at any given time. This does not imply that they will be best taught by the same methods used for normal children. Methods used with normal children often involve a "telescoping" of the learning process not appropriate for the trainable. For example, reduced capacity to transfer means that less can be left to incidental learning or nonspecific teaching; a particular disability in language, may require specified individualized attention to deal with verbal methods and abstractions.

BASIC FACTORS IN LEARNING

Most appear to agree that retarded children fundamentally differ from normal children of the same chronological age in their ability to acquire knowledge and skills. In this area they are slower and more inefficient, but we need to determine whether retarded children are slow to learn in all types of situations or whether their handicaps are worse in some areas than in others. We must also examine their ability to function under various conditions. We must know what conditions are conducive to and which interfere with learning. We should discover the length of their attention span and when it is inadequate apply remedial techniques.

The other aspects of the learning process which interfere with efficient learning are inability to retain knowledge, response to certain stimuli and indifference to other, failure to discriminate between different cues, and the need to respond on a sensorimotor basis because of difficulty to verbalize responses.

Before theorizing about the learning process in retarded children, perhaps we should acquire a basic understanding of the factors involved in learning per se. They accompany all kinds of learning and constitute the bare bones framework of the learning process. They are equally applicable to the earthworm and the doctoral candidate. According to most psychologists there are at least such basic factors: drive, cue, response, and reinforcement.

Drive (motive) is the state of tension that takes place within an organism when a need initiates an active period of restless seeking. For example, the drive (hunger) causes the organism to seek food; this leads eventually to eating and end of search. Many theorists have proposed that all drives arise from some sort of disturbance of inner equilibrium and the need to remove such disturbance.

Cue (signal) is the stimulus which guides the organisms response. A newborn baby makes sucking movements whenever certain regions around his mouth are stimulated whether or not he is hungry; the older baby sucks only when he feels something in his mouth and he is hungry. Before learning can take place the organism must respond physiologically to internal and external cues. Any child whose central nervous system has been damaged usually has problems in responding to appropriate cues.

Response (reaction or behavior) is the reaction elicited by a stimulus. Before learning can take place the essential elements of the correct response must occur. Responses are usually modified in the learning process, but the basic elements must be present before new responses can be acquired. As children increase in age so does their thinking ability increase and their responses become complex and symbolic. Therefore, we would expect the responses of the slow-maturing child to be limited in scope and complexity. We cannot teach the retarded twelve-year-old with a MA of eight years to behave like a normal twelve-year-old. A more logical objective is to expect that he may be capable of responding as an eight-year-old. A given degree of maturation is required for all children to perform certain tasks. The retarded child's ability to form complex patterns may remain absent until he is older.

Reinforcement (reward) is the strengthening of a response by the addition of another stimulus, as a reward. The principle of reinforcement has it that rewarded responses are stamped in while unrewarded responses are not learned or tend to fade when reinforcement is withdrawn. Just as drives, cues, and responses may be learned, so reinforcing stimuli may also be learned. A hungry animal placed at the entrance to a maze must learn to avoid blind alleys that do not lead to the food placed at the end of the maze. At first, all alleys are entered by chance. During a course of trial runs, the subject comes to make the correct turns more surely and to avoid dead ends. At last it learns to run through the maze more rapidly without error. The hungry newborn infant will stop crying only if he is fed. The hungry older child will be comforted by responses associated with eating, such as the sight of his mother preparing his plate. However, for a response to be learned, reinforcement need not occur every time it is made. But the principle holds for a wide variety of situations and has a major bearing on the effectiveness of learning in life situations. Parents and teachers, who invest themselves in the learning of others, are in many respects managers of reinforcement, and their skill as manager has a good deal of consequence for their children and students.

KINDS OF LEARNING

Psychologists do not agree on whether all learning follows the same laws or whether there are various kinds of learning which differ from each other basically. For example, the "stimulus-reponse" psychologists (54) maintain that automatic learning (habit formation) and insightful learning (cognitive learning, the development of understanding or insight) takes place in like manner. They suggest that the same set of concepts apply to learning at the habit level (such as brushing teeth after meals) and at the level involving thoughtful mental processes (putting together a jig saw puzzle). They resolve the seeming difference by calling attention to the role of "cue-producing responses" which function as a mediator, one response becoming a cue for the next response and etc.

Some psychologists (86) suggest that higher learning involves not only acquiring responses but the learning of cognitive structures. They contend that abstract patterns, ideas, and concepts cannot be derived from stimulus-response learning. This contention is supported by evidence gathered from maze-learning experiments with rats. Rats seem to develop a cognitive map of their experimental environment (cage or room) which enables them to find the food box regardless of where it has been placed in relation to the food. If learned responses control behavior, the rats should make the same left and right turns regardless of where it starts in the maze; if a cognitive structure controls behavior, it should adjust to responses to suit the situation.

Another point of disagreement concerns the possible distinction between the learning of instrumental responses and that of classical conditioned responses. In instrumental conditioning the reinforcement is dependent upon the subject's response. Reinforcement may be either positive or negative. For example, the student using a specially designed electrical board to do arithmetic will be rewarded by the appearance of the solution in colored lights and the ringing of a bell if he has pushed the correct buttons. If he pushes the wrong buttons, nothing happens. Classical conditioning is concerned with responses which are worked automatically by one (un-conditioned) stimulus just after the presentation of another (conditioned) stimulus. Pavlov's (160) experiments with dogs is an illustration.

Other psychologists (184) have argued about whether different principles are involved in the two learning examples, and if so, what roles do they play in human behavior. However, more recently they tend to adopt a sort of in-between or middle-of-the-road view.

ACQUIRING SKILLS

Skills that children acquire in the formal setting of a school should be widely viewed as skills which will enable them to deal creatively with the purposes and problems of living. Even, today not all educators or parents are fully aware of the nature and objectives of the skills that precede formal instruction. Orderly developmental patterns in motor, self-help, social, and academic skills can be traced to the many specific subskills that are the product of the interaction of maturation and learning. Some patterns seem to be influenced more by one than by the other. In phylogenic skills such as visual or auditory discrimination, we find the influence of maturation of sensory apparatus and the neural controls essential before learning can take place. In the ontogenetic skills such as reading, spelling, and arithmetic, we recognize the importance of experience and practice.

The development and growth of academic skills are dependent on the integrity and functioning of the child's sensory equipment. The child is made aware of the world about him through the senses of touch, taste, smell, hearing, and sight. Even though, it is generally agreed that the neural mechanisms involved in the use of the senses are ready to and are functioning to some degree in the late fetal period, infants do not have equal use of all senses. Of all the senses, touch seems to be the most highly developed at birth; the sense of hearing is present, but reaction to complex sounds and pitch discrimination is lacking; the sense of sight seems to be the least perfect of all because the muscular mechanisms which control the eyes require time to develop, and the optic nerve tracts and visual areas of the cortex are not completely formed.

The child cannot learn by sensation alone. It is doubtful whether raw, uninterpreted sensations every really exist beyond the first few hours or days of life. The human mind is so fertile that there seems to be an immediate psychological interpretation of the meaning of sensation. The term "perception" is used to describe the process by which sensations are given psychological meaning. It is an active process by which the individual constructs the world out of his sensory processes. The child's early perceptions may be weak or faulty, but the essential characteristics of learning is the constant modification and enrichment of percepts.

The child learns to perceive, and the process is developmental. Perceptions are not received ready-made, nor are they fixed and immutable. They grow and change with experience. Like other skills that the child learns, they become more accurate and precise by eliminating superfluous adjuncts, by reducing the cues necessary for meaning, and by organizing isolated activities into meaningful wholes. In the motor skills, increased skill is attained by repeating a performance, so skill in perception is increased by repeatedly perceiving.

As the child grows he is exposed to an ever expanding world from which he receives a continuous flow of stimuli. To deal effectively with this mass of external and internal sensations some selective process must be put to work. Thus, the child, consciously or unconsciously, chooses to respond to some and to neglect others. He cannot, nor does he attempt to, respond to all. This screening process, which we call "attention," is tempered primarily by the state of the psychological mechanism available to the child. This includes the state of cerebral growth at which he has arrived, his inborn pre-dispositions that are part of his biologic heritage, the muscular controls that he possesses, and the level of the sensory thresholds that he has attained. The child's needs and their gratification also play an important role in the selection of stimuli. There are relatively few needs present at birth, but the child's needs gradually expand, the secondary and tertiary ones appear. The expansion of needs is dependent on the experiences to which the child is exposed. In addition to these determiners of attention, the selective process is also affected by the motive or character of the sensation. Intensity, duration, novelty, recurrence, size, and clearness may by themselves determine whether the child will or will not respond to a stimulus.

Learning requires more than sensation, perception, and attention. Memory, association, and imagery are fundamental to this process. It appears that these processes exist in animals as well as in human beings, but in many, they have been brought to a maximum perfection. Many would be seriously handicapped in solving his daily problems or in living a creative life if he were always dependent on bare stimuli alone. Through memory he is able to rehearse events and scenes without the original stimuli and of associating immediate sensations with objects formerly perceived. Memory enables him to link perceptions together and to call up images and ideas without any apparent sensory stimulation. It makes verbal and written language possible, since a symbol (word) allows an individual to recall from memory a clear picture of an experienced event.

After careful consideration of the elements involved in acquiring phylogenic and ontogenic skills, we are better able to understand why the trainable usually profit little from formal schooling. We can immediately see that they are not able to do regular classwork because they are incapable of learning academic skills, such as reading and arithmetic, beyond the learning of some words and simple numbers. Skills are acquired through practice with progress from gross accomplishment to more refined adeptness. This is especially true in the case of muscular development and also is applicable to oral language and writing, and to personal and social adjustment.

All aspects of training must be meaningful to these children at home, at school, and in the community. The teacher must concern herself with each pupil on an individual basis in regards to his chronological age, mental age, emotional stability, organic impairment, and family attitudes.

COMPARISON OF LEARNING IN RETARDED AND NORMAL CHILDREN

Any account of problem-solving that fails to consider the similarities between the thinking of normals and most retardates would be incomplete. On the other hand, it is certainly true that any account of problem solving that did not go on from trial-and-error thinking to intelligent and purposeful reasoning would be even more incomplete.

A comparison of the learning ability of normal and retarded children as found by the writer points out the clear superiority of normal children. The main differences may be summarized as follows:

1. Normal children are more readily motivated toward a specific task. They respond to a wider range of incentives.
2. Normal children have better control of their emotions. They are less likely to become confused. They use more deliberation and management in attacking a problem.
3. Normal children are better observers. They see many characteristics of things, people, and situations that lie beyond the retardates perceptive scope. The normal child is more likely to see relevant associations, and to discriminate between parts of a whole.
4. Normal children are more adept in use of symbols — language, numbers, maps, models — they are better able to weigh alternatives verbally without having to go through actual physical movements. All four differences noted above enable normal children to learn more rapidly than retarded children. The last two are rather more important, in that they open up the opportunity to solve problems by the method of reasoning. Retarded children are deficient in ability to reason.

IV

DISCIPLINE FOR THE TRAINABLE CHILD

THE retarded child, like all children, may show undesirable behavior of various kinds. There are many different causes for the way he acts, and often it requires the help of an expert in understanding and handling the child's behavior.

Ask any classroom teacher of normal or exceptional children what her biggest problem with students is, and she will tell you that discipline is the major problem. Furthermore, they will add that getting achievement from children is a big task.

Teachers have informed the writer that much of their time must be spent to minimize noise, to get the children to settle down, to repeat assignments, to get attention, and to stop squabbling. Some feel they spend more time scolding their students than they do in teaching. Not because they want to, but because it seems to be necessary. Many dedicated, sincere, pleasant, and interesting teachers are worn to a frazzle when the day is over.

The problem? Discipline. The answer? Better discipline. With better discipline comes increased achievement and better mental health of students and teachers.

What is discipline? The writer agrees with Louis La Grand's (141) definition of discipline and his description of its nature. His definition is the following: "Discipline is the habit of teaching, through measures of restraint, orientation, and organization, those essentials necessary if learning is to prevail. Discipline has as its objective education on both individual and collective basis. It sets the stage for learning. It seeks to educate toward self-discipline — that indispensable foundation of character."

"Discipline is like a jellyfish — it changes shape as it moves, yet retains a definable form. It is a form of methodology; of effective direction and stimulus for learning; of reward and punishment. It is based on what happens here and now in the classroom, not the stories colleagues pass on to each other about particular students. Prejudging students has no foundation. The teacher's own face-to-face relationships are the basis for action. Discipline implies approval as well as disapproval" (141).

IMPORTANCE OF DISCIPLINE

The entire world needs discipline. This country needs discipline. All types of children need discipline. No group of people can share anything or work together without rules and regulations. A family, a business, a school, or a community cannot function efficiently without discipline. So is an effective classroom full of students preposterous without good discipline. Good discipline is a way of achieving teamwork toward goals. It is a way of helping the individual rise to his potential.

Discipline is not old-fashioned. It is as modern and up-to-date as nuclear weapons and supersonic jets. One of the most important jobs of the classroom teacher is to work for discipline. Without good discipline the school room is a waste of everybody's time — no wonder the teacher who has to spend so much of her time on behavior problems cannot teach children the academic subject matter they are expected to learn. We can readily see why the teacher is worn out from the daily tugs-of-war between herself and the students. Furthermore, we may expect the appearance of mental health problems which are usually associated with undisciplined atmospheres.

A few people — some parents, some teachers — have mixed feelings about discipline. Some take the attitude that it is really not very close to the child's needs, and therefore, he should grow up doing whatever he pleases whenever he wishes. Others look upon discipline as a necessity to good education and good mental health. Often the real point about good discipline is missed. It is misunderstood and undersold. The writer contends that there is nothing modern, nothing psychological, nothing progressive, nothing good about the lack of discipline. If discipline is weak, we can be assured that something somewhere, somehow has failed: home, church, school, community. When discipline is weak, the child is unhappy, and *everybody* is in danger.

James L. Hymes, Jr. states (116):

> Discipline is the whole base of society. Humans cannot exist together if people lie, if they cheat, if they steal, if they hurt, if they think only of themselves. This has always been true: Stone Age, Roman days, in the Renaissance, during our pioneer period. Today it is more true than ever.
>
> We live closer to each other than people ever have before. We have nowhere to hide, nowhere to escape, no place where we can stay by ourselves. We have to talk with people. We have to work with people. We are a thousand times more a *society* today, and we are going to become more and more and more so. Our age simply must have discipline.
>
> In a million little affairs all of us are at the mercy of experts: the television repair man, the auto mechanic, the dentist and the doctor, the man who says he will fix the oil burner. The experts know. We don't. They can lie to us, they can cheat us, they can fail to keep their word. If they do we are victims. Today we have to count on the other fellow's honesty, on the other fellow's peacefulness, on his reliability.
>
> In bigger affairs the identical condition exists. This world has atomic bombs and hydrogen bombs, poison gas, poison bugs. We possess every means for torture, for pain for disturbance and disruption. We can make the Inquisition look kind. We can make the lions of the Roman Arenas look like pussy cats. Our

modern undisciplined fellow drives a death machine at 70 miles an hour. He breaks the plate glass window of the store display and walks off with a fortune. If ever a world had to be good, we are that world.

So, once again, the point: when you work for discipline your are doing a good deed. Hold your head up high, and feel proud as a peacock and useful.

All in positions of responsibility, the teacher, the coach, the public leader or the army general are by necessity strong disciples of discipline in their own way. They fully realize that they must create those conditions in which their actions can be successful. The teacher's objective — education for daily living — demands order, the very foundation upon which discipline rests. Without order, chaos results and education is impossible.

WE MUST PLAN FOR DISCIPLINE

Learning to adjust and make changes is essential in meeting the problems of everyday living. Adjusting to differing circumstances and making changes necessary to achieve a goal often require immense self-discipline. The most effective discipline is self-imposed. Those who learn early that they must make decisions they would rather avoid and complete tasks they would rather forget have grasped the fundamental principle of personal growth. However, we must recognize that such discipline is learned behavior. Children must learn from parents, teachers, and other adults the need for discipline.

Teachers must conduct their classes in such a manner as to point out that control is necessary and personally profitable for the individual. Learning to take the bad and the good, unhappiness and happiness, defeat as well as victory; realizing that real success seldom is attained without experiencing failure; these are examples in which a discipline imposed from without may well have to be called upon as a learning method.

In the absence of discipline, whether self-imposed or imposed from without, the individual may fail to use his potential or become more vulnerable to enticements which have a strong attraction for the un-disciplined — drugs, alcohol, and other forms of escape from reality. They are likely to show little or no respect for authority, cooperative effort, awareness of organization, respect for the dignity of the individual, and the need for doing things which are unpleasant.

Teachers can prevent many problems within the classroom and enhance the student's future at the same time if they teach discipline. Much of what students learn is a by-product of the teacher's preparation and procedure.

Because there appears to be a great deal of delinquency among the mentally handicapped children, some have reached the conclusion that low intelligence is in itself a predisposing factor in delinquency. The writer disagrees with this view. Mentally handicapped children are highly suggestible, and if environmental circumstances are favorable to delinquency, they are likely to become delinquent. On the other hand, the normal child from a good moral family, who is given care and supervision and every material necessity, may react against all and seek adventure in delinquency; the mentally handicapped child in a similar environment is more likely to appear stable and law abiding. Because mentally handicapped children have less inherent ability to determine their own course, we believe that environmental conditions are even more important to them than to the normal child.

Unfortunately the environment of a mentally handicapped child is often very unsatisfactory. Many homes are poor; parents fail to understand the child; often there is dirt, drunkenness, and quarrelling; the children are allowed to roam the streets, making social contacts at will. Sometimes they become dupes of the intelligent delinquents from regular schools, who use these highly suggestible children as catspaws.

Children who come from homes of this type are usually discipline problems in the classroom. In such cases the teacher's plan for discipline will of necessity be structured to meet the needs of the individual child.

GOOD AND BAD DISCIPLINE

Judging by what has been said, so far in this chapter, it seems that discipline in one form or another is with us to stay. It is not a matter of whether we shall have discipline; it is a matter of getting the best discipline we can.

Discipline that is too harsh, too negative, or self-defeating is referred to as "bad" discipline. Good discipline has some positive characteristics along with the avoidance of negative extremes.

Discipline that is too strong for the acts it seeks to correct is considered to be harsh. For example, if the teacher refused a child the privilege of eating lunch in the school cafeteria for the period of two months because he threw his tray on the floor in a fit of temper, this would be too harsh. To be meaningful to a child the corrective measure should fit the infraction.

Sometimes discipline is too negative in its effects. Discipline should serve to correct an error. As a corrective device it should point out the positive alternatives that are available to the child. In telling a child he cannot do his arithmetic assignment during reading time, it is constructive to say that arithmetic may be resumed when the reading lesson is finished. This is not a "no-no" which could bring forth a negative attitude and lack of cooperation from the child. Instead, it says that is all right in its time and place.

Another characteristic of poor discipline is its defeating nature. This occurs when the teacher tries to get the child to conform to the acceptable standards of behavior, and when he fails to do so, becomes overly critical of him. If he is admonished too much, is accused of not being able to get anything into his head, has his whole personality included in the accusations, he may be overwhelmed.

This is damaging to a child's self-respect. He may feel that there is no use to try if the teacher thinks "I'm no good." The teacher means well in such instances, but she has used "poor strategy." We ordinarily want to use corrective measures which will touch upon the error lightly, then go on to emphasize the positive and acceptable alternatives.

We must conclude that two techniques of discipline that have not been found very satisfactory are discipline based on too harsh measures and discipline based on permissiveness or ambiguous measures.

HOW TO OBTAIN GOOD DISCIPLINE

It is not enough to know that a child is retarded when you are trying to help him. We must know as well as we can the child's present level of achievement, his abilities, and his interests. We must know the family and the family background. To know the parents and siblings enlarges the scope of one's ability to help. It also assists in assessing the degree of defect with more certainty than otherwise. To a limited extent the question of heredity must play some part. For example, habits are inherited as well as imitated, and the inherited habit is as strong in a retarded child as in any normal child, and knowing this helps to assess its importance. A habit can be controlled, if it does not disappear entirely, once the child learns the art of self-control, one may suspect an underlying cause which needs different treatment before any self-control can be used. Self-control is one thing that can be inculcated in the earliest of stages. The later it is left, the harder it is for the child to acquire self-control. It is an attribute which is an essential to the mental health of every child.

Let us return to the inherited habit: These include such things as tempers, reserve, and inherent ways of walking and talking. There are also the habits picked up from observation. For example, father may have the habit of scratching his head when thinking and the retarded child notices and acquires it. So many retarded children are like putty in this respect.

Furthermore, we must know something about the general personality characteristics of retarded children before we can plan effective, sensible discipline.

PERSONALITY CHARACTERISTICS OF THE RETARDED

At this point it would probably be helpful to mention certain characteristics of the personalities of retarded children which are involved in the creation of problem situations.

In the beginning, it is important that the teacher always takes into consideration the lower intellectual functioning of a retarded child and remembers that this lower intelligence will affect his judgement and interpretation of many relationships in his environment as well as his general understanding of himself. The teacher must remind herself that the mental retardate often shows immature personality characteristics. The immature personality characteristics of a child may very definitely cause him to be on the defensive most of the time because he lacks self-control and confidence in himself, and he tries to find ways of justifying his behavior, his actions, and how he thinks about things.

The retarded, like normals, use certain defense mechanisms. Defense mechanisms are psychological ways of handling and adjusting to what appears to be threats to one's self, and one's feelings of security and status. For example, a retarded child might use the defense mechanism of *projection,* in other words, he might project in his mind, the real cause of the problem or, the problem itself to persons or things outside himself. He might say that there are persons or forces over which he has no control that are creating problems for him, and therefore, he is not to blame. He might use the defense mechanism of *rationalization,* that is, he attempts to explain away his behavior even though his reasoning may not be sound. He might also use the defense mechanism of *denial* when faced with an unpleasant fact, he will simply deny that it is true. In all defense reactions just mentioned, the individual avoids assuming and accepting responsibility for his behavior. It must be remembered that the child is often unaware that he is projecting or rationalizing or denying.

Another system of psychological defense that is used at times by retarded children is emotional insulation, or *withdrawal,* in which the child isolates himself from involvement with other persons or problems. He lives in his own world of preoccupation and avoids the company of others, thereby protecting himself from the stresses and strains of living in a social setting. Extreme withdrawal from social contact is often a symptom of very serious mental disorders in which the individual may begin to deny the existence of reality, creating for himself a substitute imaginary world in which he lives. Some forms of this type of childhood mental disorder are autism and schizophrenia. They are very serious forms of mental illness. The quiet, withdrawn child may really be in more need of attention and care than the child who is more aggressive and readily displays his feelings and problems.

Another defense mechanism which displays itself on occasion with retarded children is *regression.* The individual goes back to patterns of behavior and adjustment that brought him love and attention when he was younger, but that are no longer appropriate. His behavior becomes more immature; he becomes more dependent on adults and more demanding of their time. He becomes more infantile in approaching and adjusting to problem situations. In severe forms of regression, the child may even resort to such infantile behavior as losing control of bladder and bowel functions.

Another form of defense is that which manifests itself in a constant need for reassurance. The individual will assume no responsibility for his behavior unless he has constant reassurance from those around him. Insecure children want the teacher to tell them continually that what they are doing is right, that everything is going well, that there is no need to worry, and that they are still loved.

In summary, it should be pointed out that these defense mechanisms are not common only to the retarded, but in fact, everyone uses various defense mechanisms at times to protect himself from the stresses of interpersonal relationships and the general problems of daily living. Everyone wishes to maintain status, to be important, to be respected, to be recognized, and to belong. When we feel strongly that our status and self-esteem are being threatened by a stressful situation we use defense reactions to bolster our egos, to sustain ourselves, to defend ourselves, and to carry on in face of a problem.

The question that comes to mind at this point: Are the mentally retarded more likely to use defense mechanisms than other people?

It would be very difficult to answer a question of this nature. However, it must be kept in mind that the majority of retarded children come to school from poor home conditions and backgrounds of stress. These children probably feel more insecure than those who come from good home situations. Furthermore, classroom living is probably more stress-provoking than life in the good home situation. With these facts in mind we might conclude that as a total group retardates are no more likely to use defense mechanisms than average children with similar backgrounds.

METHODS AND PROBLEMS OF GUIDANCE

What can teachers do to help children who are having difficulty in adjusting?

There is much they can do but, first, it is important to realize that there are limits to the amount and depth of guidance the teacher should undertake. They should always remember to bring to the attention of their administrator, the school psychologist, or other designated persons in authority all chronic behavioral problems or acute problems which seem to be beyond the ordinary. Unusual or bizarre behavior should be reported immediately and in detail, with a description of exactly what the child did and said.

Harm could be done to the child by the teacher if she becomes too involved in counseling. Namely, the teacher should avoid getting involved in what is called psychotherapy. Children who have serious emotional problems need treatment by competent, professional persons who are specially trained for this sort of work. However, there is much the teacher can do and should do to maintain a healthy psychological environment for the children.

During the normal course of the day in the classroom, the teacher will be responsible for aiding the children in their adjustment to the school situation. First, it is important to realize that perhaps one of the greatest difficulties faced by teachers, as well as others working with the mentally retarded, is the problem of communication: Does the child actually understand the instructions, advice, and counsel being given to him so that he can absorb it and put it into action?

TECHNIQUES FOR OBTAINING GOOD DISCIPLINE

There are certain techniques that the teacher can apply in counseling or guiding the child.

COMPREHENSION. It is necessary to make certain that the child is able to explain to the teacher who has given him counsel, his interpretation of what the teacher has said. When the child is being counseled, it is necessary for the teacher to ask him, "Do you understand what I have said?" and, "Tell me in your own words what I have just told you."

ABSTRACTNESS. The teacher must be careful to avoid words and concepts which are obviously too abstract or demand more intelligence than the child possesses.

OBSERVATION. The teacher should be very observing of the students. She should be alert as to whether a child by motion or sign is showing agreement or disagreement with her.

SIMPLICITY. The teacher must realize that she is responsible for directing the child's behavior. She should keep these directions simple and concrete, and they should be such that, hopefully, the child can attain some immediate relief in his problem situation by following the advice that is given.

SINGLE PROBLEMS. The teacher in guiding the child in some phase of daily living should devote his attention to one problem rather than bringing into the discussion several problems, some of which may have occurred some time before and which the child may have forgotten.

RELATIONSHIPS. It is often difficult for the retarded child to understand that there is a relationship between what happened yesterday or a week ago and what happens today. He needs to understand what happened today, at this time, because this is what his problem is in so far as he sees it.

RESPONSE. Children respond differently to different adults and different approaches. No one teacher and no one teaching approach is the best for all children. A positive skepticism is the best attitude to have after reading a former teacher's report on a child.

PERSONALITY. The personality of the teacher has an effect on the child. Teachers differ in personality makeup as much as children. While we suggest that teachers use firmness, clearness, follow-through, etc., we are also aware that the conscientious teacher may want to question the manner in which she carries out the firmness. The writer is convinced that most teachers, in nearly all their relationships with children, will become better teachers as they become firmer ones.

GROWTH DIFFERENCE. We know that individual children differ greatly in their particular patterns. When growth patterns differ, teachers must consider these differences and realize that we cannot expect the same amount of work or the same quality of work from all children. Each child's assets and weaknesses must be taken into account. Discipline alone will not do much to accelerate or slow down growth tendencies in our classroom activities. But the teacher can apply the disciplined learning more judiciously and constructively if she knows the idiosyncrasies of each child.

IMPRESSIONS. First impressions are often the most vivid and lasting. We can take advantage of this common psychological fact to get off to a good, firm start with a new child or a new class. Teachers should "mean business" from the first day of school onward. The sooner they start such a regimen, the less disciplinary trouble they will have. It has been noted that many outstanding regular class teachers start the year with statements similar to the following:

"This school is in the 'teaching-learning' business. I am an employee who has been hired to teach. You are students who have been sent here to learn. So all of us are expected to work. If we work together, I am sure we will find some time for fun, also. But we must remember worktime comes before fun time." Firmness is not unfair, and the teacher must realize this and carry this meaning to the children in words and in deeds. The purpose is not to threaten children, but to let them know the business of school and to clarify their role in it.

FORMING PATTERNS. Give children tasks commensurate with their ability, achievement, and interest, note their strong and weak points, and proceed to build from there. While children are achieving in this simple way, gradually add tasks so that a pattern of successful completion is established. This should be applied on a minute-to-minute, hour-to-hour, and day-to-day basis to enable children to form habits which contribute to a pattern of success.

RELUCTANT PARTICIPATION. We must accept the fact that many children are reluctant to or even refuse to participate in some classroom activities. This technique may be used to get teacher attention or to relieve the child of his responsibility. It would be nice if children would respond with 100 percent cooperation, but we must not naively assume that this will happen.

One way of being prepared for the negative child is to understand there will always be some children who are hard to manage. We must realize that individual differences in children and in teachers may necessitate extra-ordinary persistence and vigilance in some cases.

FOLLOW-THROUGH. Making requirements and giving attention to children's responses may be an indefinite procedure. Many children need constant attention, otherwise they feel the teacher no longer cares.

Often we assume that if we explain something to a child, or show him what to do, he will carry on without further attention. According to the modern scientific viewpoint there is a tendency for human skill, attitude, efforts, and behavior to wane. We all need support for our attitudes, our skills, and our knowledge. Logically, then, we must expect to support the child's efforts at learning and at self-control. It is obvious that the retarded child needs more support.

Studies of memory and learning suggest that forgetting of skills takes place soon after practice has terminated. This implies that any child in a classroom will become "nil" in his attitudes and skills if he is not kept actively using these skills and attitudes. They must find support in their environment.

SELF-RELIANCE. As children become more mature they begin to rely upon themselves and to do their work with less outside prompting. At home they have usually learned to accept emotionally their parents' standards and values. They will take over their learning and discipline in the same manner when intellectually capable of doing so.

After all, learning is the acquiring of new behaviors. The less mature child whose intellect is low will not be able to take on new behaviors which are expected of his normal peers with like chronological age. Their acquisition of behavior will correspond to their mental age.

SATISFACTION. A sense of satisfaction comes when one is able to meet his tasks and problems and conquer them. The unhappy and unsuccessful person is one who has not been able to cope with the problems that face him.

Likewise, children learn to measure themselves against their obligations. They generalize about themselves — "I'm stupid." "I can't read." "I can do my arithmetic." — just as adults do. They judge themselves by their experiences, just as we judge them. By their experiences they evaluate themselves. Teachers can do much to remove inadequacy feelings and replace them with successful habits for daily living.

Emotions are not something apart from living. They are not separate aspects of a child that must be sorted out and worked on. The emotional evaluations of one's life are by-products of one's overall success in living or the lack of it. If we can encourage better and more successful living in the classroom, at home and elsewhere, then we can encourage emotional development.

"Security" is also a much used word today. Security is a feeling of oneness between self and one's surroundings. Insofar as the classroom experiences are constructive, a child will feel secure with himself and his teacher if he continues to meet his daily obligations in a reasonable, adequate manner.

In the emotional area teachers can foster a more adequate preception and appreciation of reality factors by the retarded child. They can help him gradually to develop traits of independence and feelings of confidence. Through careful programs of management they are able in many instances to forestall many of his problems before they reach serious proportions.

Many retarded children come to school from homes where careless parents do not give a feeling of security to them. The teacher must satisfy their need for security, for being wanted and accepted.

Teachers should be cautious about expecting that his counseling or guidance will result in immediate improvement. Changes in behavior usually take much time and advice, and counsel will probably have to be repeated many, many times. The retarded have little foresight, i.e. they have difficulty understanding how present behavior can have any effect on the future.

We must be very careful when counseling the retarded not to offend him by using terms which may reflect upon his mental status, such as "too slow," "that was a stupid thing to do," or "don't act so silly." These and other like terms, when used, are often interpreted by these children as being judgments. Because these judgments are coming from an important adult in their lives, they will tend to tear down the confidence these children have in themselves. Confidence is very necessary for their adequate adjustment. In counseling the teacher should attempt to give specific advice as to ways of dealing with problem situations. She should further suggest alternate modes of behavior which are in keeping with the child's ability and which may greatly assist the child in making a more adequate adjustment. The teacher should be calm, friendly, and objective.

Being objective means that the teacher should attempt to accept a child as he is, regardless of her own personal feelings about him. The teacher must overlook her own feelings and not allow them to interfere with her judgement and counsel.

To be objective one does not have to be cold. Being objective means to view the situation fairly and honestly and with due consideration to persons and things involved. To accomplish this, it is necessary to view the problem situation without involving one's own emotions and biases, since these can affect one's judgement as to what truly happened. Objectivity is difficult to acquire, but teachers should strive to acquire this characteristic in working with children. It is understandable that teachers cannot be objective all of the time in their relationships with the children nor should they be. There are times when emotionally based reactions are helpful and desirable in the relationship between the teacher and the children. The teacher should know when it is important to be objective and when it is not.

It is very necessary that the teacher work out a relationship with each child which is consistent and predictable.

As teachers of retarded children, many of us have found the multitude of little complaints, the trivial things which occur from time to time, or those which are constantly brought to our attention to be the exasperating aspects of working with retarded children. The teacher must evaluate each of these as to their importance and the source from which they come. It is certain that some children consistently bring to the attention of the teacher unimportant, trivial matters just for the sake of getting attention. It is important for teachers to realize that even though they are ready and willing to listen to complaints and problems, they are not obliged to solve all of them. Part of the training and growing-up process of the child is helping to face the hardships and tensions of life in a competitive society. To over-protect the child from this sort of experience would do him an injustice and ill-prepare him to meet life in the future.

GROUP GUIDANCE. Sometimes it may be a good idea to allow children at level III to get together for group discussion in which problems can be discussed freely and openly. With severely retarded children the involvement of the teacher as discussion leader will be necessary at all times. This is opposite of the practice when working with the educable retarded. Here the teacher acts as discussion leader in the beginning sessions but in successful group participation, teacher involvement becomes much less as time passes, and she finds her role becoming that of bystander.

It has been noted by experts that in the first few sessions of group discussions the retarded express individual personal problems or complaints. Later discussion gradually moves away from focus on individual problems, and more attention is given to problems of general interest and importance to the class as a whole.

THE EFFECTS OF GUIDANCE. No doubt the greatest problems that the retarded have in school stem from the fact that the rules and regulations or reasons for conforming to limits have not been adequately explained to them, or they have not understood the explanations given. There is a great need to gain more understanding of the factors which motivate these children to direct their lives in such a way that they will be acceptable and meaningful to themselves as well as to others.

Teachers can contribute greatly to the development of more mature and less self-centered children if they learn to see each child as he sees himself and the problems he faces. By guiding and counseling the child directly, the teacher can help bring about behavior changes. However, she must be sure that the child can clearly see that the change is truly something of value which will add to his happiness and well-being. The mentally retarded usually accept guidance and leadership without much question. Very often they have difficulty distinguishing between good and bad guidance and leadership.

Often retardates are shy, self-conscious, and lacking in self-confidence. One of their greatest needs is to belong, and they are constantly seeking reassurance from people around them. Many of them feel rejected by their family, and these feelings are intensified when they are surrounded by other children who feel the same way.

The school has a great deal of influence on the direction of the personality development of these children. Question might be raised as to whether this influence is of positive value. Perhaps one of the greatest values of the special class is that it does permit retarded children to develop more fully their potential. Here he finds a predictable routine; this may increase his feelings of security, because he knows more or less what to expect from day to day. They all share to varying degrees, one common problem — mental retardation; so within limits, there is commonness of interests, ambitions, social endeavors, and problems. Within the social structure of the class a trainable child might enjoy, for the first time, the experience and joy of having friends and being accepted by his peers.

GOALS OF GUIDANCE. In counseling and guidance, there should be certain basic, general goals which the teacher is attempting to achieve. She will want to see that the child develops social skills to enable him to enjoy successful social relationships. Aside from providing social experiences, the teacher must help children to interpret these experiences and evaluate their ability to get along with others.

Another goal should be to help the child acquire a positive attitude toward life. Understanding that he is an individual, that he has worth and status will promote his general happiness. This will add meaning and purpose to his life. It is also very important to give him opportunities to demonstrate his capacity to work, as well as to play and maintain social relationships with his peers.

The teacher also should help the child expand his interests through exposing him to many experiences which deal with normal social needs and demands.

In summary, it might be said that the counseling and guidance practiced by the teacher, is a very valuable and important part of her general responsibility. Counseling and guidance can be used to support the child and assist him to understand and accept himself.

In guidance, advice can be given in which definite recommendations are made to the child, advising him as to what action he should or should not take, or what course to follow so as to avoid certain problems.

Through guidance the child may be helped to develop emotional attachments and emotional controls. The teacher can assist the child to understand and control the expression of his emotions as is necessary to constructive living.

Since the mentally retarded are highly susceptible to suggestion, the teacher should make every effort to capitalize on this characteristic and offer suggestions which will help them develop acceptable ways of attacking problems.

The teacher can think through problems with the child, helping him to comprehend the logic of suggestions that are made. She can also help him to understand the need and value of having goals which are realistic and which contribute to feelings of security and happiness.

Thus, in the final analysis, counseling and guidance is one way in which the teacher can extend her influence and the influence of the school to the child. The retarded child is looking for a dependable friend. He is looking for someone who understands him, someone who is aware of his needs, his interests, and his happiness, and someone who makes him feel important and worthy, someone who accepts him as he is and likes him.

Section Two

TEACHING THE TMR CHILD

SECTION two contains four chapters devoted to the education and training of trainable mentally retarded children. Chapter V deals with activities to promote their physical and motor development. Chapters VI, VII, and VIII are concerned with behavioral objectives, learning experiences, and teacher procedures based on mental age to assist in planning a dynamic curriculum for the TMR.

Before teachers use the guides for curriculum planning, it is wise to consider the pertinent facts that follow:

1. The mental age is more useful than the IQ in planning for the training of these children.
2. A variety of handicaps is likely to exist with these children, thus producing multiple maladjustment.
3. Large bodies must be reconciled with small minds.
4. Any infinitesimal degree of improvement is cause for rejoicing, even though it may be only a slight change of facial expression.
   This improvement, small though it be, will come only after weeks, months, even years of patience — which last mentioned trait must be inexhaustible.
5. A skill apparently learned needs constant reinforcing, or it will be lost.
6. A flexible program is a necessity.
7. Periods should be short, and teachers should be ready and willing to change activities upon onset of fatigue, etc.
8. These children will not attain the capacity to become independent of the supervision and care of responsible adults — otherwise they would be considered educable. They are not able to succeed in an academic type of program.
9. We stress (whether in public, private, or institutional school) positive social interaction — *not* academic achievement. The ultimate is for the child to be so aware of his surroundings and himself that he will be acceptable to his fellow classmates, his associates at home or in a sheltered environment, and to his neighbors with whom he comes in contact. It must be realized that education has a broad meaning.
10. The whereabouts of these children must be known every moment. They have little sense of time and place.
11. Records of techniques and samples of work should be kept. Up-to-date summary records and annual pictures of the individual

child are helpful.

12. The types of training used in school must be interpreted to parents or matrons and practiced in the home or sheltered environment.

13. Help from specialists should be solicited through the school district in the following areas: speech, music, art, physical education, and dental and medical care to help broaden their social environment and to maintain good health habits.

14. Home visits can be valuable.

15. An overall public relations program is extremely important, especially in a public school situation.

16. The teacher must be sincere with the child and parent.

17. Anyone working with these children should be calm, quiet, and happy.

18. The children should learn to walk in a relaxed fashion and talk quietly, distinctly, and slowly.

19. Observation of other trainable classes is most valuable. Also observe normal children of the chronological age near that of your trainables' mental age.

20. Wishful thinking and fixed ideas should not be allowed to influence any findings. The results of the forms and methods of training should be assessed with an open mind.

21. Classes for the trainable children and the individual children are unique.

22. The "Three R's for the Retarded" are relaxation, repetition, and routine. There can be challenge without pressure.

23. No other type of training is similar to this.

24. Confidence will be developed as one conscientiously learns to understand the children and their needs. No one should be absolutely certain his program is correct.

25. This is a challenging and most rewarding type of work.

26. These pages are a guide — the material must be adapted to individual cases.

V

PHYSICAL AND MOTOR DEVELOPMENT

IT is becoming more and more apparent that specific attention must be given to developing the physical and motor skills of the mentally retarded. Some of the most important developmental tasks of the school years consist of the development of motor skills based on the coordinated use of different teams of muscles. Society expects the child to measure up to normative expectations which fail to include the retarded child.

The school curriculum should be concerned with developing specific motor factors, such as strength, endurance, agility, body flexibility, coordination, and general body health. Motor development should improve such indirect traits as self-awareness, body concept, a sense of accomplishment, and a feeling of self-worth.

Teachers should be cautious of the type of activities presented for physical and motor development. Very little development will take place if most of the time allotted to motor activites is spent listening to directions or standing in line waiting a turn. The child should be engaged in the desired motor activity with spaced rest periods.

Many of the trainable retardates have some physical handicap, and frequently muscular coordination is very poor. These children need both organized and free-play activities in their daily routine that develop the use and control of gross and fine muscles. The degree of independence a child attains in caring for his needs, the pleasure and satisfaction he derives from work and play either by himself or in social situations, and his ability later in life to perform some vocational skills successfully depends largely on his development of nerve-muscle coordination.

Note: Unless otherwise specified, the following suggested activities are applicable to both younger children and adolescents.

SUGGESTED ACTIVITIES TO DEVELOP BODY COORDINATION

Gross Muscle Training

I. Younger Children

  A. Playground activities
    Gross muscle training for beginners is provided first through active play.

Free or informal play, either indoors or on the playground, meets early physical needs because it is a natural way to play. The child runs, jumps, bends, etc., spontaneously. When we challenge him to perform new and more demanding activities, we must do so gradually so that the confidence and security built up through free and natural play is not destroyed.

Young newcomers to the school usually play by themselves or engage in parallel play. They "feel" their way in their new environment, adjusting to new physical surroundings and new friends before they are ready for group play. Large blocks, trucks, dolls, housekeeping equipment, ball, and the sand box seem to attract them.

Some of the more experienced children will use the playground equipment readily, but for most of the younger ones this is a second step. The swings, with canvas seats for safety, are the most appealing pieces of equipment. The jungle gym and the teeter-totter are next in popularity. The arched ladders and the slide are rather frightening to many of the children and are usually the last to be tried. Do not force a child, but wait until you see that he is ready to try something new; then provide security by standing nearby and encouraging him. If he looks to you for help, give him direction, physical assistance if necessary, so that he does not become frightened. The child derives pleasure, satisfaction, and self-confidence slowly and naturally when we proceed from the familiar to the unknown in carefully planned stages.

The values of organized play should not be overlooked. This form of play helps the child to learn simple rules, to socialize, and to cooperate with others.

It is most important that all play be supervised. This is the teacher's opportunity to observe the child and his interaction in the group. It is a time to look for readiness clues which can help the teacher plan future learning experiences. Furthermore, if play periods either indoors or on the playground are to provide wholesome activity which will give all the children an equal chance for development, the teacher must be on the alert to prevent objectionable habits of behavior from forming.

Painted diagrams for simple games such as hopscotch and an area for low organization team games like kickball, baseball, touch football, etc. are very useful. The following equipment has proved useful:

(1) Sliding board
(2) Arched ladders
(3) Jungle gym
(4) Teeter-totter
(5) Swings with canvas seats
(6) Bicycles and tricycles
(7) Sand box
(8) Basketball hoop, backboard, and basketball

(9) Tetherball

(10) Balls for bounding, throwing, and catching; bean bags

B. Calisthenics

Big muscle activities aid in the development of organic vitality and development of specific motor skills. A variety of calisthenics such as knee bends, body bends, and arm reflexing can contribute to both these aims by providing well-balanced exercise for the body.

(1) Simple bending and stretching exercises

Simple bending and stretching exercises can easily and pleasantly be provided through the use of records and songs. Outstanding recordings for this purpose can be found in the materials and aids section. Selections are made on the basis of low voice pitch, slow tempo, and simplicity of directions. Songs suggesting body activity are also listed.

"Simon Says" and "Everybody Do This" are games which provide opportunity for calisthenics and are enjoyed by children. They are played in the following manner: "Simon Says" — Simon says to do the things that he will do; Do this do that, do this do that. Oh, Simon tells you what to do.

Children take turns playing the part of Simon and showing the others what to do. In the beginning, it is often necessary for the teacher to make suggestions in order to provide a variety of activities. As the children become familiar with the game and the opportunities for expression, they enjoy the challenge of thinking of different exercises.

"Everbody Do This" is another version of the same game. "Follow The Leader" could also provide this type of exercise.

(2) Simple tumbling exercises on the mats. (Shoes must be removed.)

While music is not necessary for these activities, it is both encouraging and relaxing for the child and is, therefore, highly recommended.

The Ruth Evans Childhood Rhythm Series (see "Materials and Aids") is a set particularly good for mat activities. First, as an introduction until the child is familiar with the equipment, let him perform whatever "stunt" he wishes. Do this on two or three different occasions, or as often as needed for him to feel relaxed and comfortable on the mats. When a scheduled mat period occurs, again let the child do his own stunt first; this may be nothing more than crawling or tip-toeing across the mats. Then try having each child in turn crawl across the mats — this is something they can all do with varying degrees of proficiency.

Rolling is a good exercise — ask one of the better coordinated youngsters to roll across the mats for the others to watch, then allow each to take his turn individually. Some children will have to be rolled at first. Encourage and praise the child as you help him. Remember that music is helpful. The Ruth Evans "walk" record is good for this activity.

Rocking The Baby is an exercise done with the "camel" record in the Ruth Evans Series. The child lies flat on the mat, then pulls his knees up to his chest, encircling them with his arms. He rolls as far to one side as possible, then as far to the other side as he can, repeating this motion several times in rhythm with the music.

Duck Walk is another good early exercise which the children enjoy. It should be a modified version to begin; that is, walk forward in a deep knee-bend position and allow the hands to remain either on the hips or on the knees during the entire walk across the mats. Most mongoloids do this exercise quite easily. The "Duck Walk" record — Ruth Evans Series can be used.

Rabbit Hop — modified — stoop down and hop on all fours, or the hopping may be done on the feet with the thumbs held at the head, fingers extended upward, to imitate rabbits' ears. Slow 6/8 music is suitable.

Cat Walk — amble across the mats on all fours, slow 6/8 music.

Bending Fun — have the child lie flat on his back, arms extended over his head, then rise slowly to a sitting position, and touch toes with hands. Return to original position and repeat as the child is able.

Proceed with more difficult exercises as the children exhibit readiness.

C. Games

In areas of physical development training which requires group activity, such as games and dances, it is especially important to keep the prime purpose of the training before us. The emphasis should be on the individual child's improvement in general physical well-being, motor control, poise, and ability to work and play with others. The comparison or competition should be with the child's own record only. Competition among the children in group play and teamwork should be minimized, the emphasis being placed on the fun of working and playing together.

(1) Circle games

Round and Round the Circle (singing game)

Round and round the circle go the happy children

    (Children clasp hands and go round in a circle.)

Go up to the lilac bush, birdie fly away, hush, hush!

    (Children raise hands high as they walk to the center of the circle — child in center is the birdie and flies out of the circle.)

Sally Go Round the Stars (singing game)
Sally go round the stars, Sally go round the moon
Sally go round the chimney pots on a Sunday afternoon –
   Whoosh!
   (Children clasp hands and go round in a circle – unclasp hands
   and raise over heads clapping as they say "whoosh!")
Animal Fun (singing game)
Sing to the tune of "Farmer in the Dell."
Oh what does the monkey do, Oh what does the monkey do?
   (Children form a circle, clasp hands, and sing.)
He climbs a tree and climbs a tree
   (Unclasp hands and pretend to climb a tree.)
And throws some nuts at you!
   (Children pretend to throw nuts.)
Oh what does the eagle do, Oh what does the eagle do?
He whirls around and whirls around
   (Children spread arms and whirl around.)
And whirls to look at you.
   (Whirl with one arm high, the other low, then coming to a
   stop.)
Oh what does the tiger do, Oh what does the tiger do?
He creeps along and creeps along
   (Children creep around in a circle.)
   And then he jumps at you.
   (Children jump forward.)
Oh what does the elephant do, Oh what does the elephant do?
He walks along and sways his trunk
   (Walk in circle like elephants – hand clasped in front of body,
   bend forward and walk, swinging from side to side.)
And eats some peanuts from you.
   (Pretend to put peanuts in mouth with trunk.)
      Use your imagination and supply more verses!
Many singing games can be played with familiar tunes. Here is
another one to the tune of "Farmer in the Dell."
   The Goblin in the Dark (singing game)
(Children stand in a circle and act out the game in a scary manner.
One child is chosen to be the goblin. He stamps around the inside of
the circle, walking like a monster as the children sing.)
The goblin takes a witch, the goblin takes a witch.
   Hi Ho Halloween, a goblin takes a witch.
   (The witch is chosen and rides around the circle on a
   broomstick.)
The witch takes a cat, etc.

(The cat walks on all fours and meows.)

The cat takes a bat, etc.

(The bat flies around within the circle.)

The bat takes a ghost, etc.

(Ghost stand stiff and covers face with hands.)

The goblin runs away, the goblin runs away, etc.

(Child who is the goblin goes back into the circle.)

The witch, bat, cat, and ghost each go back to their places in the circle as the children sing.

Other singing circle games which are useful with the young children and also familiar to most teachers and children are the following:

(a) Bluebird

(b) Did You Ever See a Lassie

(c) Looby Loo

(d) Round and Round the Village

(e) Oats, Peas, Beans

(f) Ring Around A Rosie

(g) Here We Go Round the Mulberry Bush

(h) How Do You Do My Partner

(i) Rig A Jig Jig

(j) Pussy Cat, Pussy Cat

Directions can be found in almost any book on physical education for elementary grades.

Duck, Duck, Duck, Goose!

One player is "it". All the other players form a circle. "It" runs around the outside of the circle, taps each person gently on the shoulder, saying, "Duck, Duck, Duck." He continues to say "Duck" until he suddenly taps a person and says "Goose." "It" runs around the circle. Goose chases "it." If "it" gets back to the vacant spot in the circle, he is safe. If "it" is caught, he goes in the "basket," the center of the circle. Goose becomes "it" next.

The Monkey and the Peanut

One player is the monkey. He has a small object, like a wooden bead, which he calls a peanut. All the other children stand in circle with hands behind their backs.

Monkey walks around the outside of the circle and drops the peanut into the hand of a player. Monkey runs around the circle. The player who has the peanut chases him. If Monkey reaches the empty space, he is safe. If Monkey is caught, he is put into the cage — the center of the circle. The player who has the peanut is now Monkey.

Pass the Pumpkin (egg, Christmas toy, etc., as the season may be)

Children form a circle and sit down. One child sits inside the circle. Children pass the object around the circle as music plays. When the music stops the child in the center goes to the one holding the object. He takes that child's place in the circle, and he also then takes the object from him. The child who had the object sits in the center of the circle.

Kitty Hide

Children sit in a circle with one child in the middle who takes the part of mother or daddy kitty. The child in the center pretends to be sleeping as the other children say these words:

Mother kitty is fast asleep

But little kitty wants to play

Up he jumps and looks around

And then he runs away.

The child who is chosen to be the little kitten jumps up, looks around, and then hides quietly somewhere in the room. When the children have said the rhyme, Mother Kitty wakes up and goes to find her kitten.

(2) Skill games

Teacher Ball — skills: throwing, catching, bouncing.

Children form a circle or arrange themselves in a straight line. The teacher stands in the circle or in front of the line of children. She calls a child's name and throws the ball to him. He throws it back to the teacher who then throws it to another child. The activity can be varied by bouncing the ball. When the children become more proficient, simple directions can be followed, such as, "Bounce the ball; then throw it to Sue."

Circle Ball — skill: rolling a ball.

Children sit in a large circle, legs apart, feet touching. A child with a ball pronounces the name of the person to whom he is going to roll it. After several rolls, divide the class into small groups and repeat the game in smaller circles.

Touch — skills: listening and following directions.

Indoors this game is best played in the following manner: Use flash cards with children's names or simply say a child's name and give him a direction to follow, such as, "Touch the doll." "Touch the highchair." "Touch the door."

Outdoors all the children can take part at one time. The children must understand that listening is part of the game. Directions such as "Touch the fence," or "Touch the jungle gym," can be given. They should return to the original spot before a new direction is given.

Cut the Pie — skill: passing a runner going in the opposite

direction.

Children form a circle and clasp hands. The pie-cutter stands inside the circle. He clasps his hands between any two players and says, "Cut the pie." He then returns to his place in the center of the circle. The two players run in opposite directions around the circle, pass each other, go through the space which they left open in the circle, run up, and join hands with the pie-cutter.

Chase the Animals Around the Corral — skill: handing an object to another player.

Children and teacher form a circle. Teacher sends around the circle an object to which she has given the name of an animal, such as "rabbit." Each child must handle the "rabbit" as it is passed around the circle. When it gets back to the teacher, it is sent around again, and a second "animal" (fox) is sent after it. If an animal is dropped, it must be picked up by the child who has dropped it and passed on to the next person before the second animal is received. If the second animal overtakes the first, the former is captured and is out of the game. This game can be made progressively more difficult by increasing the number of animals being sent around and by variation in the size and the shape of the objects used.

String Along — skill: catching.

Children sit in a circle. The teacher throws a ball of yarn or string to a child, calling his name as it is thrown and keeping hold of the end of the string. The child calls another child's name and throws the ball of yarn to him. Continue until everyone has caught and thrown the ball. As the children become more proficient, try having each child hold onto the string as he throws the ball. With younger children, the teacher will have to rewind the string.

Cat and Mouse — hunting game.

A cat hides behind a chair or any suitable place at one end of a room. A number of mice creep up to the desk and scratch on it. Immediately the cat gives chase to the mice, who run for safety to their holes (seats). Any mouse caught becomes cat for the next game.

Run, Rabbit Run — hunting game

One group, rabbits, are safe in their homes. The other group, foxes, walk through the woods. The old mother rabbit takes her young ones out in the sunshine to look for food. They go softly because they fear the old fox may see them. Suddenly the leader of the foxes cries out "Run, rabbit, run!" at which all the rabbits try to reach their homes before the foxes catch them. All who are caught become foxes and on venturing out next time help catch the remaining rabbits.

Spider and Flies — hunting game.

Two goals are marked off, one at each end of the play area. The players form about a circle, which is drawn an equal distance between the two goals. One player is chosen to be the spider and sits very still in the middle of the circle, while the flies walk or skip around, clapping their hands as they go. When the spider jumps up and chases them, they run toward either goal. If the spider tags them before reaching the goal, they become spiders and must go into the circle, sit down with the first one, and must not run to help tag until the original spider again gives the signal. The last fly caught becomes the first spider for a new game.

Ball Passing — a good beginning team game.

Divide the players into two teams, each team forming its own circle. Each team has a ball which is passed around the circle from player to player. When a player drops a ball, it scores against his team. The game can be made more challenging by using two balls of different sizes for each team.

Carry and Fetch — team game.

Children are divided into two teams. A circle about fifteen inches in diameter is drawn directly in front of each team about twelve feet away. At a signal, the first child in each team runs forward, places a bean bag in the circle, and runs back to the rear of his row. The next child in line then runs forward, secures the bean bag, and gives it to the third player as he passes. Continue until every child has run. The team which gets back to its original place first wins.

Snake — Skill: developing agility.

Children form a circle. The "starter" zigzags around the circle, weaving in and out around and between the children until he returns to his starting place. Once he reaches this spot, the child on his right begins to snake around the circle.

Jumping — Skill: jumping.

Use three objects of different heights. Space them so that the child will have to walk to each one and jump over it with both feet. This seems more fun and also more beneficial to younger children if it is done individually with the rest of the group watching. Later is can be played as a "follow-the-leader" game.

Races — Skill: running, tiptoeing, hopping, skipping.

Children form a line facing a "base." One child who is the leader will say, "Run to base." All the children will run to the base at the same time and then return to the starting line. The child who is leader will select someone to take his place. The new leader will say, "Tiptoe to base," and the children will follow directions continuing the game in the same manner.

Tightrope Walking — Skill: balancing.

Lay a string along the floor or ground in a straight line. Have the children walk along the string, one foot after the other without falling off. The teacher will need to take the hand of a child who has a poor sense of balance to encourage his efforts. This game can be varied by having the children walk in the same manner around a painted circle. When coordination seems to be somewhat better developed, use a balancing board. First let it rest on the ground or floor; later raise it one or two inches.

(3) Team games

Very few team games are used with the younger children, but if they were kept simple and understandable to the children, these games can contribute to their social development. It is an opportunity for them to feel the satisfaction that comes from helping others and contributing to a common goal. "Hunting" games have an appeal to the young child, and because of their simple organization, they can sometimes be used preliminary to teaching team games at a later time.

D. Body action rhythms

Basic locomotor skills are natural ways of moving to normal children.

   (1) Variations of walking, skipping, and marching are the following:

       (a) Walking
       (b) Running
       (c) Tiptoeing
       (d) Sliding
       (e) Hopping
       (f) Jumping
       (g) Skipping
       (h) Marching
       (i) Galloping
       (j) Bending
       (k) Stretching
       (l) Swinging and swaying
       (m) Twisting and turning

While most of the retarded can walk, run, or march even though awkwardly, there are many who must be taught to skip, jump, and perform other more difficult body movements. They must be helped to see and feel their rhythms in relation to the songs they sing and music they hear. Music is again a helper here as it is in so many other activities. It provides the relaxation which reduces body tension and permits the child to move more freely and easily. A child should have many experiences in clapping and tapping in time to music before he can try the more difficult activities of marching, skipping, etc.

When the child exhibits readiness, each unfamiliar rhythm must be taught separately — very slowly, step-by-step, and without accompanying music at first. As an example:

(2) Skipping

    (a) Child stands with feet a few inches apart.

    (b) He bends one knee in hopping position. Teacher may have to put child in this position.

    (c) Child hops. (Show him what to do, and support him if he is unbalanced.)

    (d) Child puts raised foot down, stepping forward slightly and bending the other leg in hopping position (Teacher must give step by step directions and at the same time physically assist the child.)

    (e) Repeat the above steps exactly the same way several times then hold the child's hand and skip with him in the same slow way described above. Do this many times for very short periods on different days.

    (f) While the child is learning to skip without music, he should be exposed to "skipping" music during "listening" periods so that the rhythm of the music becomes familiar to him. When he has learned the skipping motions unhesitatingly, the music can be used successfully.

The Ruth Evans Records are excellent for these rhythms. The American Book Company Music Series, Ginn and others have good piano selections. Please refer to the Material and Aids section.

(3) Mimetics

Mimetics are imitative movements of familiar activities usually without props. "Let's play a game," can be an introduction. Teacher can start by saying, "I wonder if you can guess what I'm doing?" She should imitate brushing teeth, washing hands, or some equally familiar activity. After the children have guessed two or three mimetics, select a more able member of the group and say, "Missy, can you think of something for us to guess?"

Some beginner activities would be washing, eating, combing hair, brushing teeth, putting on clothes, playing ball, raking leaves, etc.

Story plays are more difficult, but a few of the younger children are sometimes able to dramatize something simple. It could be the Easter Bunny filling Easter baskets, Santa filling the stockings, a part of some story, such as Goldilocks waking to find the three bears staring at her, or the pig in the little brick house waiting for the wolf.

E. Dancing
   (1) Simple folk dances
      Folk dances in the usual sense are not used with the younger
   children. They cannot be expected to follow a pattern involving
   several steps. A foundation for future experiences in folk dancing can
   be given through singing games, a few of which have already been
   described under the heading "Circle Games." Ring Around A Rosie is
   an excellent beginning dance for children. Since the children do not
   drop hands until the end of the game, it is easier for them to remain
   in a circle. The tune and the timing are easy to follow, and the dance
   ends with an action with which they are all familiar — falling down.
   (2) Social dancing
      This is not taught to the younger children.
   (3) Creative dancing
      Since imagination and creativity are largely lacking in the retarded,
   these abilities must be developed through many different kinds of
   experiences. Experiences through expression in art by the use of
   crayons and finger paints and through music by opportunities to
   listen and to take active part in rhythmic activities are basic to the
   child's development of the ability to interpret creatively. Picturesque
   music with definite rhythms and appealing melody as well as story
   records, such as "A Visit To My Little Friend" and "Nothing To Do"
   are helpful. Please refer to the Bibliography. Physical training
   activities which reduce tension are necessary. A rigid child cannot
   express his feelings.

II. Adolescents

A. Playground activities
   The rapid physical growth of adolescence places a new importance on
play activities. Excessive energy needs outlets which normal children find
in highly organized, competitive sports. Because of the wide diversity of
abilities within a trainable class, the competitive angle must be de-
emphasized. Each child must be made to feel that he is winning.
   Playground equipment, such as sliding boards and swings, still have
their place, especially for the child who was too timid in his earlier age to
use them. Bicycles and large orthopedic tricycles offer a good opportunity
for large muscle development within the safety of the school property.
   When the basketballs, baseballs, tetherballs, and kickballs are used,
"rules" have to be modified to meet the comprehension of the group.
Basketball may be no more complicated than allowing each person to have
a turn at throwing for a basket, then dribbling back to a starting line.
"Teacher ball" may ignore the failure in throwing or catching and permit

each person to serve as teacher and throw to each person in the entire line.

Leadership and cooperation find natural channels for development on the playing field.

(Note: See suggested list of equipment under "Playground Activities" for younger children, at the beginning of this chapter.)

B. Calisthenics

(1) Many of these large muscle activities can be continued indoors when a gym is available. However, when space is limited, modified exercise can be gained by classroom calisthenics or by tumbling routines on a mat. Simple action must be taught one step at a time with much repetition. In calisthenics, wands often give directions to arm action and seem to help stabilize muscular control.

Later music can be adapted to the routine, helping by its rhythm to make the action smooth flowing and more pleasurable. An advanced group may even "invent" an exercise to do to new music.

(2) A mat-work program for trainable children providing gross muscle activities

Precautions: Children should wear slipper socks or an extra pair of heavy gym socks. Girls should wear slacks or leotards. Pockets should be emptied. Glasses or hearing aids should be removed and put in a safe place.

There is a distinct advantage in having the teacher demonstrate the exercises. However, slowly explaining the exercise to one of the better coordinated youngsters will bring the same results. Do not aim for such perfection that the fun is taken out of the program. The program can be started by asking that someone volunteer to do a "stunt" then having the class try to copy it.

The children sometimes become so interested in their gym program that they begin cutting pictures of exercises out of newspapers and magazines and ask to try them in class.

Stunts and Tumbling

Duck Walk

Stand with feet about eight inches apart. Bend down into a deep knee position and place the hands on the heels, preferably with arms between legs. Walk or waddle in this deep knee position.

Seal Crawl

Body is in a face down position with all the weight on the hands. Walk on the hands, dragging the toes on the mat. Keep the ankles and knees together, resembling a tail.

Rabbit Hop

Bend to a deep knee bend position with hands on the floor in front of the feet. Hop forward first with hands and then with the feet, imitating the hop of a rabbit.

Kangaroo Jump

Bend to a deep knee position, keeping the back straight. Carry the hands in front of the chest like the front feet of the kangaroo. Take hops forward by stretching and bending the knees.

Crab Walk

From a sitting position, place hands on the mat in back of the body. Bend the knees so the feet are flat on the mat. Raise the body so that it is parallel with the mat and as high as the knees and shoulders. Walk forward and backwards without letting the body sag.

Lame Dog

Take the same position on the mat as for the rabbit hop, but lift one leg high in the back. Go forward down the mat by moving the two hands forward together and by jumping the one foot up to the hands.

Mule Kick

From a standing position in the middle of the mat, place hands on the mat and kick both legs up at once.

Log Roll

Lie down across the end of the mat, with arms extended above the head. Keep the legs, arms, and body in a straight line. By pulling with the hips and stomach, try to roll down the mat in a straight line. Avoid bending the arms or legs.

Sit Up

Lie on the back and fold the arms across the chest. Press heels against the mat and try to come to a sitting position without raising the heels or legs. When this has been mastered, try to move to a standing position without aid from the hands and arms.

Human Rocker

Lie on the mat, bend knees and raise feet. (This is from a face down position.) Grasp the ankles with the hands and raise shoulders and head from the mat. Rock back and forth from the shoulders to the knees.

Stump Walk

Kneel on the mat with the knees slightly apart. Keep body erect. Grasp one ankle by the hand and walk on the knees for the length of the mat.

Push up

Lie on the mat, face down, and place the palms of the hands on the mat, under the shoulders. Raise the entire body off the mat until just the hands and toes are touching the mat. Keep the body in a straight line. Slowly lower the body to the mat.

Exercises for Two Children

Wheelbarrow

Two children stand at the end of the mat, one in front of other. The front one places both hands down on the edge of the mat and keep arms straight. His partner grasps his extended legs by the ankles and raises them from the mat. They walk forward down the mat with the front person walking on his hands and the back person carrying his legs.

Rowing

Two children sit on the mat, facing each other with knees flexed. They will grasp a dowell stick or similar instrument with their hands. By alternately pulling back, they will imitate the action of a rowing boat. Be sure to keep the soles of the feet on the mat.

See-Saw

Two children stand in the middle of the mat, facing each other. They will stand at a comfortable arms' length from each other, holding hands. Alternately, they will make a deep-knee bend and return to the upright position.

Leap Frog

Two children stand at the end of the mat. The front one will kneel on the mat making himself as small as possible and protecting his head with his arms. The second child will leap over him and then assume the kneeling position. Continue this for the length of the mat.

Many of these exercises can be done to music. Often it is helpful to have a background of rhythmatic music for the entire program. Especially adaptable to music are the Rowing, See-Saw, Human Rocker, and Bicycle exercises.

C. Games

(1) Circle games gradually lose their appeal to the adolescent retarded.

(2) Skill games

Many adolescent retarded have not yet developed a proficiency in throwing, catching, and bouncing a ball. In throwing and catching, the achievement of a degree of skill in handling a bean bag usually precedes a satisfactory performance with a ball.

In learning to bounce a ball, the repetition of self-directions (such as, "Bounce, hold, bounce, hold") helps the child concentrate on what he is doing. Later, music (such as, the Ruth Evans Series − "Childhood Rhythms" − vol. V, Record 503) can be introduced. Here again, the child may chant self-directions to the rhythm of the music. At this point, the less the teacher interferes, the more readily the child finds the rhythm.

Skill with the basketball and tetherball is gained through experience. Too many directions and too many rules take the fun out of the game.

(3) Team games

Often the adolescent retarded will say, "Let's choose teams," mainly because they know that sports are generally played in teams. They seldom choose their teammates for their skills. By letting the teams have "captains," responsibility, self-direction, and initiative can be cultivated. In having gym teams for mat work, the captains can choose the stunts to be performed by his team, along with disciplining his teammates; thus the program becomes more child motivated.

(4) Modified team games

Kickball

Opposing teams face each other. Position A on Team I kicks to Position A on Team II — who kicks to Position B on Team I. Otherwise, some members never get a chance to kick and lose interest.

Basketball

Each team lines up at a given line. The teams alternate in turns at throwing for a basket. A score is kept.

Throwing a ball for distance

Each team stands in line at a given point. Each team has its own ball. Two members at a time throw for distance. Each thrower must retrieve his own ball and return it to the next contestant. A score is kept.

Circle Kickball

The entire class stands in a circle fairly close together, holding hands. A soccer ball is placed in front of one child, who gently kicks it across the circle. The group keeps the circle intact by continuing to hold hands. The object is to keep the ball going back and forth across the circle. If it gets out of the circle, the person missing it must drop hands, chase the ball, and bring it back into the circle. This game can be played for quite some time before interest wanes.

Leader Soccer

A large playing area is needed for this game. When it is properly motivated, it can be a fast, active game. Since it is played on a "turn" basis, it also gives the slower children a chance to participate. A leader is chosen who stands at one end of the field or gym. The rest of the class forms a line at the other end of the field or gym. The leader kicks a soccer ball to the first child in line, who kicks it back to him. The leader then kicks to the second child, and so on down the line. When every child has kicked it back to the leader, a new leader is chosen. Using hands is forbidden. Each child is urged to move out of line to meet the ball, and he is urged to direct his kick toward the receiver. A great deal of action can be developed during the game.

D. Body action rhythms

Body action rhythms in a class of trainable children is a continuation of the marching, skipping, and walking done with the younger children. These activities are usually used for relaxation. It is assumed that, by this time, a degree of proficiency has been attained in these areas, making these activities success experiences.

Wand rhythms have proved highly successful with the older retarded. In a sense, they simulate the baton twirling they see on television. The holding of the wand seems to give direction to their arm movements. At first the teacher will create the movements, explaining and demonstrating them. Later on, advanced pupils can assume the role of teacher. These wand exercises for gross muscle development were built around Ruth Evans Record, Series V, no. 503.

Exercise 1 — First position: Hold the wand in front of the body in a relaxed position. Continuing positions: Pass the wand behind the body with the right hand, grasp it with left hand, and bring it to the front of the body and pass it into the right hand. Continue this action throughout the first movement of the music.

Exercise 2 — First position: Place feet slightly apart. Hold the ends of the wand in a relaxed position in front of the body. Second Position: Swing the wand upward to the right, shifting body weight to the right foot. Third position: Swing the wand downward, then up to the left, shifting body weight to the left foot. Continue throughout the second movement of the music.

Exercise 3 — First position: Hold the wand in front of the body in a relaxed position. Second position: Raise rod in front to shoulder height. (Count 1.) Third position: Bend knees, keeping back straight and maintaining rod. (Count 2) Fourth position: Return to standing position keeping wand at shoulder height. Same as position 2. (Count 3.) Return to position 1. (Count 4.) Continue throughout movement three of the music.

Any music with a definite rhythm can be adapted to simple calisthenic routines. The use of wands seems to help concentration on the routine. The wands also seem to give direction to muscular action.

E. Dancing

    (1) Simple folk dances

        Since most folk dances depend upon a repetitive body movement set to a definite rhythm, they readily appeal to retarded children.

Sometimes the routine needs to be modified since these people rarely can master complicated patterns or intricate steps. When a dance calls for a change of partners, it is well to ignore that process. It is usually less confusing if the same pair remain together throughout the dance.

In teaching a dance, it is best to present one routine at a time. The children may chant self-directions as they practice the pattern. It is usually more successful if the music is withheld until the entire dance is learned.

Here are some examples of dances that have been successful with adolescent retarded:

(a) Record: "Childhood Rhythms," Ruth Evans, Box 132 P.O. Branch X, Springfield, Massachusetts:

Series Six

601 MEXICAN SOCIAL DANCE (Individual Partners)

Take hands, jump in place, alternating right and left feet, pointing the toe forward for eight measures. One jump per measure. Walk in circle to right eight measures; walk in circle to left eight measures; stop. Repeat three more times.

602 RIG-A-JIG JIG

Directions as in album with one exception: only one couple in the circle at a time.

603 SEVEN AND THREES

See directions in album.

603 CLAP AND TAP

Form a circle facing in one direction; walk four steps; clap three times. Repeat to end of music sequence. Next walk four steps; jump three; walk four; jump three, and continue to the end of music sequence. Next repeat part one, clapping over head; then repeat part two.

604 SKIP AROUND YOUR PARTNER

See directions in album repeating first movement for the fourth set.

605 WALKING WITH MY PARTNER

See album directions. We use walking, skating, swinging — stretching arms high. Repeat this series once.

(b) Record: "Childhood Rhythms," Ruth Evans, Box 132 P.O. Branch X, Springfield, Massachusetts:

Series Seven

701 BAA BAA BLACK SHEEP

Form a circle facing the center; directions as in album.

703 TWO LITTLE BLACKBIRDS (Done with partners.)

"Two little blackbirds sitting on a hill" (Both stoop down.)

"One named Jack" (Boy jumps up.)

"One named Jill" (Girl jumps up.)

(Take hands and skip in a circle.)

"Fly away Jack, fly away Jill" (Reverse direction.)

"Come back Jack, come back Jill."

#705 ACH? YA!

(Partners form a double circle facing counter clockwise, walk forward.)

"The mother and father paid a visit to the fair, Ach Ya, Ach Ya."

(Turn to partner and bow twice. Take hands and walk forward again.)

"They hadn't any money, nor did anybody there, Ach Ya, Ach Ya."

(Bow as before.)

(Chorus) Tra la la, etc. (Join both hands and slide four slow slides) Tra la la, etc. (Reverse slides.)

"Ach ya, Ach Ya." (Bow twice.)

(Repeat twice more.)

#706 LOOBY LOO

Use album directions. We use right hand in, left hand in, both hands in, whole self in.

#706 BOW, BOW, BELINDA

(Partners facing each other, a short distance apart. Step toward partner.)

"Step, step, and bow, Belinda." (Step toward partner.)

"Step, step, and bow, Belinda." (Step backward.)

"Right hand around and bow, Belinda."

"Left hand around and bow, Belinda." (Turn the other way and sing, sing.)

"Round and round, Oh, Belinda." (Bow at finish.)

(c) Record: Children's Dance Time for Primary Children
    Rhythm Record Co.

Follow printed directions for three dances on side #1. Modifications can be made if the group have any difficulty with the routine. The movements are simple, repetitious, and of slow tempo.

(2) Social Dancing

Social dancing in the life of a retarded person will generally be done only within a peer group; hence ballroom procedures and excellence of technique will be of little importance. When it is part of the school program, it should be for fun. It can be enjoyed during a free period or during a party. It can be introduced by inviting the children to bring favorite records to school to share with their friends.

As in Junior High School social dancing events, often it begins with the girls dancing together and the boys watching. Gradually the boys are drawn in. Often it is well for the teacher to remain in the background. Where a child is unusually slow in being drawn into the activity, the teacher may offer herself as a partner. With today's television-oriented child, the teacher often finds that her class has to teach her.

(3) Creative dancing.

Creative dancing must be a spontaneous thing. The classroom teacher can do little more than create the atmosphere for its nurture. It is most easily developed with another musical or rhythmic experience. Perhaps during a rhythm instrument session she may ask a particularly expressive child to dance. The results become very contagious. Particularly shy, inhibited children may be invited to follow a body rhythm routine done by the teacher. The entire body rhythm program, starting with the youngest child, helps build toward a creative expression program.

Fine Muscle Training

I. *Younger Children*

Some basic motor functions such as grasping and releasing with the hand develop without specific practice provided the child is not too handicapped. The teacher must provide the motivation to do things in everyday play periods which will strengthen these functions. The other motor responses of fine muscles require specific, systematic training. This area of training is especially difficult for the retarded. Have patience and make their experiences pleasurable. When the child tires, stop the activity and go on to something else. Praise him. Help him to feel successful.

A. Finger plays

Finger plays are a way of helping the child develop an image of himself and control over the movements of his fingers, hands, and arms. There are many additional values which are discussed in the proper context in other sections of this guide.

Young children enjoy finger plays and often respond quickly to them than to other activities. The following suggestions will help the teacher in presenting finger plays:

(1) Remove distractions — toys, etc.

(2) Sit or stand directly in front of the group.

(3) Speak clearly and in a well-modulated voice.

With young retarded children it is generally better to eliminate finger plays with left and right motions. (When teaching left and right, the teacher should stand in back or beside the child.) As an example, the following rhyme is a good one for developing the left-right concept:

With my right hand I do a salute
With my left hand I brush off my suit
With my right hand I wave goodbye
With my left hand I point to the sky.

This idea can easily be reinforced each day when the children salute the flag. Simply say, "With my right hand I do a salute." Accompany the remark with the physical act of placing the child's right hand in position. Use the action suggested in each line of the rhyme as it is recited. When the child knows left hand and left foot from right hand and right foot, he is ready for more involved rhymes, and activities embodying this concept. The following may be helpful.

(1) Ask the children to do as you do. Say the rhyme slowly as you perform the correct actions. Be enthusiastic. Make it a real "fun game."

(2) Repeat the rhyme a second time, again asking the children to do as you do.

(3) The third time suggest that they say the words with you. Some will be able to respond.

(4) Provide for many repetitions at different times. The more familiar the children become with a finger play, the more they enjoy it. Give them frequent opportunities to suggest the finger plays they would like to do.

Ball for Baby

Here is a ball for baby. (Cup hands to make a ball.)
Big and soft and round!
Here is baby's hammer. (Pound fists together.)
Oh, how he can pound!
Here is baby's music. (Clap hands.)
Clapping, clapping so!
Here are baby's soldiers. (Hold up all ten fingers.)
Standing in a row.

Ten Little Fingers (Follow suggested actions.)

I have teen little fingers, and they all belong to me!
I can make them do things, would you like to see?
I can shut them up tight or open them wide,
I can hold them in front or make them all hide;
I can hold them up high or put them down low,
I can hide them in back, then fold them just so!

Here is a Beehive

Here is the beehive. Where are the bees? (Make fist; swing from side to side.)

Hiding away where nobody sees.

Watch them come creeping out of their hive. (Continue above action.)

One and two and three, four, five. (Raise thumb then first finger, etc.

Bzzzzzzzzzzzzzzzzzzzzzzzzz. (Make fingers fly around.)

Where is Thumbkin?

Where is thumbkin, where is thumbkin? (Hide hands behind back.)

Here I am! Here I am! (Bring one fist forward — wiggle thumb; then bring second fist forward — wiggle thumb.)

How are you this morning? Very well, I thank you. (Make thumbs bow to each other, one at a time.)

Run away, run away! (Put hands one at a time behind back.)

(Follow same actions substituting "pointer" for the first finger, "tall man" second, "ringman" third, "pinky" for fourth, and then "all men" using all fingers.)

On My Head — (Follow suggested actions.)

On my head my hands I place;

On my shoulders, on my face,

On my hips, and at my side;

Then behind me they will hide.

I will hold them up so high;

Make my fingers quickly fly;

Hold them up in front of me,

Swiftly clap, 1, 2, 3!

Ten Little Fingers

Ten little fingers, (Arms resting on elbows, hands made into fists.)

Show them all to me! (Open fists, show all fingers.)

Helpers — (Use appropriate actions.)

Little fingers, Little fingers

Helpers all are we,

We pick up toys and hang up clothes,

Busy as can be.

Up and Down the Stairs

Thump, thump, thump-thump-thump.

Down the stairs we go!

Climb, climb, up-up-up.

Going up is slooooow!

(Make stairs with ten blocks have children take turns going up and down with the "pointer" and "tallman" fingers.)

Open, Shut Them — (Use appropriate actions.)

Open, shut them; open, shut them;
Give them a clap.
Open, shut them; open, shut them;
Lay them in your lap.
Creep them creep them, slowly upward
To your rosy cheeks.
Open wide your shiny eyes
And through your fingers peek.
Open, shut them; open, shut them;
To your shoulders fly.
Let them like little birdies
Flutter to the sky.
Falling, falling, slowly falling,
Nearly to the ground,
Quickly raising all your fingers,
Twirling them around.
Open, shut them; open, shut them.
Lay them in your lap.

Readiness Game — (Use appropriate actions.)
Make one eye go wink, wink, wink;
Make two eyes go blink, blink, blink;
Make two fingers stand just so;
Then ten fingers in a row.
Front and back your head will rock;
Then your fists will knock, knock, knock;
Stretch and make a yawn so wide;
Drop your arms down to your side.
Close your eyes and let us say
Our very quiet sound today —
Sh. . . . .sh. . . . .sh. . . . .shhhhhhh!

Touch your Nose — (Use appropriate actions.)
Touch your nose;
Touch your chin;
That's the way this game begins.
Touch your eyes;
Touch your knees;
Now pretend you're going to sneeze.
Touch your hair;
Touch one ear;
Touch your two red lips right here.
Touch your elbows where they bend;
That's the way this touch game ends.

Finger Fun — (Make fingers run along the table or in the air.)

Fee, Fie, Foe, Fum;
See the little brownies run.
Fee, Fie Foe Fum;
Four fingers having fun.
Fee Fie, Foe, Fum;
My brownie is my thumb.

A House for Everyone

Everyone has a house.
Here's a nest for Robbie Redbrest, (Cup hands.)
Here's a hive for Bessie Bee, (Cup hands, bring finger together.)
Here's a hole for Jackie Rabbit, (Pointer and thumbkin together, point to hole with pointer of other hand.)
And here's a house for me. (Hands overhead for pointed roof.)
Everybody has a house.

Touch Game — (Use appropriate actions).

Hands on shoulders, hands on knees,
Hands behind you if you please;
Touch your shoulders, now your nose,
Now your hair, and now your toes;
Hands up high in the air,
Down at your sides; now touch your hair;
Hands up high as before;
Now clap your hands, 1, 2, 3, 4.

A Birthday — (Fill in the child's name and number of candles. Make appropriate gestures for each line.)

Today is_____'s birthday;
Let's make him a cake;
Mix and stir,
Stir and mix,
Then into the oven to bake.
Here's our cake so nice and round;
We frost it pink and white;
We put_____candles on it
To make a birthday light.

Tall and Small

Here is a giant that is tall, tall, tall; (Children stand up tall.)
Here is an elf who is small, small, small. (Children sink slowly to the floor.)
The elf who is small will try, try, try (Children slowly rise.)
To reach the giant who is high, high, high. (Children stand tall, stretch, and reach arms high.)

Funny Bunny

This is the bunny (Pointer finger.)

That hops so funny. (Make finger hop.)

And this is his home in the ground. (Make hole by putting pointer and thumbkin together.)

At the slightest sound he hears, (Hand to ear.)

He pricks up his ears, (Put hands over head for tall bunny ears — wiggle them.)

And hops right in with a bound. (Pointer of one hand hops into hole made by putting tip of pointer and thumbkin of other hand together.)

Ten Little Snowmen

Same as Ten Little Indians. End with "Ten Little Snowmen Bright."

Raindrops . . . or . . . Snowflakes

Down the little raindrops fall,

Down — down — down to the ground.

Falling falling — oh, so softly,

They never seem to make a sound.

(Fingers in relaxed downward position for raindrops — use floating motion for snowflakes.)

Little Christmas Tree

I am a little Christmas tree (Hands outstretched.)

I'm standing by the door; (stands up very straight.)

And I'm so full of presents

I can't hold any more. (Shake head.)

Here's a ball for Ricky (Hands together to form circle.)

A doll for Nancy Beth (Rock imaginary doll.)

Brian has some carpenter tools, (Hammering motion.)

There's a sewing set for Jane. (Sewing motion.)

I'm just a little Christmas tree, (Hands outstretched.)

Up here there is a star; (Point to top of head.)

I have many good gifts too,

Like wisemen from afar. (Hands to forehead as if looking into distance.)

B. Manipulative activities

It pays to emphasize here, again, that though there are exceptions, most trainable children are encumbered with other handicaps in addition to their mental retardation. Motor responses are usually awkward and uncoordinated and the disability is more pronounced in the finer muscles. The manipulative activities suggested here are helpful in the development of small muscle facility.

The first basic motor pattern of fine hand muscles is to grasp and release. To develop good coordination in these responses, suggested or partially directed play experiences are helpful to the young child. More formal learning experiences can follow this beginning phase. Suggestive manipulative activities follow:

Water play

Squeeze sponges, push boats, and chase soapsuds.

Damp sand or sawdust play

The beginner enjoys making mounds and digging tunnels. With suggestions he will later use such things as plastic molds, wax paper cups, pails, shovels, etc.

Dry sand

The use of dry sand requires close supervision, but very young children enjoy and benefit from running their hands through the sand and sifting it.

Ball play

Use different ball sizes. Practice throwing, catching, rolling, and bouncing. See suggestions under gross muscle training.

Paper punch

Have the children punch holes in paper at random. Try spreading paste or glue on colored paper. Have the child hold the paper he is punching over the pasted paper instead of the waste basket. The white disks will stick to the colored paper and look quite pretty. Paste can be put on the corners of the paper from which he has punched holes. This paper then can be laid on another paper of contrasting color.

Puzzles

These can be introduced as group experiences and can later be included in free time activities. Give individual attention only to those who really need it.

Bead stringing

Use large wooden beads. Assist those who need help. When a child has developed readiness, use the smaller one-half inch wooden beads. This can be followed by the use of costume jewelry beads or buttons, using the appropriate size needle and thread. Variety can be provided by stringing one-half inch wooden beads or painted macaroni on flexible wire or pipe cleaners. Interest can be held during the large wooden bead stringing stage by varying the procedure. Have the children string beads of all the same shape, one square and then one round bead; string a red bead then a blue one until the string is completed, etc.

Pegs

Let the children fill the boards at random. This will be difficult for some and will require the assistance of the teacher. When a child is able to do this easily, provide variety by giving him an animal and suggesting that he make a cage for it by putting pegs all around the edge of the board. Parking lots for cars and trucks can be made the same way. Simple designs can be made by the teacher for the child to reproduce.

Put-together toys

There are a variety of theses toys on the market. Cars, trucks, trains, and tracks are a few. Putting these together and guiding them around the floor requires the use of the fine finger muscles and eye-hand coordination. Encourage the children and help where it is needed.

Blocks

Beginners will simply make random piles of blocks, or put blocks in a truck or wagon and possibly pull them around the room. Later they will try to construct something. Express verbal interest in each child's activity no matter how simple it might be. At appropriate times show the child how to match edges to make a straight line with the blocks, etc. Provide and encourage the use of props, a doll for a house, a truck for a garage, a fire truck for a firehouse, etc.

Tinker toys

Let the child tell you what he has made or say "This looks like a road." – or a car, as the case may be. He may need suggestions. Show how he can make wheels by using round pieces, etc.

Plastic put-together blocks

Use these at a table or a desk. It is helpful for the child to keep them on a tray while he is playing with them.

Plastic bead stringing

These are sold in the toy shops and most of the supermarkets. The child fits the pieces together. No string is needed.

Tops

The push-screw type seems to be the most effective.

Colored sticks

Use for making designs or matching the stick with the correct colored paper. However the child's interest is held, the benefit is in his learning to handle the sticks precisely.

Nests of rings or boxes

Use your imagination to provide variety.

Winding

Give the children empty spools with one end of short yarn attached to the spool by tape. Have the children wind the yarn on the spools. Give help where needed. Give attention to neat winding. Practice with string, jumping ropes, and extension cords. When children show some comprehension of what is expected and some ability to perform this skill, it can be used in many ways. Perhaps they would like to take a gift home. Apply paste or glue to a straight sided jar. Secure an end of yarn just below the mouth of the jar on the outside and help the child to start winding. Show him how to keep the yarn flat and how to lay it side by side. The finished jar makes an attractive gift.

Play a game. Have the children sit in a circle. Throw a small ball of yarn to a child, keeping hold of the end of the yarn. Have a child rewind the short piece. Help with the rewinding when a child shows need. Proceed around the circle giving each child a turn.

Folding

Do not use construction paper at first. Poster paper is more pliable and less likely to crack. Give the child a square of paper. Place the child's hand in the correct position for each step as you proceed. Take one corner and match it to the opposite corner on the same side of the paper. While holding these two points together with the pointer finger, take the pointer finger of the other hand, and starting at the point where the two corners meet, press down and at the same time draw the finger down the paper to the edge of the paper next to the body, producing a fold. Press to the right if you are working on that side, making a firm crease. Release the fingers. Match the two other corners as suggested and hold them with the pointer as before. Follow the same procedure, drawing the pointer finger of the other hand along the edge of the paper to fold near the body. Release the fingers. Press gently on the paper with one hand (corners will be together and the creases at each bottom edge will help to hold the paper). Take the other hand and firm the crease. Follow the same procedure with all paper folding. Practice folding paper napkins, etc. The child also should have experience in folding towels, rest blankets, and clothing.

Sewing

See "Arts and Crafts." Sewing boards can be used, but are not especially recommended.

Button cloth

This is a square of cloth with buttons sewn on it. Accompanying swatches of material with buttonholes can be fastened to the cloth. This is an excellent beginning for teaching buttoning. Later, place the child's coat or sweater on the table in front of him. Be sure to lay it in the same position it would be if he were wearing it. When he is at ease with the procedure, try having him button it after he has put it on.

Cloth with snaps

Use the same way as the button cloth.

Zippers

Use a jacket with a heavy zipper. Be sure to lay it on the table in the same position it would be if the child were wearing it. It is easy for a child to pull a zipper, but to lock it and hold it in place as he pulls it up requires more dexterity than a beginner at a training center usually posesses. He should have many manipulative experiences before this is attempted. It is difficult, and the child should be ready for the experience.

Shoe training board

Wait until the child shows readiness before this is attempted. Nail shoe lace and a buckle-type shoe to boards. This helps to keep them firm while the child is working. Place a board on the desk or table in front of the child, being careful that the shoe is in the same position it would be if he were wearing it. Whether it is buckling or tying that is being taught, the teacher must proceed slowly, one step at a time, verbalizing as she holds the child's hands and guides them into the right movements. Switch to another activity at the first sign of fatigue. Do not frustrate the child. It takes at the very least months of effort. Have patience.

C. Arts and crafts

Training in the use of tools and materials in arts and crafts is as much a manipulative activity as the arts and crafts projects designed for use after rudimentary training. Here we are concerned with the basic training and experiences in handling various tools and materials which relate to the development of finger dexterity and motor coordination more than for the finished product.

Coloring

Use one simple form, such as a square, heavily outlined. Give direct help to the child who needs it, guiding his hand. As interest and performance improve, draw verbal attention to the child's results and make suggestions. From the simple forms used in the beginning, progress to single forms of more complicated design, such as kites, Halloween cats, and pumpkins, etc. Let the season be the inspiration. When some degree of success has been attained, pictures with one or two uncluttered figures can be colored.

Finger painting

Focus the child's attention on covering the paper with the color of his choice. After many experiences, when interest and participation are good, begin to point out forms in the painting. "This looks like a ball," or "This looks like a cloud." Show how different forms are made by using finger tips, palms, and arms. Encourage free expression using finger, hand, and arm muscles. Let the child tell the story of his completed picture. Print the story with an indelible marker at the bottom of the picture, with his name. Display it.

Drawing

Use pencil first (the child will be more careful); later crayons, chalk, and brush can be used. Allow the child to experiment. Try to find something familiar to him in his picture. Point it out and talk about it. Draw around it with an indelible marker.

As a group lesson, draw a circle on the board. The teacher can say, "What does this make you think of?" Answers might be "ball," lollipop," etc. The teacher can show how to make a lollipop by putting a straight line under the ball. Let the children come to the board and make "lollipops." Then let the child select a color from his crayon box and make a lollipop on his paper. At Halloween the children might draw a pumpkin and color it orange. At Thanksgiving the drawing might be a wigwam, etc. With beginners and young children keep to basic forms and repeat frequently with slight variations. A snowman could be two circles; a truck, one rectangle with two small circles added; a house can be made from a square, etc. While these formal lessons are needed in order to teach retarded children the use of tools and to develop their eye-hand coordination, they should have ample time for free expression.

Pasting

Begin with pasting a colored circle on a background color or the child's selection. Take a pencil, and make a few short strokes in four places around the edge of the circle. Tell the child that his "pointer" finger is the one that does his pasting. "Pointer is going to put paste on each pencil mark, then you must wipe the paste off pointer onto the scrap paper. Then turn the circle over and put it on the paper you selected." Help will be needed. Continue pasting of simple objects in the same manner. Try pasting circles without pencil guide marks. Then other single objects without pencil marks. As the child's ability develops, try having him paste two or three objects on a background, forming a picture. Use pencil marks at first as a guide, then dispense with them. Cards, magazines, wall paper figures, or scraps of colored paper can be used for additional practice. Let the child form his own picture by pasting two or three things he has selected.

Clay

The beginner will pound, pat, poke, pinch, squeeze, break, pull, and roll the clay. After many experiences the child may attempt to make shapes. He will be receptive to suggestions. A ball, snake, hot-dog are familiar to him and easily made. A rolling pin can be used to flatten and spread the clay. Take cooky cutters and encourage the children to press into the clay to cut out cookies. Let the children remove the cookies they have made and put them on a tray. Another time the child might try making cookies without the cutter. Having had the formal experience, he may be inspired to reproduce shapes he remembers or he may invent one.

Cutting

While most children are fascinated by scissors, few retarded children have any idea how to use them. Through finger plays and songs develop an interest in the fingers as helpers. Through the finger plays the child learns a name for each finger which is helpful to him in learning to cut as well as in learning to do other manipulative tasks. The teacher can say, "Middleman and thumbkin are going to hold the scissors for you. They will make the scissors open and close. Pointer will help the scissors to cut where you want them to cut." Put the child's fingers on the proper places on the scissors and have him practice the motion. Make a game of it; have fun. Next, cut paper at random. The teacher may have to hold the paper. Another lesson may be fringing paper and making long hair or grass. Learning to cut properly on a line or around a design usually takes years of practice. Much time and attention must be given to the beginning steps of holding scissors and the paper properly. A small piece of colored construction paper with a line drawn across in crayon or with an indelible marker makes a practical and interesting cutting lesson. Later, the lines can be wavy or zigzag, or the children can cut around a circle. The cut pieces can be pasted or stapled to a pretty background and displayed. The teacher can draw a snowman for each child. The children can paste in place the eyes, nose, mouth, buttons, etc. which they have cut. Designs or pictures can be cut from wall paper or magazines and then pasted on paper the child has selected. A bulletin board can be the result of a group cutting effort; leaves for trees, fruit, colored eggs at Eastertime.

Sewing

Fiber board sewing cards are not recommended. A child should be proficient in bead stringing before sewing is attempted. Follow the theme of the season in selecting a simple form for sewing. As an example, use a heart design for Valentine's Day. Make two large ones (but not too large for the children to handle easily) from construction paper. Place the hearts together. Punch holes with a paper punch around the edge of the hearts. Tie contrasting colored yarn in place. With a blunt end, raffia needle, show the child how to insert the needle in the hole, turn the heart to the other side and observe where the yarn comes out. Ask the child to put his finger on the next hole, the one alongside of the yarn. Tell him to insert the needle in that hole. Turn the heart over and repeat the process until the heart has been outlined. The brighter youngster will, in time, show readiness to put his needle in the hole and bring it out the next hole without turning the material. Encourage him to do this. Continue this type of sewing until the child has gained some facility. The next step would be sewing on cloth or other material. Use simple objects, mark both sides with a pencil dot where the needle enters the material. Try to point out to the child what happens when he pulls too hard with his needle — it comes off the yarn. Show him how to hold the needle and the yarn so that this does not happen.

Hammering

Educational toy workbenches with wooden pegs are a good

beginning for this experience. Give verbal attention to aiming at the peg and what is to happen. Later, when working with metal nails and wood, the teacher should start the hole with an awl. Hold the nail while guiding the child to hit it with the hammer. When he shows readiness for the next step, start a number of nails, and let the child hammer through two pieces of wood and observe the results. The children enjoy this; give them plenty of opportunity to practice.

Nail board abstracts can be made by the child winding bright telephone wire or string from one nail to another, indiscriminately.

Wrapping

Provide packages for the child to unwrap. Wrap packages while the child observes. Then allow the child to try wrapping. Help the child by placing the article to be wrapped squarely on a piece of paper. Assist him as he folds the paper. Help him to secure the package by using a rubber band or tape. Gifts for parents can be wrapped and sent home. Attractive wrapping paper can be made with sponges or other printing forms dipped in paint or, preferably, colored ink and applied to ordinary tissue paper.

Rolling paper

Start with teacher participation. Roll the paper for the child, having him hold it while the teacher secures it with a rubber band. When the roll is completed, remove the rubber band and help the child to reroll the paper. To make the experience of rolling meaningful, help him to roll a painting or drawing he wants to take home. The rolling skill can be used in handcraft projects, such as megaphones, movie strips, or cardboard tubing, cornucopias, May baskets, or other holiday ornaments.

II. Adolescents

A. Finger plays

Finger plays as related to fine muscle training. As the retarded child grows older, finger plays, as such, are generally discontinued. However, they may take the form of mimetics: "Let's pretend we are playing the piano; the flute; the violin; the drum; etc." or "Now we are sewing; knitting; stirring soup; etc."

B. Manipulative activities

(1) common manipulative activities – The use of puzzles, pegboards, sewing cards, bead stringing, etc., can be continued as long as the child shows interest and he appears to be benefiting from their use.

(2) With adolescents these materials are generally given a new emphasis based on improving spatial relationships.

C. Arts and crafts for adolescents

Training in the use of tools and materials: Training at the intermediate level in the use of media needed for arts and crafts work is merely an extension and refinement of the training already outlined in the beginner program. (See beginning techniques for teaching the use of scissors, crayons, paste, clay, paint, and simple woodworking tools.)

(1) Water color painting

In the older group, water color painting can be done with some success as long as the introduction is made slowly and gradual steps. For example, a large soft brush should be used at first. In so doing, the pupil can see the action of the bristles when used properly in a stroking rather than a scrubbing motion as he might have done at a primary level.

At first, large, individual pans of color should be given each child. This is preferable to a box of mixed colors, which may be distracting. The following sequence of progressive water coloring has proven to be helpful.

(a) Wet the entire paper with water with even strokes of the brush.

(b) Apply one single color in the same manner.

(c) Fold the paper in half and then open flat. Paint the top one color, the area below the fold line, a second color.

(d) Fold the paper in four horizontal sections. Open flat to paint the sections four different colors. The folds are the dividing lines, and the child learns not to overlap colors.

(e) When attempting creative scenes, remind the pupil to "fill in the picture" rather than have a few isolated spotty objects.

(f) Figured wall paper can be used in developing control of a finer brush by outlining the pattern in a contrasting color. This is very satisfying to pupils who lack creative imagination.

Sewing

Sewing requires a carefully structured procedure. Use a large eyed needle and heavy thread, preferably colored at first. If burlap is used, threads can be pulled to leave an easily recognizable guide line to follow with a running stitch of colored thread or yarn. Fringing is good training in finger dexterity and also in learning the limits of the project being attempted; that is, to stop when an inch fringe has been obtained. Later, smaller needles can be used for hemming such articles as aprons or towels. It is still helpful to use a contrasting colored thread.

Large buttons can be sewn on scraps of cloth until the technique is learned. Then buttons of various sizes and colors can be attached to felt or other materials to make eyes, nose, and mouth for cats, dogs, and puppets.

(3) Woodworking

Only the most elementary woodworking skills can be successfully taught to trainable retarded. Learning to sand, learning to hammer nails at random on a board held in a vise, and practicing screwing cup hooks in a prepared hole in wood can be used later in making simple gifts for the home.

D. Movement exploration

Influenced by the contention that a great part of a child's learning comes from and through body movement, a friend of the writer has included movement exploration in the curriculum for the teenage trainable mentally retarded students which he teaches. The activities which follow are included in his program, "Movement Exploration in "TMR" Curriculum." The author is Joseph Garcia (80), teacher of the trainable mentally retarded, Grant Union High School, Sacramento, California.

"To Explore – Movement exploration is experienced by every human being from infancy to adulthood – it is sequential and developmental experience in motor and sensory awareness and control. Motor exploration is not new but its widespread popularity as a concept lies in the fact that we have been made aware that it exists, we have all experienced it, and we believe the possibilities for advancement are worthwhile-through conscious application, concentrated effort in programs based on freedom to explore, to create, and to grow.

"Movement exploration is widely commended for many reasons. It is used within physical education programs, as a total physical education program, and in readiness programs. Correlations between motor development and academic achievement as well as social adjustment provide excellent opportunity to incorporate movement exploration activities.

"Movement exploration in group situations provides those participating with optimum opportunity. Everyone responds simultaneously to the challenge given – each "doing his own thing" in an effort to develop the common task. The goals of movement exploration are fitness, motor development, mental and social-emotional growth just as they are in education. The goal provided by any single challenge is for the individual to explore and experiment within his own realm and to gain awareness as well as ability. Each individual must meet the challenge in his own way; there is no pressure to meet the standard, no competition that might be stiffling. There are so many phases and areas of movement exploration activities and tasks there is very little chance that one could be best or worst in everything – there will always be degrees of agility, inclinations on a continuum from positive to negative. The atmosphere should always be one of exploration, try things that are new and different, everyone else is; fear of failure would ideally be non-existant the task being only to see what you can do and how it feels to do it.

"To Elicit – The task for the instructor of movement exploration is to build an atmosphere in which students are motivated to respond creatively to challenge given. The atmosphere, environment must be positive to successfully elicit free response. To implement movement exploration it is essential that the teacher identify the activities appropriate for class experience. Fitness results from the teacher's challenge to the child to respond in multiple movement patterns. The curriculum should include locomotor skills as well as large muscle activities. Goals of a movement exploration program for the TMR might include:

1. Increased flexibility of posture and large muscle coordination.
2. Body awareness, specifically in relation to laterality.
3. Spatial orientation and positioning exercises involving the entire body, and similar exercises with arms and legs.
4. Directionality — concepts of up-down, forward-back, sideways, in-out, work on walking boards, limited chalkboard exercises.
5. Increase motor control.
6. Balance training using square boards and walking boards games.

"Teacher techniques in movement exploration as I have indicated, may be the most important single factor in the program. The following is a very brief but indicative outline which may be of value to the beginner:

I. Signals
   A. Whistle — have a whistle and get the children used to a stop, look, and listen response when blown.
   B. Accompany hand or body signals by voice — make the challenges specific and to be taken literally.
   C. Give a challenge — blow the whistle, immediately give another. Keep repeating through multiple patterns. (If this is unclear refer to questions and Challenges in Movement Exploration, end of paper)
II. Question Phrasing
   A. Who Can?
   B. Can You?
   C. What Can?
   D. Show me . . .
   E. Try to . . .
   F. How high can you climb the rope as opposed to climb til you are even with a specific mark.
III. Demonstrations
   A. Do a particular task (teacher)
   B. Have some students perform
IV. Discipline
   A. Give the child something to do with a particular piece of equipment while you pass out the same to other children.
   B. The whistle should be met with an eagerness to hear the next challenge, try to avoid the connotation that it is a negative signal to end all activity.

"To Use — I have tried to write what follows in a form that would be functional to those who wish to use it. An explanation of Movement Exploration could never be accomplished in a paper of this length just as it would be futile to attempt to cover thoroughly even one specific area of activities in this field.

"What follows is a very brief mention of some areas of skill and perception: body image, balance agility, ball handling, swimming, and for most of these one or two movement exploration activities that could be applied in each area. Though the activities are specific you will see how they each can be applied to practically any of the above mentioned areas of skill and perception as well as many not mentioned — they are classified as they are just as examples and illustrative purposes.

"At the very end of this paper are some diagrams of equipment which might be useful in understanding activities as well as in setting up programs. Also there is a section on Questions and Challenges in Movement Exploration which I hope will help those unfamiliar with this subject to gain some perspective in actual administration of the theory involved.

"I sincerely hope this paper will in someway be functional to you.

. . .

PERCEPTUAL MOTOR CHARACTERISTICS OF THE TRAINABLE MENTALLY RETARDED AND CORRESPONDING MOVEMENT EXPLORATION ACTIVITIES

"Body Image

The typical trainable mentally retarded seems to have no concept of left and right and will fail to identify his left or right sides, hands, and body position as related to an object. The trainable mentally retardates at our school (age group 13-21) exhibit very good left-right awareness; however, most trainable children around the ages of 10 or 11 will possess the coordination of four year olds. Therefore it would seem that training these children in perception of body image would be basic to the acquisition of more complex motor and cognitive skills.

"Routines to establish awareness of parts:

A. HOPPING
  1. Hop on first one foot and then the other.
  2. Hop quietly.
  3. Hop for height.
  4. Hop for distance.
  5. Who can hop in different directions?
  6. Change the level of the upper body while hopping.
  7. At the height of the hop make some striking motion.
B. JUMPING
  1. How can you jump as high as possible?
  2. Repeat, jumping high but landing quietly.
  3. Jump and turn around as far as possible.
  4. Jump as far as possible from a stationary start.
  5. Run and jump as far as possible.

   6. Jump and make some kind of striking motion.
   7. Jump backward.
C. SKIPPING
   1. Practice skipping while moving in a particular direction.
   2. Skip among group; change directions, avoid collisions.
   3. Skip as lightly as possible.
   4. Lift as high off the ground as possible while skipping.
   5. Do something different with the hands while skipping.
   6. While skipping, lean from side to side from the waist.
   7. Skip backward.
   8. Skip in a circle.
   9. Skip in a square.
   10. Can you skip in many directions while facing one way?
   11. Take as few skips as possible to get from one point to another.
   12. Skip as quickly as possible from one point to another.

"Balance

The problem of balance seems to often focus on whether or not the child fully comprehends the task he is asked to perform. For instance, I have asked children to stand on one leg and all but three children managed this task; those that found balancing on one leg very difficult had their feet spread apart but when instructed to stand with feet together they performed without difficulty. By being observant and supportive of the children an instructor can help his students hurdle fundamental skills that will enable him to expand and explore as an individual. A fundamental task like standing on one foot opens the way for numerous activities.

   Routine for enhancing balance:

   A. two, three, and four point balance problems on the mat:

Hand and knee balance, *two points* (cross pattern) right arm and left leg in the air.

Hand and knee balance on *three points*, lifting either one hand or foot from mat.

Hand Knee balance, *four points* touching the mat.

B. HOPSCOTCH VARIATIONS:

"Italian Hopscotch

This game, played with a puck, is a variation of Ladder Hopscotch. A number of players form a line and take turns in the several activities.

The game proceeds as follows:

1. Toss puck into area 1; then hop into area 1.
2. Kick puck into area 2; then hop into area 2; and continue hopping and kicking puck on, finally reaching area 8.
3. In area 8, both feet may be put down. Pick up puck and hop out.
4. Hop backwards through all squares from area 8 to area 1 in turn.

5	4
6	3
7	2
8	1

A foul or a miss is charged when:

1. Player steps on any line.
2. Puck stops on any line.
3. Both feet are put down in any area except area 8.
4. Touching ground with hands.
5. Changing feet. (the penalty for a foul or miss is loss of turn)

"Finland Hopscotch

Arrange a number of boys and girls in a single line facing and three feet away from the No. 1 area of the court. The first player in the line takes a position in front of area No. 1. Holding a puck, he tosses puck into area No. 1 and proceeds to play the game as follows:

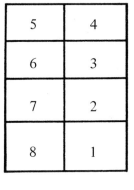

1. Hop into area No. 1; pick up puck; and hop out of court.
2. Hop into area No. 1; then hop into area No. 2; pick up puck and hop out of court.
3. Continue up through all the area and back out again. NOTE: In areas 4-5-7-8-both feet may touch ground, with one foot in each area.

The following fouls or misses result in loss of turn:

1. Touching a line with feet at any time.
2. Using two feet anywhere except in straddle position in areas 4-5 and 7-8.
3. Changing feet while hopping.

"Snail Hopscotch

Arrange a number of boys and girls in a single line opposite and facing the first area in the court. The first player in the line takes a position at starting line (last outside block of spiral) and begins as follows:

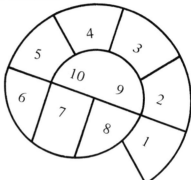

1. The player starts on one foot.
2. Player tosses puck into area No. 1; and hops over area No. 1 into area No. 2.
3. Player picks up puck and hops into area starting area via area No. 1.
4. Player then tosses puck into area No. 2. and hops over area No. 2 into area 3.
5. Picking up puck, player hops into area No. 2, into area No. 1, and hops out.
6. Player continues to progress around the spiral and back to the first area.

The following fouls, misses or errors result in lost of turn:

1. Tossing puck while not in proper hopping position at starting line. Leaning over starting line is permissible.
2. Puck when thrown comes to rest on any area line. In this case the puck is not in designated area.
3. Failure to hop in or out correctly.
4. Any irregularity in progression through the spiral areas.

"Question Mark Hopscotch

Arrange a number of boys and girls in a single file in front of, and three feet away from the circle marked "start". The first player advances to the "start" circle and with both feet in the circle proceeds as follows:

1. Hop to end of question mark.
2. At end of question mark reverse and hop back to starting circle.
3. Succeeding players hop into every space except those spaces having initials. Each player completing a successful trip through the question mark may place his initials in any space except starting circle. All players then follow same procedure.
4. Use the same procedure as for Snail Hopscotch except that two feet are placed in the starting circle or "dot" of question mark.
5. Each player may rest in the space marked with his own initials. Encourage the placing of initials in

spaces for "rest" purposes.

The following fouls, misses or errors result in loss of turn:

1. Stepping on any line in the court or question mark and dot.
2. Putting feet on the pavement or ground while hopping.
3. Touch any line on pavement or ground with any part of the body other than the feet.
   C. Balance Beam and Balance Board — please refer to diagrams and challenges listed on pages 117-19.

"Agility

Most trainables evidence good extension patterns when asked to crawl or jump in unstructured tasks. Considerable difficulty is encountered, however, by mental retardates when asked to hop and jump within particular lines or in squares. Observe a TMR girl playing hopscotch and you will notice the lack of "exact" control. Agility is a very broad field: all of us are more agile at some tasks than others and we know the degree of agility achieved is seldom constant. Being an agile tight-rope walker does not preclude agility on a soccer field or vice versa. Movement exploration offers a wealth of activities to experience motor movement, control, and coordination. In every challenge offered is exploration; every challenge repeated will hopefully increase the individual's agility in that specific task. The following activities are, perhaps three in a million.

"Routines in agility experience:

A. Hula Hoop Activities (really fun) — please see QUESTIONS and CHALLENGES section in back pages.
B. Ladder Activities — please see QUESTIONS AND CHALLENGES section in back pages. (Ladder: inclined position)
C. Hopscotch — please refer to rules and illustrations in *Balance* section.

"Throwing and Catching Balls

The trainable retardate exhibits what I call lack of "hands". He is usually able to catch a large soft ball bounced to him; however, the vast majority of children in my class cannot catch a softball thrown with medium velocity. Throwing for accuracy is almost an impossibility at their present level of achievement. I sincerely feel, however, their very low functional level is more a product of inexperience and lack of opportunity than a physical inadequacy. I have listed 32 activities under Ball Handling in the Questions and Challenges section of this paper. These exercises, I hope, will give you a start — take-off point for your imagination and creativeness to swell into an endless list of challenges that I believe can improve the functional level of our students.

"Swimming

This summer the Grant High School District TMR program included an hour of swimming daily, which as you can imagine opens up an extensive area in every phase of movement exploration. All of us are probably familiar with the weightlessness sensation of being held up by water — if the children could relax they would be free of awkwardness, free to float and to glide. Once fear is abated, or at least curtailed, movement in water — at whatever level of proficiency — is a total sensory experience. It provides avenues to explore, excel, experiment, and become aware. Our students found swimming to be a very positive experience and it did prove to be a highlight in our summer program. Many schools or centers for the Trainable Mentally Retarded do not provide swimming experience for their students because they lack personnel or facilities but I would encourage instructors to do whatever possible, perhaps contact the American Red Cross, in an effort to incorporate swimming into their programs.

QUESTIONS AND CHALLENGES IN MOVEMENT EXPLORATION

"Ball Handling
1. Can you bounce the ball keeping it waist high?
2. Now can you take the ball down to a very low bounce?
3. Can you change hands and keep the ball bouncing just as low with this hand?
4. This time, how low can YOU go while bouncing the ball? Keep it bouncing as you get into that low position.
5. Bounce to a standing position and repeat this with the other hand.
6. Can you go down lower while bouncing with this second hand?
7. Come to a standing position again while bouncing the ball.
8. Try bouncing the ball while looking away from the ball. Try not to peek.
9. Change hands many times while doing this.
10. Can you bounce the ball very low while doing this?
11. Now can you move among your friends without bumping, while bouncing the ball? You may have to look around now and then to avoid bumping.
12. Change hands many times while doing this.
13. Who can bounce the ball with a different part of the body? Remember that to bounce the ball means to strike it downward.
14. Find another part of the body with which you can bounce the ball.
15. Can you bounce the ball on the ground and catch it before it bounces again.
16. Now can you bounce the ball on the ground and jump to catch it before it bounces again.
17. How high can you toss the ball, catching it before it bounces?
18. If you are successful, try to toss it even higher.
19. Place the ball on the ground. Find a way to go over the ball without

touching it.
20. Try this several times, changing the way you go over the ball each time.
21. How can you get the ball from your feet to your partner's hands?
22. Can you find another way to get the ball from your feet to your partner's hands?
23. Show me if you can volley the ball with your hands many times.
24. Count the most number of times that you can volley the ball in succession.
25. Now try to volley the ball with different parts of your body, using your hands only when it is necessary to regain control of the ball.
26. Place the ball on the ground and gently kick it with the inside of one foot then the inside of the other foot. Try to keep the ball quite close to you at all times. Walk as you do this.
27. Repeat this, walking faster if you can. Look up to see where you are going.
28. If you have been able to keep the ball quite close to you while dribbling with your feet, practice dribbling while running.
29. Throw the ball down the field, retrieve it and sit down.
30. Now throw it back this way and retrieve it.
31. Try to kick the ball straight ahead of you down the field. Retrieve it and sit down.
32. Do the same thing coming back this way.

"Hula Hoops
1. Can you roll your hoop and keep it from falling over?
2. While it is rolling, can you make it turn without having to stop it.
3. Who can spin his hoop like an egg beater?
4. How can you throw the hoop on the ground so that it will return to you?
5. Can you throw the hoop high in the air and catch it before it lands?
6. While rolling your hoop, can you jump through it?
7. Can you climb in and out and around your hoop?
8. Who can make the hoop turn circles while it is on his arm?
    . . .while it is around his neck?
    . . .while it is around his foot?
9. While holding the hoop, can you use it as a jumping rope?
10. Who can jump into a hoop held by his partner? Let your partner try.
11. Can you and your partner throw a hoop back and forth to each other?
12. Find some different ways to get it to your partner.
13. See if you can throw your hoop so that your partner is in the middle of it.

"Ladder (Inclined Position)
1. Can you go up the ladder using your hands and feet?

2. In what other way can you use your hands and feet to go up the ladder?
3. Can you weave in out of the rungs?
4. Can you go up the ladder without touching the rungs.
5. Who can use just his feet to go up the ladder?
6. This time while using your feet can you touch every rung?
7. Can you skip every other rung?
8. Who can go down the ladder using his hands and feet?
9. Can you go down head first?
10. Can you go down feet first?
11. Can you walk down each rung?
12. Can you walk backward down each rung?
13. How else can you get from one end of the ladder to the other?

"Walking Board — Balance Beam
1. Who can walk slowly across the board touching heel against toe?
2. Can you go across the board backward while touching heel against toe?
3. Can you cross backward and not look at your feet?
4. Who can cross the board moving slowly sideways?
5. Can you walk across the board, turn without stepping off, and walk back sideways?
6. Who can cross to the middle, stop, bounce and then go on?
7. Can you go just halfway, turn and come back?
8. How many steps do you need to go across the board? Can you count them?"

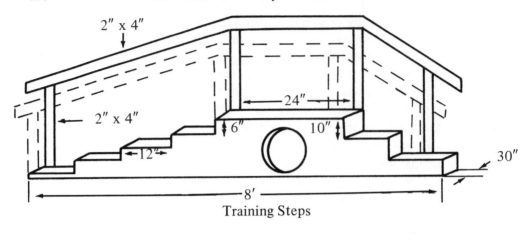

Training Steps

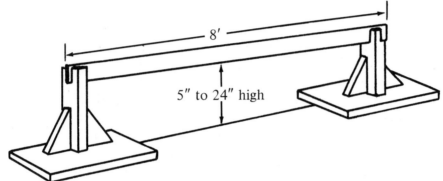

Balance Beam

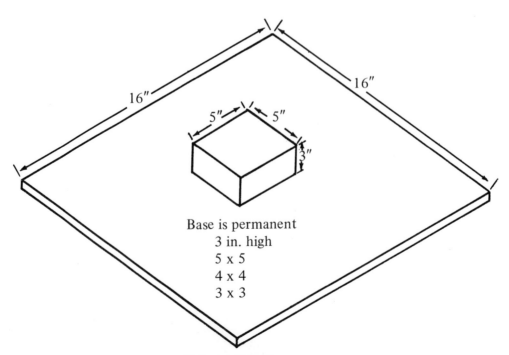

Base is permanent
3 in. high
5 x 5
4 x 4
3 x 3

Balance Board

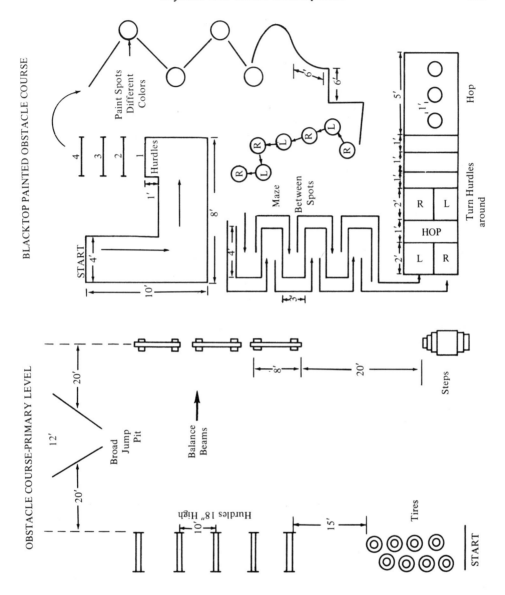

MATERIALS AND AIDS

Music Books

1. The Magic of Music. Ginn and Company (Kindergarten).
2. Bregman, J. K.: 33 Rhythms for Children. Vacco and Conn, Inc., 1956.
3. Ginglend and Stiles: Music Activities. Abingdon Press, 1965 (for retarded children).
4. Arthur, Sister Mary, and Elaine, Sister Mary: We Speak Through Music. Stanborn Productions, 1959.
5. A B C Music Series (Book I). American Book Company, 1963.
6. Songs Children Sing. Hall and McCreary Company.
7. Childrens' Favorite Songs, Haskin Service.
8. Pitts, L.: Singing On Our Way. Ginn and Company, 1949.
9. A B C Music Series. American Book Company, 1959 (Kindergarten).
10. Carter, J.: Twenty Little Songs. Willis Music Company.
11. Groetzinger, I., and Gode, M.: Play and Sing, Action Song Book, Hayes School Publishing Company.
12. Wood, L., and Scott, L.: Singing Fun. Webster Publishing Company.
13. The Kindergarten Book. Ginn and Company.
14. Miessner and Beattie: Melodies to Play and Sing. McCreary Company.
15. Miller, M., and Zajan, P.: Finger Play. G. Schirmer.
16. The First Grade Book. Ginn and Company.
17. Our Singing World. Ginn and Company, The Kindergarten Book, The First Grade Book, The Second Grade Book, Singing and Rhyming (Third Grade), Singing Every Day (Fourth Grade).
18. Ginglend, D.: Music Activities for Retarded Children. Abingdon Press.
19. King, S., and Presser, T.: Party Piano Book. Bryn Mawr.
20. Seeger, R.: American Folk Songs for Children. Doubleday.
21. Whelan, F.: All Through The Year. Hall and McCreary Company.
22. This is Music — #3. McCall, Allyn, and Bacon, Inc., 1962.
23. Wiechard, A.: Today's Tunes for Children. Paul Schmitt Music Company.
24. Perkins and Vernon: The Silver Book of Songs. Schmidt, Hall, McCreary Company.
25. Tobitt, J.: Promenade All. 1947.
26. Day, R.: Rhythm and Song. The Willis Music Company.
27. Kuhn, J. C.: Rhythms for Children. Bregmann, Vocco, and Conn, Inc., 1956.
28. Current sheet music for familiar show tunes.

Records

1. Spin-O-Rama Records, 356 West 40th Street, New York, New York.
   "Jesse Crawford At the Organ"
   "Christmas Sing Along"
2. Bowman Records, Los Angeles, California.
   "Listening Time I"
   "Listening Time II"
3. Decca Records.

"Babar"

"The Magic Record"

"Songs of Safety"

"Health Can Be Fun" (Children's Records)

"A Child's First Record" (Sung by F. Luther.)

"The Three Billy Goats Gruff (Sung and told by F. Luther.)

"Twas The Night Before Christmas" (Fred Waring and his Pennsylvanians, 3 records.)

4. Sound Book Press Society, Scarsdale, New York.

"Musical Sound Books"

"Musical Sound Books for Dancing"

"Musical Sound Books," C L 512

"Music to Remember" ("March of Toys," etc.)

5. Picnick International Inc., Long Island City, New York.

"Happy Birthday"

6. Miller International Records, Media, Pennsylvania.

"Songs of the Golden West"

"Symphony for Lovers"

7. Mercury Record Company.

"Kiddie Hit Parade"

8. Radic Craftsmen Col., Los Angeles, California.

"Strauss Waltzes"

9. RCA Victor, Camden, New Jersey.

"Music for Relaxation"

"Howdy Doddy's Do's and Don'ts"

"Peter Rabbit, Goldilocks, and other tales"

"If You Catch A Little Cold"

10. Columbia Record Company.

"Anniversary Songs, C L 586

"The Tap Dance Record"

"Let's Have A Rhythm Band"

"Peter Cottontail and The Funny Little Bunny" (Sung by Gene Autry.)

"Rhythm Band"

"Dance Along Zoo — Captain Kangaroo"

"Songs from Walt Disney's Magic Kingdom"

"Doctor Sniffiswiper and The Fox and His Friends"

11. Affiliated Publishers, Inc., Rockefeller Center, New York, New York.

"Romper Room"

"Peter Cottontail" (a Golden Record)

"School Days" (a Golden Record)

"Easter Parade" (a Golden Record)

"Baby's First Record" (a Golden Record)

"When the Red, Red Robin Comes Bob, Bob Bobin' Along" (a Golden Record)

"From Walt Disney's Perri-Together Time" (a Golden Record)

12. Sing "N" Do Company, Ridgewood, New Jersey.

"Sing N Do Songs"

13. Ruth Evans Records, Box 132, Branch x, Springfield, Massachusetts.

"Childhood Rhythms I"
"Childhood Rhythms III"
"Childhood Rhythms V"
"Childhood Rhythms VI"
"Childhood Rhythms VII"

14. Folkways Record and Service Corporation, 117 West 46th Street, New York, New York
    "Adventures in Rhythm"
    "Call and Response" — Rhythmic
    "Songs for Kids" (By Marcia Berman)
    "American Folk Songs for Children"
    "Group Singing"
    "Learning As We Play" — Album #FC 7659
    "American Folk Songs"

15. Stanborn Productions, Valhalla, New York.
    "We Speak Through Music"

16. Ginn and Company, New York, New York.
    Let's Listen (Auditory Training for Speech Development)
    "Our Singing World" — Kindergarten Album KA
    "Our Singing World" — Kindergarten Album KB

17. Bowmar Records, 4921 Santa Monica Boulevard, Los Angeles, California
    "Songs for Children with Special Needs" (3 records)
    "Listening Time Album #1" (4 records)
    "Rhythm Is Fun!" (3 records)
    "Songs From Singing Fun" (4 records)

18. Bowmar Records, 10515 Burbank Boulevard, North Hollywood, California.
    "Singing Games Album #1"
    "Folk Dances #5" (American)

19. Bowmar Educational-Children's Music Center, 5353 West Pico Boulevard, Los Angeles, California.
    "Patriotic Songs"

20. Children's Record Guild, 27 Thompson Street, New York, New York.
    "My Playful Scarf"
    "The Little Puppet"
    "Noah's Ark"
    "Animal Supermarket"
    "Grandfather's Farm"
    "Nothing To Do"
    "A Visit To My Little Friend"
    "Train To The Zoo"
    "Eensie-Weensie Spider"

21. Concept Records, P. O. Box 524, North Bellmore, Long Island, New York.
    "Concept Records I" (Basic Songs For The Exceptional Children) N-C 2457

22. Stanley Bowmar Company, Inc., 12 Cleveland Street, Valhall, New York.
    "Songs For Children With Special Needs"
    "Singing Games For Primary Grades"

"Rhythm Is Fun"

"Childhood Rhythms" (arranged and recorded by Ruth Evans — three records), Series I

23. Childcraft Records.
    "Let's All Join In"
24. Pioneer Records, Houston, Texas.
    "Folk Dance Tunes"
25. The Record Guild of America, Inc.
    "March Militaire"
26. Pickwick Sales Corporation, 33-34th Street, Brooklyn, New York.
    "When You Wish Upon A Star"
    "Happy Birthday"
27. Peter Pan Records, Synthetic Plastics Company, Newark, New Jersey.
    "Frosty the Snowman"
    "Puff 'n' Toot"
    "Easter Parade"
    "The Lord's Prayer"
    "Circus"
    "Santa Claus Is Coming to Town"
28. Capitol Records.
    "Bozo on the Farm"
    "Bozo at the Circus" (a "Reader" record)
    "Learning to Listen"
29. Alma Records, Inc., 4705 Elmwood Avenue, Los Angeles, California
    "Favorite Hymns" (Paul Nickelson)
30. Pram Records.
    "Nice and Bye-Bye"
    "Where Are Your Eyes?"
31. Horizons Records Series, Silver Burdett Company.
    Victor Record Guild.
    "La Golondrina" (Waltz)
32. Audio Education Inc.
    "Primary Music — Rhythm"
33. Young Peoples Records
    "My Playmate, The Wind"
    "Jingle Bells and Other Songs for Winter Fun"
    "The Little Fireman (sung by Thomas Glazer)
    "Every Day We Grow I-O" (sung by Thomas Glazer)
    "Swing Your Partner"
    "When the Sun Shines"
    "Little Gray Ponies" (told and sung by Thomas Glazer)
    "I'm Dressing Myself (written by G. Lowell and P. List)

VI

GUIDES FOR TEACHING
THE TRAINABLE MENTALLY RETARDED
LEVEL I

SOCIAL COMPETENCIES

M.A. 1 to 3 years

In the School

Behavioral Objectives	Learning Experiences to Develop Behavior	Suggested Teacher Procedures to Develop Behavior — Level I
✗ Child develops the ability to take turns.	Take turns playing with toys, playhouse equipment, being leader, getting a drink at fountain, washing hands.	Structure situations where child takes turns.
		Discuss and demonstrate situations, such as waiting while others are having their turn in classroom activities and on playground equipment. Always be sure each child has a turn.
		Have aggressive child assist a shy child by being "teacher" and helping that child.
		Utilize existing friendships between children to encourage cooperative behavior.
	Play with building blocks on 4′ x 6′ throw rug. Keep toys on rug.	Assign portion of day or week for specific child to play in certain area or do certain tasks.
Child develops the ability to share.	Bring items from home to share with classmates.	When children bring items from home, give opportunity for sharing with other children, i.e. candy, toys, etc.
	Play cooperatively with duplicate or similar toys.	Provide toys for construction by several children within a small group, i.e. building blocks, Tinker Toys, etc.
	Share sandbox space and toys while playing in sand.	Provide sandbox with toys.
		Show filmstrips (FS-001, FS-002).

Child develops the ability to cooperate.	Cooperate in group activities, such as "Let's pretend we are Popcorn or Bacon."	Schedule ample time at end of each activity for cleanup and to put away all equipment and materials. Each item should always be returned to same place.
		Have children pretend to be kernels of popcorn, slowly opening little by little, making loud popping sounds as they become "delicious" popcorn. Have children lie still and straight on floor pretending to be strips of bacon cooking in a frying pan.
	Take turns with room duties, such as cleaning table, delivering messages, turning off lights, feeding pets, etc.	Make job chart listing "jobs" and corresponding illustrations. Use Child's photograph to identify assignment. Rotate daily.
Child develops the ability for good grooming.	Look in full-length mirror to see if face is clean, hair is combed, clothing buttoned, etc.	Checking by means of full-length mirror needs to be done several times a day, i.e. morning, before and after lunch, and whenever appropriate.
		Teach song "Look in the Mirror" (B-001).
	Take turns being Good Grooming Monitor.	Stress that Good Grooming Monitor checks self first, then sees that others are tidy.
	Wear appropriate apparel for special days, i.e. slacks, shorts, play clothes, etc.	Notify parents beforehand what special day's activities will include so dress will be appropriate.
	Hang coats, sweaters, hats on hangers or hooks.	Make certain all apparel is labeled with children's names.
	Brush teeth at school. Wash hands and face before and after meals.	Always demonstrate how activity should be done.
Child develops good eating habits.	Practice proper eating habits during meals.	Be consistent in having children hold cup correctly, keep mouth closed while chewing, sit in chair properly, keep fingers out of food, milk, etc.
	Place chair close to table, sit up straight, put napkin in lap, use spoon and fork.	Use verbal praise for correct use of utensils, napkins, etc., and good manners.

	Eat at least a small portion of everything at lunch time.	Serve lunch at school and eat with children. Children enjoy eating lunch seated around small tables. If meals are served family style, children can be taught to pass food and learn to serve themselves, taking only small portions at a time.
Child develops good manners.	Take small bites of food. Chew properly. Eat food in proper sequence (dessert last). Clean up eating area.	Praise child taking small bites, chewing food, etc.
	Wait until everyone is served and "host" or teacher says, "You may eat now."	Always use same manners, considerations, and expressions expected from class.
	Say, "Thank you," "Please," "No thank you," "Your welcome."	Comment on "turn for all." Be certain each child has opportunity to participate.
	Serve at snack time, clear table, and pass wastebasket.	At snack time, present various kinds of food.
	Peel a banana, crack an egg, use spoon to eat cereal, knife to butter toast, etc.	Demonstrate how to peel banana, crack an egg, spoon out sugar, etc.
Child develops an awareness and acceptance of authority.		Develop positive interpersonal relationship with each child so child will accept other authority figures.
	Identify teacher, bus driver, etc. from photographs.	Show photographs of people who represent authority figures in the school: teachers, matrons, principal, drivers, etc.
	Take turns assuming duties and authority of "teacher," i.e. flip flashcards, distribute and collect materials, choose songs, and form lines for recess.	Keep directions simple and consistent. Follow through and make certain child carries out instructions. Be firm and structured. Have other personnel follow through using same approach.
	Practice following directions on signs, i.e. "Enter," "Exit," "Walk," "Don't Walk," etc.	Place painted plywood signs and signals in appropriate areas in classroom. Praise children who follow directions.

In the Home

Behavioral Objectives	Learning Experiences to Develop Behavior	Suggested Teacher Procedures to Develop Behavior
Child develops an awareness of membership in the family.	Bring photographs of members of family to school.	Make home visit in order to become familiar with the family constellation.
	Identify by name older or younger siblings.	
	Mount photographs as gifts for siblings, parents, grandparents.	Provide cardboard, construction paper, other backing materials to mount photographs.
	In playhouse corner take turns helping "mother" clean house, feed baby, and do other household chores.	Provide playhouse corner with kitchen equipment and household furniture.
	Boys and girls assume family roles in helping each other.	During free activity observe children's interactions in playhouse area and verbally reinforce examples of cooperative and supportive behavior.
Child recognizes his limitations.		Require of child only what he can perform. Set tasks within ability so child will understand high performance in all areas is not always expected of him.
	Practice daily activities, i.e. going to bathroom, fastening clothing, handling toys and equipment in classroom and on playground.	Be near enough to prevent any mishaps and to assist child having difficulty.
Child requests help when needed.	Accept help from another child or adult in putting on coat, rolling up sleeping mat, folding blanket, etc.	Structure situation in which assistance might be exchanged by either peers or adults.
Child develops an awareness of others and their needs.	Offer a "share time" item to another child	Call attention to donor's feelings and recipient's feelings.

Guide child to choose activities requiring cooperation.

Provide' activities for small groups, working children into natural pairs or utilizing existing friendships.

Have one child pass crayons, paper, straws, etc., or distribute surprises and treats.

Make certain all children verbalize to the utmost of their capabilities, indicating, "One" or "Two" and always saying, "Please" and "Thank you."

Cut out large octopus from butcher paper, add eyes and wide smile. Mount on bulletin board. Place bubbles leading from octopus to large sign. "Mind your Manners." Print a phrase on each arm, i.e. "Please," "Thank you," "I am sorry," "Excuse me."

Make small fish from different colored paper. When child uses one of the phrases, print his name on a fish.

Help a classmate with clothing, take another child's hand while marching, help work simple puzzles, etc.

Use verbal expressions "For you," "Would you like?" when passing, sharing, or offering food or materials.

Help another to carry out a task with which he is familiar, i.e. water plants, shut window, put away crayons.

Take turns being host or hostess for snacks. Ask, "How many would you like?" Other child responds, "One, please," "Two, please." "Thank you." "You're welcome"

Child develops simple verbal courtesies.

Pin fish to appropriate arm.

Behavioral Objectives	Learning Experiences to Develop Behavior	Suggested Teacher Procedures to Develop Behavior
Child develops an awareness of routine daily living.	Tell about daily activities when at school and home.	Display pictures on bulletin board illustrating activities, i.e. getting dressed, brushing teeth, eating breakfast, riding school bus, classroom routines, washing hands, hanging up coat, eating dinner, taking bath, sleeping, etc. Display (SP-001).
		Make paper plate clocks with movable hands and mount on bulletin board. Set hands at time children have recess, lunch, dismissal.
	Observe clocks on wall.	Call children's attention to position of hands for corresponding activity.

In the Neighborhood

Behavioral Objectives	Learning Experiences to Develop Behavior	Suggested Teacher Procedures to Develop Behavior
Child develops an awareness of the neighborhood.	Take walk with class around school neighborhood.	Prior to walk, discuss with children some of the things they will see and behavior expected of them. Point out fences, lawns, flower beds, crosswalks, homes, garages.
Child becomes aware of neighborhood restrictions.		Emphasize following rules: Stay in own yard. Never go into neighbor's home, garage or yard uninvited. Play away from streets and cars. Always follow parents' rules.
	Set up model of neighborhood.	Reinforce rules through games, cutout pictures, etc. (Mics-001, Misc-002). Display (SP-002).

In the Community

Behavioral Objectives	Learning Experiences to Develop Behavior	Suggested Teacher Procedures to Develop Behavior
Child develops an awareness of the community – stores, school, parks, swimming pool, etc.		Take field trips around town. Visit fire station, police station, post office, another school, grocery store, park, bowling alley, restaurant, gas station, bank, zoo, barber shop, drug store.
	Identify pictures or models of buildings and places visited as teacher gives name.	Set up toy model of community, in large enough area for several children to play or work together. Utilize (Misc-001), (Misc-002). Display (SP-002).

COMMUNICATIVE SKILLS

M.A. 1 to 3 years

Oral

Level I

Behavioral Objectives	Learning Experiences to Develop Behavior	Suggested Teacher Procedures to Develop Behavior
Child develops the ability to make needs or ailments known.		Work toward use of recognizable language rather than guttural sounds or gestures to communicate wants or needs.
	Raise hand and verbally indicate omission.	Distribute snacks, treats, paper, crayons, etc., deliberately overlooking one child. Ask, "Did everyone receive _____?"
	Communicate to teacher need to go to bathroom.	Respond with immediate cooperation when child indicates need. If need is obvious but not verbalized, ask child if he has to go to the bathroom.

	Inform teacher when feeling ill or an accident or injury has occurred.	Recognize signs of illness. Let child know his ailments are understood. Help child find adequate ways to verbalize problem.
	Make simple requests using one or two words for drink of water, snacks, toys, etc.	Avoid granting child's request until attempts are made to verbalize needs or wants.
		Do not interrupt or correct when child is attempting to speak.
Child develops the ability to obey simple commands.	React appropriately to "No."	Specific commands must be taught as early as possible for child's protection. An appropriate response to the word "No" is imperative. Immediately upon infraction, capture child's attention by taking his hands or shoulders and directly facing him. To establish eye contact, take child's chin in hand and gently guide until child looks squarely into teacher's face. Say softly but firmly and authoritatively, "No!" while shaking head.
	Understand and obey simple commands, i.e. "Please sit down, stand up, wash your hands," etc.	Start with basic, one-step directions. First demonstrate each and repeat in classroom situations until proper response is learned.
	Form circle around teacher. When called by name, carry out teacher's request and return to seat.	Ask each child by name to "Please come to circle." "Bring your chair." "Please get me the book." "Please bring me my pencil."
	During cleanup time, collect scissors, crayons, scrap paper, etc., and place in appropriate container. Carry wastepaper basket to each child for scrap paper. Pick up paper that has been dropped on floor.	Assign one child for each task. When necessary, accompany child collecting materials and papers. Children will sometimes not want to stop activity.
	Play "Bean Bag Game." Put bean bag on table, on chair, under table, etc., as directed.	Give each child an opportunity to participate even if it is necessary to provide some assistance.

	Look in mirror and listen to name.	Provide full-length mirror. Repeat name of child several times.
	Acknowledge name by raising hand or standing up.	Give each child time to respond to name before continuing with morning roll call.
	Listen and respond to name by taking place in line, choice of toys, etc.	Use child's name at every opportunity throughout day. Encourage children to use each other's names.
	Return greeting of teacher or another child.	Accept and praise any response made. Teach "Greeting Song" (B-001, B-002).
Child develops ability to say name.	Look in mirror and say name.	Repeat name with child.
	Sing, "Who's that knocking at my door?" At end of song, respond with, "It is _____." (Say own name.)	Point to child who is to respond.
	Play "Teacher-Ball." Form circle around teacher.	Roll ball to each child in turn, calling out name first.
	During opening exercises, step forward and tell name to class.	Gradually increase identification to include last name.
Child develops the ability to identify main parts of body.	Face mirror while following teacher's directions.	Direct child to put hands on head, touch nose, raise arms, etc.
	Take turns being leader.	Play "Simple Simon" game with children, using appropriate movements.
	Sing songs about parts of body.	Teach song, "Put Your Finger in the Air" (B-001).
	Respond to directions.	Give directions orally without gestures.
		"Hands on your hips, hands on your knees, Hands, behind you if you please, Touch your shoulder, touch your nose, Touch your ears, and your toes.

	Place features on face.	Mount outline of face on flannel board. Provide removable eyes, nose, etc.
	Identify missing parts.	Place picture of doll with a missing part, i.e. arm, leg, head, on flannel board. Furnish large mannequin puzzles. (Misc-003).
Child develops the ability to name simple objects on sight.	Observe each object, feel shape repeat name.	Present only three-dimensional objects at first. Say names slowly and clearly.
	Name object.	Re-present each object without naming. If child has difficulty recalling name and exhibits frustration, add two more objects, one of which he can identify and allow him to name that one. Urge another attempt to name original item immediately following successful response.
	Reach in box and without looking, select item. Name object. If correct, may keep for part of school day.	Assemble a "Surprise Box" containing several familiar toys or objects, i.e. ball, car, spoon, key, lock, etc.
	Watch teacher's mouth and repeat name.	Display picture of a single object. Place picture directly under mouth and say name. Use pictures from magazines and books. Utilize (B-003) and Peabody Kit flash cards (Misc-004).

Raise your hands high in the air,
At your side, on your hair.
Raise your hands as before
While you clap 1, 2, 3, 4.
My hands upon my head I place,
On my shoulders, on my face,
Then I raise them up on high,
And make my fingers quickly fly,
Then I put them in front of me
And gently clap 1, 2, 3."

Child recognizes and identifies familiar objects in room.	Touch object as teacher says name.	Set aside time during morning circle period to identify familiar objects in room.
	Look at pictures and point to corresponding object. If possible, say name.	Display pictures of objects in classroom.
	Play "What is Missing?"	Place three familiar objects on table. Have children close eyes. Take one object away and ask, "What is missing?"
Child develops the ability to use simple sentences.	Sing or chant simple songs. Recite nursery rhymes with teacher.	While teaching or reciting nursery rhymes point to appropriate pictures depicting rhyme. Display (SP-003) or (Misc-005).
	Watch filmstrips. Try to retell story or event that occurred.	Show filmstrips of fairy tales with which children are familiar. (FS-003), FS-004, FS-005).
	Join in refrain each time with, "Who's that walking over my bridge?"	Retell "Three Billy Goats Gruff." Say, "The Troll heard the clip-clop, clip-clop and roared in his big troll voice . . ." Wait for the children to complete sentence.
	Say as a group or when pointed to "I'll huff and I'll puff, and I'll blow your house down!" in the Wolf's voice.	Follow same procedure with "The Three Little Pigs."
		Provide variety of puppets either commercial or teacher-made, i.e. stick, paper bag, sock.
	Listen to puppet and respond to greeting.	Manipulate puppet, greeting each child individually.
	Reply through puppet.	Direct question to puppet that child is holding.
	Two or more children stage puppet show.	Blanket-covered table can be used as stage.
	Hold conversation between puppets.	
	Shake hands with classmate and ask "How are you?"	Arrange children in circle. Encourage complete responses, i.e. "I am fine."

Behavioral Objectives	Learning Experiences to Develop Behavior	Suggested Teacher Procedures to Develop Behavior
	Raise hand and say, "I have the lion," "I have the apple," etc.	Use two boxes of Lotto Game cards. Distribute two cards from one set to each child. Hold up card and wait for child to indicate he has matching picture.
	Look at picture and answer, "The horse is eating" or "He is eating grass," etc.	Use action picture to elicit responses in simple sentences. Ask, "What is the horse doing?" "What is the horse eating?"

Word Recognition

Behavioral Objectives	Learning Experiences to Develop Behavior	Suggested Teacher Procedures to Develop Behavior
Child recognizes name.	Look at Polaroid picture of self with name printed underneath.	Take Polaroid pictures. Mount and print names. Display in prominent place.
	Raise hand when own name is shown.	Prepare individual flash cards with each child's name. Hold up card and wait for child to recognize name.
	Select own chair or table and attach name tag and photograph.	Place names of children on clothes, hooks, toothbrushes, crayon boxes, etc. Encourage child to look at label and repeat name.
	Play "Going Home." Sit on floor in front of teacher at dismissal time.	Hold up name cards one at a time. If child recognizes name he may get his coat. If child cannot recognize name, read it aloud.
	Find object on which own name has been printed.	Cut shapes or figures of animals and objects from construction paper, i.e. circle, square, pumpkin, Christmas tree, heart, rabbit, etc. Print each child's name on one cut-out.
Child recognizes simple words or cues of safety.	Look at and talk about posters.	Display large, colorful safety posters and explain meaning. Emphasize safety concept.

Listening

Behavioral Objectives	Learning Experiences to Develop Behavior	Suggested Teacher Procedure to Develop Behavior
	Look at picture books to strengthen recognition of safety cues.	Encourage children to identify safety cues in posters. (Misc-006, Misc-007).
		Provide picture books that reinforce concepts of safety.
	Recognize simple safety words.	Build vocabulary, i.e. "Hot" (H), "Cold" (C), "Go," etc.
Child develops the ability to listen attentively to short stories.		Tell flannel board stories so that children can see as well as hear stories.
	Place character on flannel board as it is introduced in story.	Use stories with enough characters so each child can participate, i.e. "The Gingerbread Boy" and "Chicken Little."
		Teacher-made puppets are another means of visual presentation. Resource (B-004).
	Listen to picture book stories. Sit in circle around teacher so each child can see pictures they are shown.	Tell, rather than read, stories at this level. Hold book so illustrations are facing children. Maintain attention by use of different voices for characters in story. Keep story time short. Make it enjoyable.
	Watch filmstrips of fairy tales.	Repeat filmstrips often. (FS-003, FS-004, FS-005).
Child develops the ability to identify sounds of nature.	Listen to records or recordings. Imitate sounds.	Acquaint children with common sounds, i.e. running water, rain, wind, thunder, etc. Make a recording or utilize (R-001 through R-004).

Objective	Child Activity	Teacher Activity / Method
		Familiarize children with common environmental sounds, i.e., whistle, bell, clock, telephone, door bell.
	Point to appropriate picture when teacher makes sound.	Place pictures representative of sounds on chalkboard, i.e. whistle, bell, telephone, etc.
	Select desired picture by correctly imitating sound of animal.	Mount several large pictures of animals and give corresponding sounds. If correctly identified, allow child to keep picture for part of school day.
	Play "Barnyard Game." Hold toy behind back and give sound for class to identify, then show toy.	Distribute toy animal to each child, i. e. horse, duck, chicken, dog, etc.
		Make certain each child has a turn, even if assistance is needed in making sound.
		Introduce songs, "Old MacDonald Had a Farm" and "Sounds I Hear" (B-001).
Child develops the ability to identify sounds of danger.	Identify sounds from tape.	Tape record sounds of danger to play in classroom.
	React to sound of car horn, "stop and look."	Introduce idea that some sounds require immediate action.
	Tell parents when warning sounds are heard.	Include sounds of a siren, train whistle, and railroad crossing bells.
		Music chosen should have clear, simple melody and strong rhythm easily felt by children.
		Note response shown by body or facial movements as child is listening.
Child listens to music.	Rest and remain quiet/still while listening to music.	Set mood for rest period by playing soft, soothing music.

	Sing and follow actions with fingers or sticks.	Sing song, "One, Two, What Shall I do?" (B-001). Lead singing and demonstrate actions. Let children take turns being leader.
Child develops the ability to listen.	Bring records to play in class.	Encourage children to bring records from home.
		Set example by listening carefully when children talk.
Child develops the ability to follow simple directions.	Perform simple drills, i.e. stand, sit, form line.	Give concise directions, one at a time.
	Respond with appropriate movements to verbal directions. May act as leader.	Action Play: Teddy Bear, Teddy Bear, Turn around / Teddy Bear, Teddy Bear, Touch the ground / Teddy Bear, Teddy Bear, Lead the band / Teddy Bear, Teddy Bear, Wave your hand / Teddy Bear, Teddy Bear, Reach the sky / Teddy Bear, Teddy Bear, Throw a kiss goodby / Teddy Bear, Teddy Bear, Climb the stairs / Teddy Bear, Teddy Bear, Say your prayers.
	Place finger on indicated object.	Select objects within child's experience.
	Hand teacher requested object.	Place three items on table. Instruct child to "Show me the ——." "Put your finger on the ——." Direct the child to "Give me ——."
	Play "Follow the Leader." Take turns as leader and give directions.	Give only verbal directions. Children will need to listen in order to follow instructions. "Put your hands on your head." "Put your hands on your nose." "Now put them on your toes."

Perceptual

Behavioral Objectives	Learning Experiences to Develop Behavior	Suggested Teacher Procedures to Develop Behavior
Child works in a defined area.	Color, draw, or paint within marked area.	Use masking tape to outline area on large sheet of paper in which child is to confine work.
	Glue bits of colored paper within yarn outline to make collage.	Glue string or yarn outline on paper.
		Provide small scraps of colored construction paper.
Child follows heavy solid lines with pencil or crayons.	Follow lines with index finger. Progress to crayon or pencil.	Tape long pieces of butcher paper to floor. Use broad felt pen to draw large circles and squares; straight, curved and wavy lines.
Child traces circles, half-circles, vertical, straight, and horizontal lines.	Draw around plastic lids and vinyl tile patterns on butcher paper.	Cut patterns for desired shapes from plastic lids, vinyl tile, etc.
	Trace over figures with large crayon.	Use Winterhaven Templates as models for size and shape (Misc-008).
Child begins working from left to right.	Look at pictures from left to right. Name objects from left to right.	Always work from left to right on flannel board when placing objects or pictures for sequence stories.
	Insert pegs from left to right.	Provide peg board and pegs. Place first peg at left so child will start on correct side.
	Play "Railroad Track Game." Starting at left, push small toy engine along tracks as teacher draws ties ahead of train.	On large piece of butcher paper, draw two black parallel, horizontal lines for railroad tracks. Starting on left fill in vertical lines to represent ties.

Child hand dominance establishes.	Draw ties for track from left to right as teacher moves train.	Reverse procedure.
		If child tends to perseverate by drawing ties one upon the other, have him change colors after drawing each tie and say, "Let's go ahead."
		Evaluate hand dominance:
		Obtain history of child's hand preference from parents.
		Observe child in play, eating, reaching for articles and record examples of hand usage.
		Test handedness by placing spoon, crayon, or book directly in front of child.
		Always present articles to child so that dominant hand is used.
		Recheck hand dominance by observing choice in using crayon, handling spoon, turning pages, etc.
	Kick large rubber ball. Step over barricade.	Test foot dominance.
		Note foot preference for first step on stairs.
	Look through small hole in piece of cardboard.	Test eye dominance. Child will use dominant eye and close other.
Child uses top to bottom motion.	Put object at top of board. Each child, in turn, places an object directly under it until a row is formed.	Provide flannel board and flannel-backed objects, figures, etc. Have first child begin at top of board.
	Draw vertical lines beginning at top and ending at bottom of page.	Color top edge of paper with green crayon and bottom with red. Say, "Let's make the lines go down, down, down, down. Start at top and go down, down, down."
	Place pegs from top to bottom in rows.	Provide peg boards and pegs.

Child recognizes own name on chair, work folder, hanger, etc.	Identify picture of self and printed name.
	Display each child's picture with name printed under it on bulletin board.
	Outline name with black felt pen to give child concept of shape.

	Walk around room pointing to each article on which own name is printed.
	Label crayons, work boxes, chairs, coat hangers, etc., in exact manner as printed under picture.
Child discriminates between gross shapes of objects.	Assemble simple wooden and rubber puzzles.
	For child's ease in handling, provide preschool puzzles of single object liftouts with knobs.
	Compare and match shapes and designs with dominoes, design blocks, etc.
	Commercial peg boards, sorting boxes, nesting cubes, etc., are readily available from catalogues or toy stores. Utilize (Misc-009).
Child plays imitative games.	Imitate teacher's hand movements while repeating words.
	Utilize finger play, jingles, and action songs.
	Finger play:
	"Jack in box sits so still"
	(closed fists)
	"Won't you come out?"
	"Yes, I will!" (fists fly open)
	"Open – shut them
	Open – shut them
	Give a little clap.
	Open – shut them
	Open – shut them
	Lay them in your lap.
	Creep them, creep them, creep them,

Way up to your chin. Open up your little mouth But do not let them get in!"	
Imitate actions of leader by waving arms, clapping hands and other body movements.	Play records of action songs, i.e. "Follow the Leader," "Looby Lou", "Did You Ever See a Lassie?" (R-005). Interpret music with appropriate motions. Give each child a turn being leader.
Child recognizes rhythm.	A child's natural response to rhythm is a body activity and movement. Initially, choose music that is direct, rhythmically strong, and uncomplicated.
Listen to music.	Replay same musical selection for a particular action, i.e. march walk, skip, gallop, to familiarize children with tempo and melody.
Perform appropriate activity indicated by musical cues.	This association enables children to change activity without verbal direction when a change of music is made. (R-006, R-007, R-008)
Place chairs in semicircle and sit facing teacher. Imitate Teacher's clapping pattern. Beat drums or shake bells in time to music.	Sit in low chair. Clap to music with strong, simple rhythmic beat or 2/2 or 4/4 time.
Remain seated and move feet as if marching.	Stamp feet to heavy beat in music. (R-009, R-010) Select music to set mood and determine activity i.e. soft, relaxing background music for rest, eating quiet periods. (R-011)
Child recognizes and chooses food by taste, smell, and visual clues. Close eyes while teacher places food on tongue. Identify.	Use individual tongue depressors to place small sample on child's tongue from jars containing foodstuffs, i.e. sugar, salt, peanut butter, jelly, etc.

Taste small sample of fruit or vegetable, i.e. grape, apple, banana, tomato, or carrot.	If child can identify food, reward with larger portion.
Use straw to sip liquid, i.e. chocolate or strawberry milk, lemonade, orange juice, or cola. Identify liquid by taste.	Provide individual straws and liquids in covered containers.
	Reward correct responses with small paper cup of child's choice of liquid.
Close eyes when tasting candies.	Provide foods contrasting in taste, but in same category, i.e. cinnamon candies and chocolate drops.
	Suggested Variations: Sweet-sour: seedless grape, blueberry. Pungent-bland: mustard, vanilla pudding. Mild-sharp: swiss cheese, cheddar.
Make verbal comparisons in response to teacher's questions.	Tape record responses and replay to reinforce experience.
	Help children to distinguish between pleasant and unpleasant odors.
	Provide egg cartons to store plastic containers and egg flats for "pleasant" and "unpleasant" scents. Paint halves of flat in contrasting colors.
Open container and inhale lightly. Replace lid and put container in either half of egg flat according to "pleasant" or "unpleasant".	In 12 small plastic containers place pieces of tissue saturated with pungent-smelling liquids, i.e. orange, lemon, peppermint and vanilla extracts, cologne, Chlorox, etc., and place in egg carton.
	Supervise children to prevent over-inhaling or eating of tissue.

Play game, "What is It?" One child is blindfolded. Another passes sample of food under his nose and asks, "What is it?" If food is correctly identified, reverse roles.	Provide tray with assortment of food samples, i.e. apple, orange, lemon, onion, banana, etc.
	When game is completed, select another pair of children to participate.
Identify food by pictures on labels.	Display empty cans with labels intact. Design chart with labels cut from boxes, frozen food cartons, etc. Make certain all food groups are represented.
Bring empty can to teacher or point to label on chart.	Request child to, "Please bring me some peas" or "Show me the jelly." May be played in form of shopping game where child is asked to "buy" peaches, Rice Crispies, milk, sugar, etc.
	Prepare soup, jello, cocoa, sandwiches, punch or other cooking projects in which children can participate.
Child develops tactile sense.	Introduce concepts of: Hard – Soft Rough – Smooth Warm – Cold Wet – Dry
Use clay to feel, roll, pack, pull, squeeze.	Provide clay, plasticene, Play Doh, or other easily manipulated materials.
Separate hard and soft items.	Furnish items, i.e. stone, block, fur, cotton, key, etc.
Place rough rocks on sandpaper and smooth rocks on plastic.	Provide rocks distinctive in texture. Prepare two box lids, one lined with sandpaper, the other with smooth plastic.

Learning Experience	Suggested Teacher Procedures to Develop Behavior
	Construct "Texture Box." Cut two 3″ x 3″ squares out of various textured materials, i.e. cloth, leather, vinyl tile, sandpaper, etc.
Select an item to be matched. Another child finds matching item from inside box by texture.	Place one square of each set inside box, the others on table.
	"Texture Box" is available commercially (Misc-010).
Reach in bag, grasp one article, and identify by touch only. Remove from bag to see if correct.	Place several familiar objects in a cloth or paper bag, i.e. ball, toy car, spoon, dull pencil, etc.
Dip fingers into bowls containing warm and cold water.	Introduce concept of warm and cold.
Touch ice cubes and feel heat from vents or light bulb. Drink cold milk and warm chocolate.	Supervise activity carefully. Make certain "warm" articles are not too hot.
	Furnish materials that will demonstrate a change in texture when wet or dry i.e. sponge, clay, flour, sugar, paper towel.
Immerse one piece of sponge in water. Observe difference in sponges when squeezed.	Divide sponge in half, giving child both pieces and bowl of water. Call attention to wet and dry sponges.

ECONOMIC USEFULNESS

Level I

M.A. 1 to 3 years

Self-help Skills

Behavioral Objectives	Learning Experience	Suggested Teacher Procedures to Develop Behavior
Child develops the ability to put on, remove, and fasten outer clothing.	Use dressing frames and self-help books for practice.	Provide frames and cloth books to develop dressing skills, i.e. buttoning, lacing, snapping, zipping, etc. (Misc-011), (B-005, B-006)

	Dress and undress dolls.	Provide doll at least 20" tall and doll clothes (Misc-012).
	Drape coat across table, lining side up with collar next to body. Place hands just inside sleeves. Flip coat over head, pushing arms completely through sleeves.	Demonstrate method of donning outer garments.
	Practice putting on and removing outer garments.	Allow ample time for practice and review frequently.
		Give recognition to children who have successfully learned task.
	"Dress up" in play clothes.	Stock "old clothes box" with hats, shoes, dresses, gloves, purses, sweaters, aprons, etc. Encourage children to put on and remove clothing independently.
Child recognizes and cares for personal belongings.	Know where personal coat hanger, locker, toothbrush, etc., are located.	Label items. Stress that "our" things are put back in "our" place.
	Place coat on flat surface. Lay hanger in coat, pull coat around hanger, and lift up by hook.	Demonstrate how to use coat hanger.
	Assume responsibility for removing and hanging up coat, sweater, hat, etc.	Furnish coat hangers or labeled hooks for each child.
	Take off one shoe and put in center of circle with those of rest of class.	Have two children at one time race to circle, select own shoe, and put on correctly. Tying is not necessary.
	Play game "It is Mine." Raise hand and/or say, "It is mine."	Hold up coat, etc., in front of class and ask, "Whose is this?"
	Place items brought to school for "Share and Tell" in designated area and show at appropriate time.	
Child develops ability to groom, toilet, and feed self appropriately.	Wash face when dirty. Wash hands after using bathroom, before and after meals, and when dirty.	Supply full-length mirror, tissue, towels, soap, wastebasket.

Pull up sleeves. Close drain. Draw right amount of hot and cold water. Wet and soap hands. Rinse and dry palms and backs of hands thoroughly. Return cloth towel to proper place. Dispose of paper towels in waste container.

Constant supervision is required to train younger children to wash and dry hands thoroughly.

Repeat constantly.

Have regularly scheduled toileting times. Encourage younger children to go to toilet even if need has not been expressed.

Younger children should have adult in attendance when going to bathroom. Show proper use of toilet tissue. Teach boys to pull up lid and stand to void.

Stress importance of keeping area dry around toilet. Have child always flush toilet and wash hands afterward.

Act only as emergency stand-by to button clothes, zip trousers, etc.

Wait until told to begin eating or drinking.

Provide place mats, paper napkins, and cups for juice period.

Before serving morning juice, make certain children's hands and fingernails are clean.

See "Develops the ability for good grooming, eating habits and manners in the group" under "In the School" in "Social Competencies," "Level I."

Help to keep lavatories clean. Put used paper towels in containers, etc.

Supervise the use of all facilities closely and help children learn proper use of each.

Child learns proper use and care of facilities, such as toilet, drinking fountains, etc.

Child learns to respect property and rights of others.	Line up at drinking fountain. Always leave space between child who is drinking and the next child in line. Turn off water when finished drinking. Use water for drinking only.	If possible, paint parallel horizontal lines in front of drinking fountain.
	Help to keep fountain clean.	Remind children to keep mouth off water spout.
	Practice "DO'S and "DON'TS."	Emphasize keeping foreign matter out of drinking fountain, i.e., chewing gum, sticks, paper, etc.
	DO	Take advantage of the many daily opportunities to teach respect for property.
	Put toys away carefully and in correct place. Treat playhouse equipment as if it were real furniture. Help keep classroom and school grounds neat. Dispose of litter in proper containers.	
	DON'T	
	Color or mark on furniture or walls. Stand on tables or chairs. Throw "trash" around classroom or on school grounds.	See "Develops the ability to share to take turns and to cooperate" under "In the School" in "Social Competencies," "Level I."

Home-help Skills

Behavioral Objectives	Learning Experiences to Develop Behavior	Suggested Teacher Procedures to Develop Behavior
Child recognizes function of household appliances.		Display pictues of common household objects, i.e. stove, refrigerator, sink, vacuum cleaner, iron, washing machine, toaster, egg beater, etc. Give name and simple explanation of function.
	Observe objects while being used.	If possible, demonstrate function using actual item.
	Use toy appliances and household objects in playhouse.	Prepare completely equipped playhouse area (Misc-013, Misc-014, Misc-015).
	With teacher's help paste pictures on sheets to make appropriate room arrangements.	Use large sheets of tag board to form a house. Have each sheet represent one room, i.e. kitchen, living room, bedroom, etc. Draw or cut out pictures of furniture, appliances and fixtures.
Child identifies family property and possessions: home, car, furniture.	Color dittoes of "house," "car," and various items of furniture. Paste on construction paper.	Make dittoes large and simple in detail.
	Assemble pictures and dittoes into personal scrapbook with teacher's help.	If possible, obtain photograph of each child's home and family car to include in child's scrapbook.
Child recognizes the dangers of certain household appliances and equipment.	Is aware that:	At this level safety precautions are learned by rote.
	Some appliances are hot and burn: stove, iron, toaster. Some items are sharp and cut: knife, scissors, tin can lids, broken glass.	
	Some objects spin and cut: electric fans and mixers, wheels, washing machine.	
	Some things are electric and cause shocks: wall outlets, light sockets, television, and radio sets.	

Community-Help Skills

Behavioral Objectives	Learning Experiences to Develop Behavior	Suggested Teacher Procedures to Develop Behavior
Child identifies places and things in his environment.		Show potentially dangerous objectives to children. Emphasize these objects must be left alone.
		Show filmstrip (FS-006).
	Take tour of school buildings and grounds.	Point out school bus, playground equipment, nurse's office, school signs, etc.
	Take short, frequent walks in the immediate neighborhood surrounding school.	Identify grocery store, dime store, gas station, bank, department store, post office, drive-in, etc.
		Show filmstrips (FS-007, FS-008) and films (M-002, M-003).
Child follows simple task-oriented instructions.	Place block on matching paper while naming color.	Keep verbal instructions to a minimum. Make certain child understands what he is to do. Emphasis should be placed on visual demonstration rather than verbal explanation.
		Provide colored blocks and matching colored construction paper. **Place block on same color of construction paper, saying, "*Red block on red paper.*"** Repeat.
	Select block and make proper placement on paper.	Hand child one block at a time.
		Give all blocks to child to make own selection.
	Select, match, or sort familiar objects or geometric forms by color, shape, or size.	Provide wide variety of materials, i.e. small pegboards, mosaic boards, colored cubes, formboards, stacking trees, etc.

Child identifies self as member of the class or group.	Point to self in group picture.	Have enough small cars, plastic boats, etc. to allow child to sort by color, i.e. 12 items, 3 of each color.
		Urge completion of each task before attempting a new one.
		Always insist materials be put in container and returned to proper place before next activity is begun.
		Take picture of class. Display on bulletin board.
	Identify as many classmates as possible.	Design bulletin board using individual pictures.
		"Pictures" could be paper plates with colored yarn to represent hair, buttons for eyes, nose, and felt or red construction paper for mouth.
	Eat at assigned tables, color or paint with several other children and play with building blocks.	Divide class into groups for activities.
Child identifies various tools and materials.	Examine objects on "feeling board" and attempt to identify.	Construct a "feeling board." Glue, nail, bolt, or staple objects onto piece of plywood, i.e. wooden spool, cork, wire screening, sandpaper, leather, lid, magnet, etc.
		Help child identify objects.
	Identify and manipulate tools.	Obtain toy facsimilies of common tools, i.e. hammer, wrench, screwdriver, saw, etc., to enable children to become familiar with tools and their function. (Misc-016, Misc-017, Misc-018).

RECREATION AND EXPRESSIVE ACTIVITIES

M.A. 1 to 3 years

Behavioral Objectives	Learning Experiences to Develop Behavior	Level I Suggested Teacher Procedures to Develop Behavior
Child enjoys listening to music, nursery rhymes, stories.	Listen to background music while resting or doing certain activities.	Use background music to develop child's appreciation and awareness of music.
		Play records that are appropriate for activity, i.e. quiet, soft, lively, etc. Background music played softly while children engage in art activities is often productive.
	Sing words when tune is recognized.	Play two or three beginning notes of song on piano.
	Use listening post or listen as a class.	Music selected should have clear, simple melody and strong rhythm easily felt by children.
		Words should be basic, repetitious, easily understood and remembered. Play record (R-005).
	Repeat rhymes after teacher.	Obtain illustrations of nursery rhymes. Show pictures and repeat rhymes slowly.
		Keep pictures on display around room so children will become familiar with them (SP-004).
	Point to picture of rhyme being played on record.	Play records of nursery rhymes and have children identify matching pictures. Utilize (R-012, R-013).
		Read or tell short, interesting stories to children. Condense longer stories to not more than five minutes.
	Use puppets to act out parts as teacher retells story.	Provide puppets to play characters, and repeat story.

Child enjoys looking at pictures, television, colors, shapes, forms, etc.		Tell flannel board stories using cut-outs to represent characters.
		For additional activities see "Develops the ability to listen attentively to short stories" under "Listening" in "Communicative Skills," "Level I."
		Show sound filmstrips of children's books. Limit viewing time to not more than five minutes.
	Choose book to look at pictures. Turn pages following story sequence.	Have corresponding books on display at table, so children can turn pages and look at pictures at own pace or interest.
	Request story by showing book to teacher.	Show filmstrip of story selected by child. Make certain each child has turn to hear favorite. Show and play (SFS-001).
	Sit in circle around television set. Watch quietly or act out activities being demonstrated on program.	Utilize educational television for programs geared to primary level of interest, i.e. "One, Two, Three, "Sesame Street."
		Arrange class schedule to allow for program times.
		Some commercial programs are also appropriate, i.e. "Captain Kangaroo," "Romper Room."
		Do not have children watch entire program. Begin with five minutes and gradually lengthen time. Television should not be substituted for individual attention.
		Display colorful pictures and identify each color.
	Point to colors in picture as teacher identifies.	Name objects in room, always including color as adjective.

Take turn naming color of own clothing.	Call attention to color in children's clothing, i.e. red sweater, blue pants, yellow blouse, etc.
	Provide different shapes and colors of paper, cloth, wood for children to look at, play with, and handle.
Paste colored paper of various shapes on heavy paper.	May be done on individual sheets or one large roll of paper to make border around room.
Child experiments with arts and crafts media.	*Finger Painting* Class works with one color, and each child has individual container of finger paint.
Spread finger paint using palm of hand in full circular motions.	Smearing in finger paint can progress from full hand to more directed and controlled use of finger tips. This control can be transferred to ability to hold crayon or chalk.
	Scribbling First stage for child will be disorderly scribblings over which there is little motor control.
Name or tell what scribbling is.	Praise child's response even though there is no recognizable relationship. This is highly significant step, as child is beginning to think imaginatively in terms of drawing.
Practice making long up-and-down strokes. Progress to circular motions.	Assist child in gaining control of arm and hand motions, so what has been performed physically can be experienced visually.
	Chalk Take one or two children to chalkboard. Allow sufficient space and chalkboard surface for each child.
Use white chalk to scribble on board.	Place chalk in child's hand and guide arm in desired movements. Encourage large, free actions.

Play expressive, lively music to stimulate motor response.

Scribble on wet or dry paper towels in time to music.

Coloring

Distribute dark-colored construction paper and two or three large, light-colored "No-Roll" crayons to each child (Misc-019).

Color with light-colored crayon on dark-colored paper.

Provide crayons, finger paint, and paper. Give one color of finger paint at a time to each child.

Color on finger painting paper with wax crayon. Press hard to make deep colors. Finger paint over coloring.

Trim away uncovered areas, mount on contrasting paper. Print child's name and date on back.

String Painting

Fold sheet of white or pastel paper in half. Use premixed tempera.

Open paper and place flat on table. Dip string in liquid tempera.

Help child refold paper and press halves together. Open and carefully remove string. When paint has dried, mount design on contrasting paper. Label with child's name and date.

Arrange string on one half of paper in desired design.

Pasting

Give each child small refillable jar of paste.

Cut scrap material, chips of paint colors, wallpaper samples, etc, into random shapes.

Create design by pasting shapes on bright contrasting paper.

Cutting

Require child to cut with scissors for an activity only after he has learned to use them successfully. Full attention can then be directed to project rather than process of cutting.

Begin with exercise of opening and closing hand.

Practice until an even rhythm is developed.

	Attempt to pick up large cotton balls with tongs.	Provide scissor-type kitchen tongs.
	Practice opening and closing scissors.	Furnish both right and left-handed blunt-edged scissors. Help each child use correct fingers and motion.
	Use scissors to cut up "snake."	Roll "Play-Doh" or modeling clay into long narrow strip.
	Practice by cutting up old magazines, newspapers, or scrap paper.	Furnish paper for cutting and continue to help child with scissor technique.
	Cut along black frame.	Use wide black felt pen to draw a square frame around picture to be cut from magazine.
Child walks, skips, marches, and claps to rhythm.		Select music distinctive in both rhythm and tempo so children can determine what to do without verbal instructions. Play (R-009, R-010).
	Walk with heel touching floor first. Jump with both feet. Hop on one foot.	Demonstrate desired activity and instruct children to imitate movements.
	Walk, skip, or run to record, piano, or tom-tom.	Ask, "What does the music tell you to do?"
	March around room in time to music.	Join in activities with children. Do not require children to march in formation. Play (R-014, R-015, R-016).
	Sit on floor in semicircle around teacher. Join in clapping. As song becomes familiar, take turns leading clapping.	Use clapping as a "sit in place" activity. Sing words, clapping as indicated. Repeat song (B-001).
Child participates in finger and imitative play.		Before introducing finger play, talk about names of fingers, i.e. thumb, index, middle, etc. Point out differences in size of fingers.

The Trainable Mentally Retarded Child

Child participates in singing games.	Say, "Jack in the box, sitting so still." "Won't you come out?"	Close hand into fist, thumb inside. "Yes, I will!" Pop thumb up.
	Suggested variations are "Eency Weency Spider" and "Where is Thumbkin?"	
	Sources (B-007 through B-012), and (R-017, R-018).	
	Many children's songs can be learned and enjoyed with slight modification as needed.	
	Farmer in the Dell Have only one child in the circle at a time.	"Cat" stands in center of circle and chooses child to be "rat," then joins children in circle while "rat" remains to choose "cheese."
	Looby Loo Verses should be taught one at a time.	Hold right hand out and put left hand behind back. Reverse procedure for left hand.
	Old MacDonald Had a Farm Provide wide variety of reproductions, and let child make selection.	When name of animal is sung, hold up visual facsimile, i.e. picture, or stuffed, plastic, wooden, or rubber toy.
	Jack-in-the-Box Use toy music box with pop-up clown as introduction. Sing: "Jack-in-the-box is out of sight, When the cover's fastened tight. Touch the spring and up he goes," (Release lid.) "Jack-in-the-box with his long red nose."	Take turns cranking box and releasing the lid.

Child learns to use playtime equipment and apparatus.	Take turns being "Jack-in-the-box." Listen for cue to jump up.	Have children form circle around "Jack-in-the-box" and sing.
	Rock in chair while teacher and classmates sing.	*I am Rocking* Provide small rocking chair. Teach "I Am Rocking" (B-002).
		Demonstrate and reinforce correct method of using equipment.
		Provide each child with an opportunity to learn to use all play equipment, i.e. tricycles, wagons, swings, slides, rocking boats, etc.
	Play "Follow the Leader."	Set up maze of open barrels, boards, boxes, and sawhorses. Encourage children to change arrangement of portable equipment to build different mazes.
	Crawl through boxes. Two or three hide in boxes and call to others to find them.	Obtain large grocery cartons or cardboard packing crates from appliance stores.
	Pretend stack of boxes is a rocket which is knocked down for "Blast Off."	Stack boxes on top of each other.
		Refer to (B-013).
	Makes designs in smooth sand using hands or tools. Hide toys in sandbox for another child to dig out.	*Sand Box* Provide funnels, colanders, tea strainers, play shovels, spoons, and plastic pails for play in dry sand.
	Pour sand from small cans into larger cans.	Furnish tin cans which nest together, i.e. frozen juice, soup, no. 2, no 2½, etc.

QUANTITATIVE CONCEPTS

M.A. 1 to 3 years

Measures

Behavioral Objectives	Learning Experiences to Develop Behavior	Suggested Teacher Procedures to Develop Behavior
		Use moistened sand to build walls, tunnels, and bridges.
		Add water to sand for special projects and activities on warm days (B-014).
		Review filmstrip (FS-001).
		Level I
Child develops concept of big-little, heavy-light, full-empty.	Form group around table.	*Big-little*
		Place pairs of familiar objects of contrasting sizes, i.e. large and small dolls, toy cars, blocks, etc., on large table.
	Take turn following directions.	Call child to table and give directions. "Put your finger on the big doll." "Put your finger on the little ball." "Please give me the big block." "Please give me the little car."
		Following the same procedure, progress from concrete objects to pictures. Gradually reduce degree of difference in size.
	Walk around room and point to big or little objects.	Call attention to wide variety of objects of contrasting sizes.
	Bring objects to teacher.	Give oral directions during "circle time," so all children can observe the child following directions.
	Point to big or little object.	Place two like objects of different size on flannel board. Direct child to point to the big or little object.

Say aloud, while demonstrating actions.

"A little ball."
A bigger ball."
"A great big ball."

Source (B-015).

Heavy-light
Hand child heavy object repeating, "heavy." In other hand, place a light object repeating "light."

Use items i.e. feather, brick, cotton ball, piece of iron, etc.

Use plastic containers or cans. Fill two containers to identical levels with contrasting materials, i.e. sand/ commercial plant mixture, cotton balls/ball bearings, sugar/instant coffee, etc.

Place various items on table, i.e. rocks, scotch tape dispenser, paper weight, ball of yarn, badminton shuttlecock, croquet ball, stapler, etc.

Full-Empty
Provide six glass jars or bottles. Fill three almost to top with colored liquid and leave others empty.

Utilize liquid measure sets, small pots and pans, or plastic pitchers and cups. Use either sand or water for pouring (Misc-020).

Call attention to empty or full glasses at lunch or snack time.

Repeat words and gestures.

Make circle with thumb and finger.
Make circle with both hands.
Make circle with both arms.

Repeat "heavy" or "light" as objects are presented.

Lift containers and indicate which is heavier or lighter.

Lift and compare items, then sort by heavy or light into two boxes.

Select empty or full bottles as directed.

Point to bottles and say, "empty" or "full."

Fill small containers with sand or water and pour into larger containers. Indicate which are empty and which are full.

Time

Behavioral Objectives	Learning Experiences to Develop Behavior	Suggested Teacher Procedures to Develop Behavior
Child recognizes clocks and watches.	Point to clock when asked, "Where is the clock?"	Point to school clock. Hold up alarm clock, watch, timer. Explain all keep or tell time. Refer to clock at recess, lunch, and dismissal time.
	Select watch or clock from several items, i.e. ball, doll, toy car.	
Child discriminates between daytime and nighttime.		Explain that daytime is when it is light outside and sun shines to make light.
		Nighttime is dark because there is no sun.
		Moon and stars shine at night, but are not bright as sun.
	Point to pictures that show either daytime or night-time.	Provide pictures of daytime activities, i.e. children playing, going to school, swimming, visiting zoo, etc. Contrast with nighttime scenes i.e. children sleeping, moon and stars in sky, flashlight or car lights shining in dark, etc.
	Separate mounted pictures by day and night.	Mount on cardboard, place on table, and let children separate by daytime or nighttime scenes.

Money

Behavioral Objectives	Learning Experiences to Develop Behavior	Suggested Teacher Procedures to Develop Behavior
Child recognizes currency (coin and paper).	Sort coins by pennies, nickels, and dimes.	Take one coin at a time, name and show to class.
	Handle coins. Repeat name and tell to another child.	Provide collection of pennies, nickels, and dimes (Misc-021).

Behavioral Objectives	Learning Experiences to Develop Behavior	Suggested Teacher Procedures to Develop Behavior
	Bring empty cartons, paper bags, and containers from home.	Construct toy store. Provide play coins to exchange for objects in store.
	Use coins to make purchases in store. Say, "Here's a penny," "Here is a dime," or "Here are some nickels."	Have regular shopping time and give each child turn to be storekeeper.
	Be responsible for bringing lunch money to school.	If lunch money is collected, identify each coin child brings.
	Repeat name of each coin.	

SAFETY

Level I

M.A. 1 to 3 years

At Home

Behavioral Objectives	Learning Experiences to Develop Behavior	Suggested Teacher Procedures to Develop Behavior
Child leaves objects of danger alone, i.e. matches, knives, pins.	Repeat names.	Show potentially dangerous objects to children. Name each item, i.e. matches, knives, pins, etc.
	Under adult's close supervision, gently feel sharp points of knife, pin, nail, etc.	Tell what can happen when children play with knives. Emphasize knives are not toys and are only used by adults.
		Place same emphasis on matches.
		Explain why kitchen is not a safe place to play. Encourage parents to carry through at home.
Child seeks help when hurt i.e. mother, father, teacher.	Take turns playing role of hurt child, mother, father, adult member of family, or teacher.	Show film (M-004) and filmstrips (FS-009), FS-010).

Behavioral Objectives	Learning Experiences to Develop Behavior	Suggested Teacher Procedures to Develop Behavior
Child stays out of medicine cabinet.	Look at contents of a medicine cabinet or first-aid kit in classroom.	Display pictures of adults helping children when hurt, i.e. applying bandages, helping child up after falling, etc.
		Discuss items briefly. By showing contents, some of children's curiosity will be satisfied.
		Stress only adult should put medication on wound or give medicine.
	Try to read labels on bottles and tell whether sugar or salt.	Provide sugar and salt in two labeled bottles. Stress danger of tasting contents of "pretty" bottles when one cannot read the labels.
	Look at actual sign on bottles and cans of lye, insecticide, poisons, etc.	Place skull and crossbones sign in front of medicine chest or first-aid kit. Explain sign means "danger" and children never taste or touch.
Child stays in own yard.	Talk about homes and yards.	Use positive approach that yard protects children. It belongs to them as much as a toy or game. Tell stories of how animals were saved by being in their "own yards," i.e. Peter Rabbit, Br'er Rabbit, etc.
		Show film (M-005).

At School

Behavioral Objectives	Learning Experiences to Develop Behavior	Suggested Teacher Procedures to Develop Behavior
Child recognizes authority, i.e. teacher, bus driver.	Look at pictures of people who represent authority, i.e. teachers, bus drivers, etc.	Show pictures and explain how these people help children.
		Stress that adult present is in charge, i.e. bus driver on bus, teacher in classroom, supervisor on playground.

Cite familiar television programs where there is a definite authority figure, i.e. mother, father, sheriff, captain.

Take turns being "boss" of small chores, i.e. all coats hung up, tables cleaned, toys put away, etc.

Let children select one to be in charge, but make certain each child has opportunity to be "boss" at least once.

See "Develops an awareness and acceptance of authority" under "In the School" in "Social Competencies," "Level I."

Child begins to develop ability to follow fire drill exercises.

Arrange for fire chief or marshal to visit classroom and demonstrate fire drill procedures.

Work toward an automatic and immediate response to fire warning.

"Walk through" procedure many times.

Have fire marshal return periodically to reinforce instructions.

Demonstrate fire drill exercise.

Take turns being "Fire Chief." Wear fire chief hat and walk beside teacher.

Child develops ability to get on and off school bus.

Have each driver bring bus or car to boarding area.

Practice getting in and out of vehicle.

Demonstrate how to step, not jump, into bus, sit quietly, etc.

Develop the ability to fasten and unfasten seat belt without assistance.

Driver should always insist that each child attempt to put on and take off seat belt independently.

Use "planned" field trips or short rides as rewards for appropriate behavior.

Show film (M-006) and filmstrip (FS-001).

Behavioral Objectives	Learning Experiences to Develop Behavior	Suggested Teacher Procedures to Develop Behavior
Child begins to understand he must keep hands to himself.	Sing songs about happy hands, busy hands, clean hands, etc.	Ask children: "Whose hands are your hands?" Where do they belong?" "What are some things they can do?" "What are some things they shouldn't do?"
	Keep hands in lap during "circle time."	Be consistent in enforcing rules on keeping hands to self. Avoid having chairs too close together.
	Trace around hands on colorful construction paper. Use for decorations on folders, place mats, etc.	Cut out tracings for children.
	Press hand in plaster of Paris. When impression is set, paint plaque and take home as gift.	Prepare plaster of Paris and pour into small pie pans for individual molds.

In Traffic

Behavioral Objectives	Learning Experiences to Develop Behavior	Suggested Teacher Procedures to Develop Behavior
Child stays out of streets.		Show pictures of busy intersections, freeways, streets, roads, etc.
		Ask questions "What are they for?" "Who may use them?"
		Explain that everything has a place: streets for cars, tracks for trains, yards for children.
Respond to words on signs in relation to traffic: "Stop," "Go," "Wait," "Don't Walk."		Provide traffic signs to familiarize children with words.

(Misc-022).

Behavioral Objectives	Learning Experiences to Develop Behavior	Suggested Teacher Procedures to Develop Behavior
Child stays with accompanying adult in traffic.	Take walks around neighborhood, staying on sidewalks.	Take two or three children on short walks around school neighborhood.
	Cross streets only at corners or at crosswalks.	Demonstrate correct way to cross streets.
	Look up and down street before crossing.	Point safe play areas, and emphasize danger of running or playing in streets.
	Take walks as class in areas of relatively heavy traffic.	Show films (M-007, M-008) or filmstrips (FS-012, FS-013).
		Display (C-001) or (SP-005).
		Arrange field trip to downtown business area or other section of town where pedestrian and vehicular traffic is heavy.
		Keep ratio of children to each adult to a minimum.
		Stress importance of adult for safety and security.
		Insist that children stay with group.
		Do not allow children to wander off become separated.

In and Around Water

Behavioral Objectives	Learning Experiences to Develop Behavior	Suggested Teacher Procedures to Develop Behavior
Child begins to understand the dangers of swimming pools, lakes, rivers.		Stress first, never go near water unless accompanied by an adult. Emphasize dangers of getting too close to water without over-doing "fear tactics," i.e. slippery decks around swimming pools, loose dirt along river banks, unsteady rocks or logs, etc.

Behavioral Objectives	Learning Experiences to Develop Behavior	Suggested Teacher Procedures to Develop Behavior
Child learns water safety.	Raise hand when teacher names a water danger near home.	Name sources of potential water hazards in community, ditches, reservoirs, drainage canals, creeks, etc.
	Talk about not pushing or shoving others into water.	Explain child may not be able to swim. Surprises are not fun when they can hurt or frighten someone.

In the Community

Behavioral Objectives	Learning Experiences to Develop Behavior	Suggested Teacher Procedures to Develop Behavior
Child begins to learn the danger of accepting rides or gifts from strangers.		Explain who strangers are and why one does not accept rides or gifts, i.e. candy, toys, etc., from them.
	Role play.	Demonstrate what to do when approached by a stranger.
	Play or stay where mother or teacher has instructed.	Stress importance of staying in play area and why.
Child begins to learn the danger of petting stray dogs and cats.		Stress unfamiliar animals should be left alone. Point out dogs that are on a leash, tied up, or in a strange yard are not to be petted or approached.
		Emphasize stray animals bite or scratch for a reason. They are not people and do not talk, so cannot tell when they are frightened or hurt.

HEALTH

M.A. 1 to 3 years

Personal Hygiene

Level I

Behavioral Objectives	Learning Experiences to Develop Behavior	Suggested Teacher Procedures to Develop Behavior
Child controls toilet habits.	Remember to go to the bathroom at recess and after	See "Develops abilities to groom, toilet, and feed self

lunch.		appropriately" and "Learns proper use and care of facilities such as toilet, drinking fountain, etc.," under "Self-Help Skills" in "Economic Usefulness," "Level I."
Child keeps fingers and foreign objects out of nostrils, mouth, ears, and eyes.	Watch demonstration of possible danger to eyes and ears by fingers, sticks, sharp objects, etc.	Use models to demonstrate possible injury to ear or eye by finger or foreign objects. (Misc-023, Misc-024).
		Stress social behavior pertaining to fingers in nostrils, etc., and gently remind children when unacceptable behavior is observed.
		Show film (M-009).
Child gets adequate sleep at night.		Discuss importance of getting adequate sleep.
	Have parents keep chart showing number of hours slept each night. Bring to school periodically to show teacher and class.	Parents should be aware of amount of sleep their child requires to maintain good health.
	With teacher's help, make faces out of paper plates.	Make bulletin board display of faces to show how one looks with or without proper amount of sleep, i.e. happy, sleepy, bright-eyed, droopy, cross, etc.
		Show films (M-010, M-011) and filmstrips (FS-014, FS-015).
		Play record (R-019).
Child washes hands and face.		Remind children to wash hands and face before and after or whenever "dirty."
	Pull up sleeves. Close drain. Draw right amount of water – balance of hot and cold. Rinse and dry palms and backs of hands thoroughly. Put towel in proper place.	When hot water is available, proper precautions should be taken to prevent scalding.
		Provide constant supervision in training child to wash

The Trainable Mentally Retarded Child

and dry hands thoroughly and to use paper as well as cloth towels.

Have children look in mirror to check that face is clean.

Use individual wash cloth or wet paper towel to wash face.

Repeat procedure over and over until child can wash independently or with minimum help.

Discuss why everyone needs a bath/shower.

Have daily inspection for good grooming. Make individual "Good Grooming" charts using stars as rewards.

Demonstrate proper procedure for bathing using washable doll and large wash basin.

Child bathes with assistance.

Bathe doll, making certain all parts of body are thoroughly soaped and rinsed.

Let each child have a turn bathing doll.

Stress safety aspects, i.e. hot water, slipping, soap in eyes, etc. Emphasize water taps are only adjusted by adults. An adult should always be near or within hearing distance, and should always be present when child gets in or out of tub or shower.

Teach song to tune of "Mulberry Bush."

Sing:
"This is the way I brush my hair
wash my face
take a bath
clean my nails."

Show film (M-012).

Food and Nutrition

Behavioral Objectives	*Learning Experiences to Develop Behavior*	*Suggested Teacher Procedure to Develop Behavior*
Child begins to develop good eating habits.		More relaxed behavior during lunchtime can often be achieved by playing carefully selected background music.
	Eat with spoon and fork without spilling food. Make use of knife to spread and cut soft foods.	Whenever possible, seat children within groups at tables. Serve food on dishes with correct utensils rather than using trays and spoons.
Child eats the food on his plate.	May choose any amount, but must eat everything selected.	Periodically serve "family style" so child has experience in passing food, serving self, sharing with others, and making decisions on what and how much to eat.
	Always take at least one bite of each portion of food on plate.	Establish and explain "One-Bite Rule"
Child eats a variety of foods.	Try fresh fruits or vegetables in season and canned counterparts.	Introduce one new item a week, i.e. coconut, walnuts, pineapple, cauliflower, melons, etc.
Child chews food well.	Chew "treats" thoroughly.	Emphasize chewing food slowly and completely. Furnish snacks that require chewing.

Mental Hygiene

Behavioral Objectives	*Learning Experiences to Develop Behavior*	*Suggested Teacher Procedures to Develop Behavior*
Child begins to recognize boys and girls are different physically.	Look for pictures of boys and girls in magazines.	Make comparisons such as length of hair, clothes, activities, etc.
	Identify boys and girls by answering yes or no.	Point to child and ask, "Is Tommy a girl?" "Is Mary a girl?"

Child tells problems to teacher.

Recognize signs of emotional problems. Let child know you understand his upsets. Probe cause of child's quiet withdrawal from activity or outburst of objection.

Differentiate between tattling (to get someone in trouble) and reporting (to help).

As mediator in a conflict, make certain each participant understands what is acceptable behavior and what is not. Give verbal reinforcement for desirable behavior.

Help child find adequate ways to deal with upsets and problems. Encourage expression of feelings by means of acceptable behavior.

Express emotions in nondestructive ways, i.e. hitting punch bag clown, running, sitting quietly, and resting, etc.

Provide quiet isolated area with cot and blanket. Furnish "aggression" toys, i.e. punch bag clown or punching-bag, and "energy-expending" toys, i.e. spring-board, utility balls, tumbling mat, (Misc-025 through Misc-029).

MATERIALS AND AIDS

Level I

BOOKS (B)

001 Music Activities for Retarded Children
Gingland, David, and Winifred Stiles
Abingdon Press, 1965

002 Music for Early Childhood
McConathy, Osbourne *et al.*
Silver Burdett Co., 1952

003 Golden Book for Kindergarten
Golden Press

004 Paper-Bag Puppets
Williams, De Atna M.
Fearon Publishers

005 All By Herself
Self-help cloth book
Creative Playthings

006 All By Himself
Self-help cloth book
Creative Playthings

007 Let's Do Fingerplays
Grayson, Marion F.
Robert B. Luce, Inc., 1968

008 Finger Plays and Action Rhymes
Pierce, June, and Ruth Wood
Grosset and Dunlap, 1955

009 Finger Plays and Rhymes for Children
Cleveland Association for Nursery Education, 1955

010 One Hundred and One Finger Plays
Child Care Centers
Richmond, California Schools, 1956

011 Finger Fun
Salisbury, Helen Wright
Cournan Publications Inc., 1955

012 Rhymes for Fingers and Flannelboards
Thompson, J. J., and Louise B. Scott
Webster Publishing Co., 1960

013 Let's Play Outdoors
Read, Katherine H.
National Association for Nursery Education, 1957

014 Water, Sand and Mud as Play Material
National Association for Nursery Education
N. A. N. E. Distribution Center, 1959

014 Finger Play
Miller, Mary and Paula Zajan
G. Shirmer, Inc., 1955

CHARTS (C)

001 Obey Your Safety Patrol

FILMS (M)

001 We Play and Share Together
002 Streets and the Community
003 Let's Be Good Citizens in Our Neighborhood
004 We Make a Fire
005 Pigeon That Came Home
006 The School Bus and You
007 The Talking Car
008 Stop, Look and Think
009 Eyes Bright
010 Rest and Health
011 Tommy's Day
012 Taking Care of Myself

FILM STRIPS (FS)

001 Share the Sandpile
002 Share the Ball
003 Story Time Picture Tales Series
004 Story Time Picture Tales Series – II
005 Story Time Picture Tales Series – III
006 Safety At Home
007 After School Hours
008 Shopping In Our Neighborhood
009 Safety At Home
010 I'm No Fool With Fire
011 School Bus Safety
012 Street Safety
013 Playing on City Streets
014 Getting Ready for Bed
015 Rest and Sleep

Shape Sorting Box $5.00
Fifteen wooden blocks of five different shapes – each hole on top of box accepts only one particular shape.
Childcraft Equipment Co., Inc.

Shapes, Colors, and Forms $2.50
Three basic shapes and colors in four sizes.
Childcraft Equipment Co., Inc.

Leaning Tower $1.19
Twelve six-sided polyethelene nesting cups in bright colors.
Childcraft Equipment Co., Inc.

Nesting Cubes $7.95
Five sturdy hardwood cubes in natural finish, four open-ended, one solid.
Childcraft Equipment Co., Inc.

Postal Station $4.75
Mailbox with four different slots for twelve vari-colored blocks to fit in.
Lakeshore Curriculum Materials

Geometric Inserts $13.50
Set of eight six-inch aluminum squares 1/8" thick with matching aluminum inserts. All inserts have plastic knobs.
Lakeshore Curriculum Materials

Dimensional Puzzle $3.00
Twelve three-dimensional two-piece plastic geometric shapes, in contrasting colors set in white plastic form board.
Lakeshore Curriculum Materials

MISCELLANEOUS (Misc)

001 Guidance Town U.S.A.
     Child Guidance Toys

002 Our Town

003 Judy Wooden Inlay Puzzles
     Boy or Girl
     Lakeshore Curriculum Materials

004 Peabody Language Development Kit
     Pre-School, Level I
     American Guidance Service

005 Mother Goose Press Out Rhyme Pictures
     Whitman Publishing Company

006 Safety Poster
     Dennison Company
     Stationery, drug, variety stores

007 Safety Posters
     Primary Grades, Set I
     Hays School Publishing Company

008 Winter Haven Lions Perceptual Program
     Star Press, Winter Haven, Florida

009 Samples and Prices of Materials

Form Sorting Postbox $2.95
Six colored shapes can only be pushed through correct holes in lid.
Childcraft Equipment Co., Inc.

Shape-Sorting Box $5.00
Seven-inch cube box – hinged top with five differently shaped holes. Ten blocks for sorting and dropping through matching holes.
Creative Playthings

Nesting Wood Boxes $7.00
Four 3/8" hardwood boxes and one solid cube fit one inside other. Can be turned upside down and stacked.
Creative Playthings

Contrast Cone $3.95
Eight graduated rings, alternately light and dark wood, stack on threaded spindle. Completed cone is 7 1/2" high and locks with threaded cap.
Creative Playthings

Graded Circles, Squares, and Triangles $3.75
Twelve rubber inserts in three shapes, square, triangle, circle, and colors graduated in size from 1 3/8 to 3 inches. Shapes fit into raised-form board, 11" x 11".
Creative Playthings

Jigsaw Cone $3.50
Interlocking individual pairs of wooden squares that stack in order on nine-inch cone.
Creative Playthings

Early Learning Kit $5.00
Three basic fitting plastic toys varying in difficulty of assembly. Accompanying manual explains use and suggests games to be played.
Creative Playthings

010 Wonder Texture Box
Creative Playthings

011 Dressing Frames (5)
Snapping
Zipping
Shoe-Lacing
Large Button
Bow Tieing
Creative Playthings

012 Dress Me Doll
Creative Playthings

013 Housekeeping Furniture/Equipment
Creative Playthings

014 Housekeeping Units
Childcraft Equipment Co., Inc.

015 Susy Homemaker Toys
Blender, washing machine, iron, etc.
Topper Toys

016 Playschool Workbench
Childcraft Equipment Co., Inc.

017 Threaded Rod and Nut Set
Childcraft Equipment Co., Inc.

018 Tinker Tools
Lakeshore Curriculum Materials

019 Tru-Tone No-Roll Crayons
Kindergarten Size
Milton Bradley

020 Aluminum Liquid-Measures Set
Creative Playthings

021 School Money Kit
Lakeshore Curriculum Materials

022 Operating Traffic Light
Lakeshore Curriculum Materials

023 Model of Eye

024 Model of Ear

025 Bobo
Inflatable clown of vinyl.
Childcraft Equipment Co., Inc.

026 Heavy Duty Punching Bag
Childcraft Equipment Co., Inc.

027 Sping-o-Lene
Plywood mounted on four coil springs.
Creative Playthings

028 Utility Balls
Creative Playthings

029 Tumbling Mat
Creative Playthings

RECORDS (R)

001 Sounds I Can Hear
Scott Foresman and Company

002 Sounds Around Us
Scott Foresman and Company

003 Muffin in the Country
Young People's Record

004 Sounds of Animals
Folkway Records

005 Kindergarten Songs
Albums #1 and #2
Bowmar Records

006 Rhythm Time
Albums #1 and #2
Bowmar Records

007 Fundamental Rhythms for the Younger Set
Teacher's manual included.
Learning Arts

008 Ruth Evans Childhood Rhythm Records
Series I and II
Learning Arts

009 Rhythm Is Fun
Bowmar Records

010 Fundamental Steps and Rhythms
Learning Arts

011 Lullabies for Sleepy Heads
Lullaby Time
Learning Arts

012 Nursery and Mother Goose Songs
Bowmar Records

013 Another Mother Goose and Nursery Songs
Bowmar Records

014 Rhythm Activities
Volume I
RCA Victor

STUDY PRINTS (SP)

001 Teaching Pictures
David C. Cook Publishing Company
Elgin, Illinois 60120
Catalog available

002 Instructo Teaching Aids
Instructo Corporation
Paoli, Pennsylvania 19301

003 Teaching Pictures: Nursery Rhymes
David C. Cook Publishing Company

004 Mother Goose Nursery Prints

005 Traffic Safety
Dennison Bulletin Board Aids
Lakeshore Curriculum Materials

015 World of Marches
Bowmar Records

016 Estamae's Toy Shop
Album I
Learning Arts

017 Finger Games
Learning Arts

018 Finger Play
Learning Arts

019 Health Can Be Fun

SOUND FILMSTRIPS (SFS)

001 Picture Book Parade — 8 sets
Four stories in each set with corresponding filmstrips, text booklets and record.

VII

GUIDES FOR TEACHING
THE TRAINABLE MENTALLY RETARDED
LEVEL II

SOCIAL COMPETENCIES

M.A. 3 to 6 years

In the School

Behavioral Objectives

Child takes turns.

Learning Experiences to Develop Behavior

Take turn for each classroom responsibility.

Level II

Suggested Teacher Procedures to Develop Behavior

Make "Helpers Chart." Assign one responsibility to each child. May use child's picture instead of name.

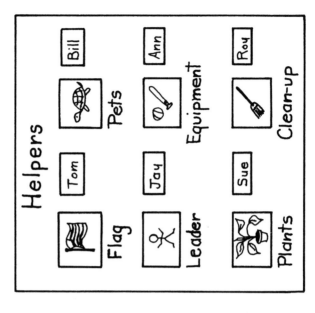

Child shares.	Share supplies and cooperate in their use.	Rotate child's assignment each morning, or weekly if task requires more time to learn. Provide one jar of paste for two children to share.
Child cooperates with others.	Two children sit back to back, feet straight out and arms interlocked. Working together, try to stand up.	Explain and demonstrate "Chinese sit-up."
	Participate in relay races. Wait for turn without pushing or shoving.	Divide class into relay teams.
	Participate in "Show and Tell." Raise hand to be recognized before speaking.	Encourage children to bring interesting items from home to show. Have several extra items on hand for children who do not bring their own.
	Play games such as "Zoo Lotto" and "Hi Ho Cherrio."	Play game with children to help them understand rules and how to play.
Child practices good grooming.	Comb hair after recess, before lunch and going home, or whenever necessary.	Provide each child with a comb. Make construction paper holder with child's name on it. Billy
	Evaluate appearance in mirror each day.	Mount full-length mirror in grooming corner.
	Make certain shirt is tucked in, buttons and zippers fastened, hair combed, hands clean, etc.	
	Wash hair once a week in classroom. Boys towel dry and comb hair. Girls set hair and dry under dryer.	Provide shampoo, creme rinse, towels, and hair dryer. Review with class procedure for washing hair.

Objective	Teacher Activities	Pupil Activities
Child practices good manners.	Encourage girls to work together in setting and arranging each other's hair. Suggest simple, neat, easy-to-manage hair styles that require a minimum of care.	
	Maintain a chart and give recognition to those who are trying or showing improvement in personal care and appearance.	
	Show one filmstrip each day from a series emphasizing good manners. (FS-101 through FS-106).	
	Keep a "Magic Word" list such as "thank you," "please" etc. Call attention to children who use words from list. Use and emphasize same courtesies when speaking to children.	Use good manners in daily snacks and at meal time.
	Invite visitors and guests to classroom so children can "practice" good manners.	Participate in "tea party" in playhouse area.
	Call attention to and praise child who has spontaneously shown courtesy toward another child or adult.	
	Provide commercial or teacher-made puppets.	Using hand puppets, role-play situation in which one puppet is polite, the other is not.
Child accepts the authority of school personnel.	At beginning of school year, tour school and introduce principal, secretary, nurse, custodian, etc.	Tour school to see where each person works and what they do.
	Show children where each person works and explain how they help in school.	
	Invite personnel individually to classroom to meet children. Help children to accept authority of these adults.	Greet guests and repeat names.

Behavioral Objectives	Learning Experiences to Develop Behavior	Suggested Teacher Procedures to Develop Behavior
Child practices appropriate behavior within the total school environment.	Talk about behavior illustrated in cartoons.	Keep room rules simple and few in number. Explain reasons for limits at school, and be consistent in their enforcement.
		Present rules graphically as well as orally in the form of stick-figure cartoons showing good and bad behavior. Emphasize difference.
	Receive prize by following rules and exhibiting good behavior.	Establish reward system. Reward each child even if additional help or reminders are necessary.
	Role-play good and poor behavior, i.e. on bus, in lunchroom, on field trips, etc.	Guide play and clearly distinguish between good and poor behavior.
		Be consistent. Review and reinforce examples of appropriate and acceptable behavior.

Level II

In the Home

Behavioral Objectives	Learning Experiences to Develop Behavior	Suggested Teacher Procedures to Develop Behavior
Child participates in activities in the home.		Determine from parents extent to which children participate in family activities.
		A brief survey sheet sent home to parents is effective.
	Share playthings, toys, equipment, take turns, follow simple directions.	
Child appreciates roles of other family members.	Find pictures in magazines that portray family members. Paste on appropriate sheet of paper.	On separate, large sheets of paper mount one picture of each family member and label, i.e. father, mother, daughter, grandfather, etc., and hang on wall.

Objective	Activity	Method
	Make a book about family. Use one page for each family member.	Pictures may be cut from chart to make individual books.
		Show filmstrips (FS-108 through FS-111) and films (M-101, M-102).
	Pantomime family member activity, i.e. mother cooking, father mowing lawn, sister setting table, etc. Classmate who guesses correct identity takes next turn.	Give assistance when necessary.
	Role-play washing clothes, ironing, cleaning house, etc. in play house corner. Boys and girls assume family roles in helping each other, i.e. putting on coat, drying dishes, etc.	Casually observe and verbally reinforce examples of cooperative and supportive behavior.
	Place each item in appropriate box, i.e. mother's iron, father's hammer, etc.	Provide toy facsimile of articles used by family members, i.e. hammer, iron, baby rattle, etc. Provide shoe boxes with picture of one family member pasted on lid.
Child participates in tasks in the home.		Provide space and furnish with bed, rug, mop, ironing board, vacuum cleaner, etc. Show filmstrip (FS-107).
		Encourage children to attempt same tasks at home with parents' assistance.
		Send home a list of self-help and home-help activities. Parents check each item that child can do, can do with help, or cannot do. Discuss completed check list at parent conference (Misc-101).
Child recognizes and finds own home.	Match picture with own house.	If possible, obtain photograph of each child and each home.
	Identify color of house.	Cut colored paper in shape of houses, selecting same colors as children's homes.

In the Neighborhood

Behavioral Objectives	Learning Experiences to Develop Behavior	Suggested Teacher Procedures to Develop Behavior
Child locates home with respect to neighborhood.	Ride home with teacher. Point out neighborhood landmarks, i.e. stores, streets, playgrounds, etc.	Obtain parent's permission to drive child home.
	Reply to questions. Help give directions to guide teacher.	Before driving child home, travel route and note landmarks.
		Ask, "Am I close?" "Am I on the right street?" "Which side of the street is your house on?"
		During parent conference point out necessity of child knowing location of home within neighborhood.
	Color and cut out houses.	Print addresses on each house and paste on large chart.
	Stand when own address is heard. When able to identify correctly, paste an ear under house.	Say an address aloud to class.
	Recognize written address and paste an eye under house.	
	Attach yarn between photograph and matching colored house.	Construct bulletin board matching children's pictures to paper houses.
	Repeat house number and name of street each day.	Provide heavy rug yarn. Help child connect yarn between photograph and house.
		Work individually with children in teaching house number and name of street.

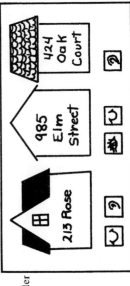

Objective	Activity	Teacher Notes
	Say address and paste a mouth under house.	Repeat address aloud with child.
Child locates key points within neighborhood.	Find pictures in magazines illustrating key points, and with teacher's help, paste on map.	Use butcher paper to construct large map of typical urban neighborhood or rural area if more appropriate.
		Discuss key sites, i.e. playground, store, fire station, police station, etc. Explain activity or purpose of each.
	Respond to each question by telling or pointing on map where activity takes place.	Ask, "Where do you go to play ball?" "Where do you find swings and slides?" "Where does Mother get sugar?" "Where does Daddy get gas?"
Child recognizes helpful people within the neighborhood.	Recognize poster on sight.	Obtain "Helping Hand" poster. Describe poster and explain it is put in windows of homes of people who will help children in an emergency.
		Ask parents if these signs are posted in neighborhood. If not, encourage their introduction and use (Misc-102).
	Identify picture of person who is "Neighborhood Friend." Tell how to find "Friend's" house.	If possible, obtain picture of neighbor, mount and set in pocket chart.
	Role-play what to do when child needs help and family is not at home.	Introduce concept of older child or teenager who can help.
✶ Child practices proper social behavior.	Divide pictures into two sets: "Places to Play," "Places Not to Play."	Discuss which areas in neighborhood are acceptable places to play.
		Provide mounted pictures of a yard, flower bed, playground, sidewalk, lawn, etc.
	Role-play situations shown in filmstrips.	Emphasize desirable social conduct in situations depicted in filmstrips (FS-112, FS-113, FS-114).

Behavioral Objectives	Learning Experiences to Develop Behavior	Suggested Teacher Procedures to Develop Behavior
Child recognizes "dangers" of the neighborhood.		Avoid "scare" or "fright" tactics to explain potential dangers of neighborhood.
	Tell where bicycles and toys are kept when not in use.	Point out hazards of toys and equipment left on sidewalks.
		Review basic but important traffic safety rules, i.e. not playing or running into street, throwing objects at moving cars, etc.
	Place small reproductions of signs in appropriate locations on model of neighborhood.	Provide two signs, "Keep Out" and "Beware of Dog."
		Explain where signs might be found in neighborhood, i.e. on fence, gate, doors, etc. When children know these signs, introduce new ones, i.e. "Keep Off," "No Trespassing," "Danger," etc. Utilize (Misc-103).
	Role-play situations portrayed in film.	Show film warning children against riding with, or accepting gifts from strangers (M-103). Emphasize safety measures "Wendy" and "Jamie" followed. Repeat film to reinforce safety rules.

In the Community

Behavioral Objectives	Learning Experiences to Develop Behavior	Suggested Teacher Procedures to Develop Behavior
Child locates home with respect to community.		See "Learns to recognize and find one's home" under "In the Home" and "Knows location of home with respect to neighborhood" in "Social Competencies," "Level II."
	Tell class about own doctor, dentist, milkman, bus driver, etc.	Briefly explain general functions and services rendered by policeman, doctor, milkman, bus driver, etc.

	Play matching game. Match objects to pictures or vice versa.	Provide pictures of policeman, fireman, nurse, etc. Provide object that identifies each helper, i.e. toy stethoscope, fire engine, police car, milk cartons, etc.
		Prepare two papers for each child. First paper has pictures of four community service helpers, i.e. fireman, postman, bus driver, etc. Second paper has pictures that identify job or activities that helper performs, i.e. bus, letter, fire, etc.
✱ Child practices proper behavior in public places.	Take frequent walks to nearby stores, markets, library, etc.	Discuss proper behavior with class before leaving. Arrange for parents to accompany class so adult/child ratio is sufficient for adequate supervision. Upon return, call attention to specific examples of good behavior.
	Relate experiences with family at restaurant, movie, or on bus.	Talk about adult expectations of children in public places. Point out good manners make outings more enjoyable for all.
	Role-play activities pertaining to each.	Arrange classroom furniture to resemble a restaurant, theater, church, etc. Demonstrate with one or two children how to enter, take seat, sit quietly, etc.
		Emphasize adult instructions and examples should be followed.
		Select from filmstrips (FS-115 through FS-120).
Child respects community property.	Tell about own property at home and school, i.e. clothing, toys, pets, etc.	Show some articles are "mine" some "yours" and some "ours."
	Respond with examples, "These are *my* crayons." "That is *your* coat."	Example: "That is *your* chair, this is *my* chair, this is *our* room."

	Share items that are "ours", i.e. playhouse equipment, playground balls, classroom toys, etc.	Explain sharing items means not only enjoyment, but care and responsibility, also. This is first step toward concept of community property.
	Take trip to park, library, public playground, zoo, etc.	Explain these places are used by everyone and are public property. Point out examples of well-kept and poorly maintained facilities.
	Keep papers picked up, trash in cans and containers, floors clean, etc.	Encourage children to become involved in care of school surroundings.
		Build responsibility on pride rather than enforcement of rules.
		Show film (M-104).
Child relates correct information when lost.		Emphasize necessity of staying with parents or adults and not wandering off alone.
	Practice saying complete name clearly.	Daily review full name, phone number, and address with each child. Child may not be able to remember phone number, and/or address, however, learning to say first and last name intelligibly is essential.
	Role-play how to attract attention, whom to ask for help, and how to give name, phone number, and/or address. Show identification card.	Type wallet-size identification card containing name, address, and phone number of each child.
		Show film (M-105) and filmstrip (FS-121).
	Respond with father's full name.	Ask each child, "Nancy, what is your Daddy's name?" Where parent and child surnames differ, make certain child knows both names.

Behavioral Objectives	Learning Experiences to Develop Behavior	Suggested Teacher Procedures to Develop Behavior
Child recognizes "dangers" in the community.	Take walk within short distance of school.	Call attention to "dangers", i.e. vacant lots, empty buildings, wrecked or abandoned cars, farm machinery, construction equipment, etc. Discuss each danger noted.
	Take field trip around community and note "dangers."	Point out warning signs, i.e. wooden barricade with flashing yellow lights or red lanterns, flags, lights. Display Study Print (SP-101) and show film (M-106) and filmstrip (FS-122).
	On field trip, ride near railroad yards and crossings.	If possible, arrange time so children can see train passing. Call attention to size and speed of train. Emphasize watching for flashing red lights and wigwag signals. Show film (M-107).
	Role-play actions when alone and approached by stranger.	Reinforce rule of not accepting gifts or rides from strangers and why. Ask, "Who are strangers?" Avoid fear tactics, but stress "must refuse" aspect. Show films (M-103 and M-108).

COMMUNICATIVE SKILLS

Level II

M.A. 3 to 6 years

Oral

Behavioral Objectives	Learning Experiences to Develop Behavior	Suggested Teacher Procedures to Develop Behavior
Child develops the ability to speak to adult or stranger.	Show visitor project or paper.	Give children opportunity to share completed work with visitors.

Objective	Activities	
	Deliver message verbally without written note.	Give each child opportunity to deliver message to another teacher or other personnel.
	Carry out duties of host or hostess.	Assign daily host or hostess to greet visitors.
	Role-play greeting adults in classroom, and in public.	Demonstrate proper way to greet visitors (B-101). Expressions of courtesy and manners can be taught through songs, i.e. "Good Manners" (B-102).
	Take field trips to store, museum, zoo, nursery, police station, fire house, etc.	Arrange field trips to provide opportunity for children to meet adults and ask questions or directions.
Child uses telephone.	Rotate role of child answering telephone and role of parent.	Provide Tele-Trainer. Have younger children answer with a simple sentence, i.e. "Hello, Mommy's coming." Emphasize laying receiver down and immediately informing parent of telephone call.
	Progress to answering, "Hello, this is Mary. I'm fine, thank you. I'll call Mommy."	Expand conversations to include courtesy words such as, "Please," "Excuse me," "I'm sorry," etc.
	Talk to classmates on toy phones, Tele-Trainer, and modified intercoms.	Stress speaking clearly, identifying self, asking who is calling, and hanging up receiver correctly.
	Give and receive messages, rhymes, numbers, etc.	Have child outside of room call child in room on phone or other connecting instruments.
	Repeat message to classmates.	Provide (Misc-104, Misc-105).
Child uses short complete sentences.		Construct loose-leaf "feel book." On each page glue a sample of different material:

silk	vinyl	fur
tweed	canvas	feathers
velvet	burlap	corduroy
leather	terry cloth	sand paper

Develop vocabulary through description of samples.	Suggest words and phrases to assist child with limited verbal expression.
Name object and tell how it is used.	Give each child object, i.e. ball pencil, napkin, spoon, etc. Ask, "What do you have, Mary?"
	For additional activities, see "Develops the ability to use simple sentences" under "Oral" in "Communicative Skills," "Level I."
Child uses own last name.	Call roll periodically by surnames only.
Introduce self giving first and last name.	When visitor arrives, ask children to introduce themselves and shake hands with guest.
	Use full names frequently throughout school day, i.e. assigning tasks, choosing leader, dividing into groups, etc.
Play "Description Game." Answer with first and last name when described.	Describe one child, i.e. "I am wearing a red sweater, blue skirt, and brown shoes. My hair is black. Who am I?"
	Explain briefly titles are terms of respect.
Child adds Miss, Mrs., or Mr. to adult names.	Remind children to use title preceding surname when referring to adult.
Say, "My father's name is Mr. Brown" or "My mother's name is Mrs. Smith."	Introduce visitors emphasizing title. Refer to school personnel and parents as Mr., Mrs., etc.
Respond with title and surname of appropriate person.	Ask for names of bus drivers, teachers, custodians, i.e. "Who teaches the class next door?" "Who drives the bus Johnny rides?" "Who brings Peggy to school?"

Child gives names of family and relatives.	Identify each person by name.	Obtain pictures of family members for bulletin board or individual "my family" books.
	Relate experiences involving relatives, designating Aunt Mary, Uncle Jim, Grandmother Jones, etc.	Print each person's name under picture. Check for accuracy at parent conference.
	Draw pictures, use paper dolls, wooden or bendable figures to tell class about family members.	Provide materials and help child with names. Utilize (Misc-106, Misc-107).
Child shares own experiences or ideas with others.	Show finished product to class. Use new words to describe how clay object was made.	Provide first-hand experiences to stimulate vocabulary development. While child is working with clay, introduce words, i.e. *pinch, roll, pull, pound*, etc.
	Select an object for "Show and Tell." Describe to class.	Display variety of objects for children to handle.
	Share events that occurred during weekend or holiday.	Sit in circle with children and also share experiences.
	Give suggestions for snacks, beverages, games, and guests.	Plan a holiday-theme party with children. List choices of refreshments, games, and guests. Use selections requested by majority of class.
Child gives name, age, birthday, address, and telephone number.	Respond with full name and age.	During morning roll call, give first name only.
	Answer roll call with name and appropriate additional information.	Rotate information to be added to response i.e. Monday, ask for name and age; Tuesday, name and address, etc.
	Play "Fishing Game."	Tie magnet on string and attach to yardstick for "fishing pole." Draw five pictures each of a birthday cake, house, and telephone. Attach paper clip to each picture. Place pictures face down on floor. Pictures may be pasted on paper shape of fish.

Child gives school name and address.	Take turns "fishing" for pictures. If "catch" picture of birthday cake, tell age and/or birthday; picture of house, give address. If picture of telephone, say phone number. When response is correct, keep picture until end of game to see who is best "fisherman."	Use school name as often as possible when referring to school activities or events.
	Respond with name of school, and if possible, street on which it is located.	Ask children routinely, "What school do you go to?" "What street is it on?"
Child names wide variety of objects used in everyday living.	Name object when card or picture is shown.	Collect pictures of a variety of objects, i.e. car, toothbrush, chair, door, spoon, bed, etc.
		Utilize cards from Peabody kit (Misc-108).
	Make booklet using magazine pictures of common objects. Show booklet to class. Name each object and tell how it is used. Ask classmates where object is found.	Provide magazines and help find appropriate pictures. Outline object with dark felt pen to guide child in cutting.
Child retells familiar stories in correct sequence.		Use filmstrips or opaque projector to illustrate familiar stories (FS-123, FS-124, FS-125).
	Act as storyteller, describing action in picture.	Repeat filmstrip and select one child to narrate.
		Darken room to lessen visual distraction and help child feel less self-conscious.
		Play single selection from record (R-101, R-102, R-103).

	Tell story as teacher places characters on flannel board.	Provide flannel cut-outs to represent main characters.
	Repeat story while placing cut-outs on board or tell a classmate when to place cut-outs.	

Word Recognition

Behavioral Objectives	*Learning Experiences to Develop Behavior*	*Suggested Teacher Procedures to Develop Behavior*
Child recognizes own name in print.	Recognize name and take turn in game, choose toy, get coat or sweater, etc.	Print each child's name on large card. When assigning activities, toys, etc., hold up card with child's name.
	Recognize possessions by means of printed name.	Print name on child's possessions, i.e. toothbrush, above coat hook, crayon boxes, table mat, etc.
	Check chart and identify name and duty.	Design "Job Chart." Print names on cards and place in slots next to assignments. Rotate daily or weekly.

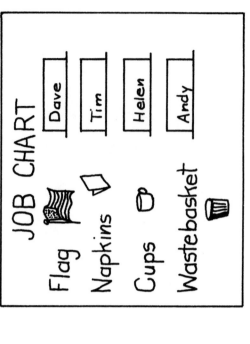

Child recognizes danger words, such as danger, poison, etc.

Cut out pictures from magazines, i.e. insect spray, detergent, bleach, oven cleaner, etc., and paste on chart labeled POISON.

Recognize printed word, "poison" and symbol "skull and crossbones," as danger signs.

Provide large sheets of chart paper. At top of each sheet print one "danger" word, i.e. fire, poison, stop, etc.

Display charts.

Child recognizes environmental labels and signs, such as "boys," "girls," "open," "close," etc.

Print words, i.e. *boys, girls, open, close,* etc., on large sheet of tagboard. Cover tagboard with second sheet and cut "doors" over each word.

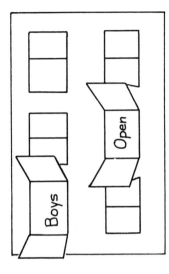

	Sit in circle in front of chart.	Point to child to be named in song.
	Chant in unison for each sign, "Door, door, open wide." will tell us what's inside."	Continue around circle until each child has opened a "door."
	Open door and read sign.	
	Boys move chairs into "Boys" "Men" or "Gentlemen" area. Girls move to area designated as "Girls" "Women" or "Ladies." No one sits in "Keep Out" area.	Post signs, i.e. "Boys," "Girls," "Ladies," "Gentlemen," "Keep Out," etc. to designate restricted areas.

Listening

Behavioral Objectives	*Learning Experiences to Develop Behavior*	*Suggested Teacher Procedures to Develop Behavior*
Child recognizes songs by sound patterns.	Raise hand when recognize song and give name.	Play verse of familiar song on piano or phonograph.
		Play one segment of "Carnival of Animals" (R-104). Explain sounds in music portray animals.
	Listen to music. Tell which of two animals music describes.	Name two animals and play one selection. Ask children which animal the music characterizes.
	Raise hand when lion "roars."	Play "March of the Lion" from same record.
	Raise hand each time sound of cuckoo is heard.	Play "Cuckoo in the Deep Woods."
Child recognizes stories from partial segments with no visual clues.	Guess name of story.	Tell beginning or ending of a well-known story. Ask, "What is the name of my story?"
		Say, "I am thinking of a story that has ———— in it" and name one or two characters.

Child distinguishes gross differences in sounds – very loud, very soft, very near, very far.		Read story written for spoken and whispered voice as designated by size of print (B-103).
		Explain loud voices are for outside and soft voices for inside.
	Recite poem in unison. Use loud (outside) voices and soft (inside) voices. Say in a whisper. Repeat, silently moving lips only. Say "mouse" in a loud voice.	Teach poem: "A big gray pussy cat, pussy cat, pussy cat, / A big gray pussy cat sat in the house. / A big gray pussy cat, pussy cat, pussy cat, / A big gray pussy cat jumped at a *mouse*."
		Play record to demonstrate contrast in loud and soft sounds (R-105).
	Beat drums to rhythm of music.	Provide drums made from coffee cans with plastic lids.
	When music is loud, beat drums heavily. When music is soft, tap gently.	Play songs on piano or use recordings with strong rhythmic beat. Alternate volume between soft and loud.
	March to music. Stop and march in place when music is played softly. March forward when music is played loudly.	Play marching music loudly and softly (R-106, R-107).
	Close eyes and respond.	Use transistor radio tuned to music at normal volume. Walk around room, varying distance. Stop and ask, "Mary, am I near, or am I far away?"
	Close eyes while child with bells walks around classroom.	Thread several small bells on a scarf and tie scarf around one child's wrist.
	When teacher calls name, tell whether bells are near or far away.	Have child stop and shake arm when another child's name is called.
Child distinguishes very high, very low pitch.	Stand and stretch arms up for high sounds, bend down for low.	Play high or low notes on piano or other instrument.

Objective	Child Activity	Teacher Activity
	Place chairs around piano. Stand for high chords, sit or remain seated for low chords.	Play contrasting high treble and low bass chords on piano.
	Raise hands for high sounds and drop for low.	Play recordings of individual orchestral instruments (R-108, R-109), or use autoharp, step bells, resonator pipes, etc. (Misc-109, Misc-110, Misc-111).
Child distinguishes specific sound within group of sounds (whistle with drums).		During school day, tape familiar sounds, i.e. bell ringing, water running, door opening and closing, children singing, playing outside, etc.
		Select pictures of sound producers to illustrate sound recorded on tape, i.e. water, bell, door, etc.
	Identify first and seconds either verbally or by pointing to picture of sound producer.	Play two sounds from tape. Show pictures of matching sound producers and ask which sound was first, door shutting or children singing.
		Display three musical instruments or soundmakers, i.e. drum, bell, whistle. Name and demonstrate sound made by each. Repeat several times.
	Cover eyes and listen to sound. Tell which instrument was used. When correct, choose an instrument to play.	Select child to play one of the three instruments.
Child responds to everyday sounds.		Impress upon children the need to listen carefully for sounds.
	Take outdoor walking trip. Listen for mechanical sounds, i.e. horns, car engines, doors closing, airplanes, and helicopters. Listen for natural sounds, i.e. birds chirping, insects buzzing, dogs barking.	Call attention to and identify sounds heard.

Behavioral Objectives	Learning Experiences to Develop Behavior	Suggested Teacher Procedures to Develop Behavior
	Crush leaves between hands and note "crunching" sound.	Provide bag of dry leaves and spread in corner of yard.
	Listen to rain on roof and window panes, wind blowing, cars moving through water on streets, thunder, drip of rain spouts, etc.	Plan "Listening Time" on rainy days before rest periods or lunch as a calming activity.
		Vary "Listening Time" activity by playing records or reading books about sounds (R-110, R-111).
Child follows directions.	Place block where directed.	Hand child one block and give each direction once, i.e. put block on floor, under chair, next to table, on teacher's desk, etc. Place voice emphasis on locational clues.
		Initially, give one direction only. Increase to two, then three: "John, will you please open the door," and add, "Walk outside," then, "Come back into room."
	Proceed when directions have been completed.	Give all three directions at once.

Perceptual

Behavioral Objectives	*Learning Experiences to Develop Behavior*	*Suggested Teacher Procedures to Develop Behavior*
Child distinguishes one missing part from whole.	Fill in missing part and color completed drawing.	Furnish materials for individual or group work. Provide puzzles, form board, games, or toys that require a minimum of explanation or supervision (Misc-112 through Misc-115).
		Design simple dittoes of partially drawn figures, i.e. dog, automobile, cat, house, etc.

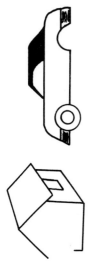

Child matches items by size, color, shape, form or pattern.	Point to or name missing part.	Show pictures of objects with missing parts. Ask, "What is missing?"
	Play game alone or with one or two others. Each player has one background card. Select cards from center pile and match to design on master card. If it does not match, return playing card to center and wait for next turn. If match is made, draw again. Player who matches all designs first wins.	Furnish Lotto background and playing cards (Misc-116). Distribute master cards. Turn playing cards face down in center of table. When played individually, limit number of playing cards to narrow choice child has to make, i.e. six playing cards for one master card.
		Matching games or cards can be teacher-made or obtained commercially (Misc-117).
	Select crayon of same color to match teacher's choice. Name color.	Provide two boxes of crayons containing eight colors. Give one box to child. Choose one crayon at random and place in front of child. Use crayons that have flat surfaces for ease of handling and to prevent rolling (Misc-118).
Child sorts by color, shape, or size.		Obtain twelve-cup muffin pan. Paste different colored shapes, i.e. red triangle, blue circle, green square, yellow diamond, etc. in bottom of each cup.
	Sort shapes into appropriate cups, matching by color and contour.	Provide additional matching shapes cut from construction paper, paint sample chips, felt scraps, etc.

Divide sheet of white construction paper into two columns. Label one column green and other red. Paste designated color at top.	Paste scraps of colored paper in correct column.
Work toward finer discrimination by heading columns with less contrasting colors, i.e. orange/yellow, blue/green, black/brown.	
Provide collection of buttons in two colors, cake pan, and two large cups or cans. Cake pan should be large enough so buttons can be spread out and not easily spilled. Buttons can also be sorted by size or number of holes.	Sort buttons by color into cups.
Trace childrens' hands on construction paper. Print "R" on right pattern and "L" on left.	Place right hand on pattern marked "R" and left hand on "L" pattern.
	Child matches right-right, left-left.
Print "R" on back of child's hand with washable felt tip markers. Use Frosting plates (Misc-119).	Place hand marked with "R" on all right hand outlines. Place hands with palms up or down to match hand in picture.
Provide pairs of gloves and mittens in various sizes and colors.	Match gloves or mittens in pairs. Put on correct hands.
Obtain pairs of shoes from rummage sales, Goodwill, etc. Place shoes in large box. Provide two smaller boxes, with right sole silhouetted on one box and left sole on other.	Put right shoes in box with right silhouette and left shoes in box with left silhouette.
Cut outlines of left and right footprints and tape to floor in natural walking pattern.	Follow footprints, placing left foot on left footprint and right foot on right footprint.
	Use right hand to shake hands when greeting guest or visitor. Shake hands when leaving at end of school day.

Child distinguishes likeness and differences in series of three.	String beads in series of three, following example.	Provide wide assortment of jumbo-size beads of different shapes and colors and plastic-tipped laces knotted at one end (Misc-120, Misc-121).
		String beads in sets of three, i.e. 3 round, 3 square, 3 red, 3 blue, etc., for children to duplicate.
		Further develop concept using pegboards and pegs, puzzles, counting blocks, and plastic counters (Misc-122 through Misc-127).
Child prints single numbers and letters.		Work with two or three children at chalkboard.
		Draw large marked-off grid for each child at individual eye level.
	Draw circles in given area. Progress to straight lines.	Let each child work at own rate. Draw letter in left line of squares.
	Proceed with first letter of name.	Draw one-inch blank squares on ditto master. Place letter for child to print in left-hand column.
	Work at desk or table using pencil or crayon to print letter.	
	Trace over sandpaper figures with fingers.	Cut set of numbers and letters out of sandpaper. Select letters in child's first name from sandpaper alphabet.
	Place paper over sheet of black-inked letters and numbers and trace.	Print letters and numbers with heavy, black felt pen. Provide each child with paper and crayon or pencil.

John   John   John
(grids: O | J)

Use paper with one-inch squares. In each square, print letters of child's first name using dotted lines.

Follow outline of dots to make completed letters.

Follow same procedure using numbers.

Child copies single designs.

Use dittoed sheets of paper with one-inch squares. On separate sheets make design across top row, i.e. color or shade every other square, alternate two colors, etc.

Fill in squares to duplicate design of top row.

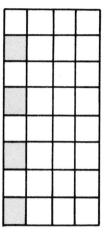

Prepare dittoes with pairs of circles six inches in diameter. Divide each circle into eight parts.

Reproduce design by filling in appropriate sections.

Shade or color in pattern on one circle of each pair.

	Place matching-colored blocks on top of squares to form design.	Color squares on graph paper to form simple designs. Provide colored cubes or blocks the same size as squares. Design cards and blocks may be obtained commercially (Misc-128, Misc-129).
Child plays imitative games.		See "Plays imitative games" under "Perceptual" in "Communicative Skills," "Level I."
Recognizes rhythm change.		Playing instruments leads to an awareness of rhythm. A basic set of rhythm instruments should include sticks, wood and/or sand blocks, tambourines, triangles, wrist bells, gourd rattles, shakers, cymbals, etc.
	Sit on chair in semicircle facing teacher and source of music. Listen and clap hands or tap toes to music.	Sit in chair of same height as children. Select music with strong, simple rhythmic beat, i.e. march or dance tune.
		Have available a set of rhythm sticks for each child. Show rhythm sticks to children and demonstrate their use.
	Play with sticks and "make music." Tap sticks in time to music, watching teacher. Tap sticks according to directions of baton. Take turn being leader.	Offer each child a set and allow ample time for sound exploration and free manipulation of instruments.
		Say, "Let us all play together."
		When children have learned to follow movements in time to music, say, "This time I will not play. I will be the leader and wave a baton for you to follow."
	Take turn playing each instrument.	Introduce and demonstrate other percussion instruments. Initially, do not combine more than two or three instruments in any one activity.

Objective	Pupil Activities	Teacher Activities
	Select instrument to play in band.	Place three or four different instruments on table. Replace selected instrument with duplicate as each child makes choice.
		Organize and lead rhythm band.
		Play records for children to accompany (R-112, R-113).
Child recognizes tactile differences.		Utilize (Misc-125). See "Develops tactile sense" under "Perceptual" in "Communicative Skills," "Level I."
Child develops likes and dislikes in foods, color, sounds, etc.		Select one day a week to use lunch menu based upon childrens' preferences.
	Choose favorite food in each category assigned.	Name four children each week to choose favorite from the four basic food groups, i.e. meat, milk, fruits/vegetables, and bread/cereal.
		Make several general suggestions so child will understand what foods are represented in his group, i.e. "Johnny, would you like apples, carrots, bananas, peaches, or celery for your choice?"
	Take at least one bite of each portion of food on plate.	Reinforce "One-Bite Rule."
	Look through paddles. Superimpose paddles to make new colors.	Furnish transparent plastic color paddles, squares, or rings in primary colors (Misc-130, Misc-131).
	Tell which sounds are pleasing and which are not.	Record familiar sounds throughout the day, i.e. door closing, bell ringing, music, etc.
		Explain pleasant sounds may become unpleasant when too loud or inappropriate.

ECONOMIC USEFULNESS

M.A. 3 to 6 years

Self-help Skills

Behavioral Objectives	*Learning Experiences to Develop Behavior*	*Suggested Teacher Procedures to Develop Behavior*
Child dresses and undresses self adequately.	Practice buttoning, buckling, and zipping vests.	Have Helpmate Vests available for independent dressing practice or dressup play (Misc-132, Misc-133).
		Collect old shirts to use for paint smocks. Replace buttons on several with zippers, snaps, and cloth tape for ties.
	Help each other snap, tie, zip, and button smocks.	Put shirts on children so fasteners are in back.
	Put on shoes and lace, crossing black and white.	Furnish shoes large enough to put on over children's shoes. Use white shoe laces for one side and black for other. Tie laces together at ends and thread through bottom eyelets.

Level II

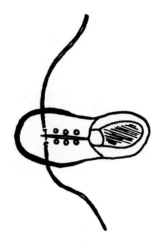

Child develops an appreciation for personal belongings.	Hang up coats, jackets, sweaters on hangers or hooks.	Emphasize importance of taking care of personal belongings, i.e. clothing, toys, games, etc.
	Polish own shoes when dirty, scuffed, or dusty.	Assemble brushes, cloths, and various colors of shoe polish. Store in wooden box with foot rest on lid. Demonstrate correct way to apply polish and shine shoes.
	Practice sewing on cloth following pencil lines.	Provide needle, thread, variety of buttons and 5″ x 5″ squares of cloth. Draw a straight line of dashes across one square. Length of dashes indicates size of stitch.
		Show how to measure and cut thread, thread needle, and knot ends.
	With teacher's assistance mend minor tears, replace missing buttons, sew torn seams, etc.	Provide sewing basket with assortment of thread, needles, buttons, and scissors.
	Practice sewing two-hole and four-hold buttons on a separate square of cloth.	
	Keep personal supplies in assigned space.	Assign areas in classroom, i.e. drawer, shelf, cupboard space, etc., for crayons, pencils, grooming kits.
	Check that no parts or pieces of games and puzzles are missing before putting away. Return books, toys, games, etc., to proper storage area.	Explain supplies and materials in classroom require special care just as toys and belongings do at home.
Child appreciates good grooming, toileting, and feeding habits.		See: "Develops an awareness of good grooming and manners in self and others" under "In the School" in "Social Competencies," "Level I." "Develops abilities to groom, toilet and feed self appropriately" under "Self-Help Skills" in "Economic Usefulness," "Level I."

Child assumes responsibility for proper use of materials and facilities.

"Develops likes and dislikes in foods, color, sounds, etc.," under "Perceptual" in "Communicative Skills," "Level II."

"Begins to develop good eating habits" under "Food and Nutrition" in "Health," "Level I."

"Starts learning proper eating habits" under "Food and Nutrition" in "Health," "Level II."

Assign more responsibile children to help prepare or serve food. Determine from food services staff exact duties, supervision, time schedule, etc.

Demonstrate procedures with child.

Appoint monitors for materials and facilities in classroom, i.e. sink areas, rest room drinking fountain, playground, and sports equipment, etc.

Make "Helping Hand" chart. Print child's name on outline of hand cut from heavy construction paper. Insert in pocket of task assignment.

Practice performing tasks, i.e. using ice cream scoop to serve portions of food, setting tables, stacking dishes, folding chairs, cleaning tables, peeling vegetables, etc.

Assume lunchroom duties.

Perform duties indicated on "Helping Hand" chart. Rotate responsibilities weekly.

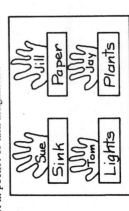

Home-help Skills

Behavioral Objectives	Learning Experiences to Develop Behavior	Suggested Teacher Procedures to Develop Behavior
Child develops skill in carrying out simple household tasks: Carries out garbage, tidies, etc. Child appreciates use of family property and possessions.		See "Assists in routine of daily living in the home" under "In the Home" in "Social Competencies," "Level II."
	Cut pictures from magazines i.e. appliaances, tools, toys, cars, etc. and place under appropriate heading.	Make headings on bulletin board of "Mine," "Brother's," "Dad's," "Mother's," etc. When complete, name and explain use and care of each item.
	Ask permission before borrowing another's belongings both at home and school.	Introduce concept of borrowing and lending among family members. Encourage sharing and stress responsibility for borrowed items, i.e. replace if lost or broken.
	Name one "house rule" practiced at home.	Discuss reasons for and give examples of "house rules," i.e. television and radio sharing, keeping room neat, possessions in their place, obtaining permission before taking food from refrigerator or cupboard, keeping yard and house uncluttered, etc.

Community-help Skills

Behavioral Objectives	Learning Experiences to Develop Behavior	Suggested Teacher Procedures to Develop Behavior
Child appreciates community facilities.		Arrange schedule of field trips to various community recreational facilities, i.e. bowling alley, roller skating rink, children's museum, zoo, etc.
	Talk about community helpers in each facility and tell what they do.	While on field trip, point out fire and police stations, post office, hospital, etc. Explain these are community facilities that help people.
	Eat lunch, use equipment, play games, walk on paths, etc.	Plan picnic in park when weather permits.

Child appreciates completed task: (feels pride in achievement).	Construct individual "How I Help" book.	Furnish construction paper for covers and newsprint for pages.
		Ditto pictures of objects to represent housekeeping duties, i.e. broom for sweeping, cloth for washing dishes, towel for drying dishes, stove for cooking, etc.
	Complete housekeeping task in classroom. Paste picture of task in book. Receive star to put on picture.	Give colored stars as reinforcement for completed task.
	Make gifts to take home for special occasions, i.e. Mother's Day, Father's Day, family birthday, etc.	Assist children with projects. However, encourage working independently.
		Provide each child with Tote Tray containing toothbrush, toothpaste, wash cloth, hand towel, comb, brush. Label trays with children's names and stack in grooming area.
	Brush teeth in front of mirror.	Place mirror over wash basin.
	Show clean teeth to teacher.	Compliment child on clean teeth.
Child contributes toward group accomplishment.		Talk about preparing salad, i.e. ingredients, utensils, types or methods of preparation, and how to serve.
	Taste and identify each ingredient.	Display ingredients for vegetable salad.
		Name and describe each step, i.e. wash vegetables, tear lettuce, grate carrots, chop parsley, combine ingredients and add dressing.
	Prepare salad for lunch. Work in groups of two or three to prepare ingredients as instructed.	Assign children to specific area of preparation.

Bake cake or cupcakes, prepare soup, meat loaf, sandwiches for field trip, etc. Follow same procedure as with salad making. Assign groups and responsibilities.

For recipes and cooking suggestions see (B-104).

Serve in individual bowls.

Construct tool board with outline or shaded shapes of tools.

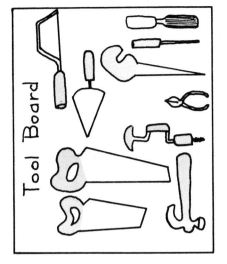

Tool Board

Identify and handle various tools.

Child distinguishes between appropriate and inappropriate materials and tools for a given job.

Discuss name and use of each tool. Provide opportunity for children to remove, use, and replace tools on rack.

Display block of wood in which a nail is firmly set. Ask, "What tool is used to pound this nail in the wood?"

Select hammer from tool board; pound nail into wood; return hammer to proper place.

Learning Experiences to Develop Behavior	Suggested Teacher Procedures to Develop Behavior
Remove saw from tool board. Saw wood in half; replace saw on tool board.	Clamp a 2 x 4 piece of wood to work table. Ask, "What tool is used to cut this wood in half?"
Choose sandpaper and smooth edges.	Hold up rough-cut piece of plyboard. Ask, "What is used to make this smooth?"
Use hand drill to bore hole in wood.	Clamp piece of wood to work bench and ask, "What tool is used to make a hole in this wood?"
	Repeat procedures with various tools until all children have had opportunity to handle various tools.

RECREATION AND EXPRESSIVE ACTIVITIES

Level II

M.A. 3 to 6 years

Behavioral Objectives	Learning Experiences to Develop Behavior	Suggested Teacher Procedures to Develop Behavior
Child enjoys listening to music, stories, etc. of own choosing.		See "Develops the ability to listen attentively to short stories" under "Listening" in "Communicative Skills," "Level I," and "Enjoys listening to music, nursery rhymes, stories" in "Recreation and Expressive Activities," "Level I."
	Choose records to listen to during free activity time.	Provide record players with listening posts. Provide wide variety of records (R-114 through R-118).
	Choose and check out books to take to classroom or home. Select story for "read-aloud" time.	Take children to library. Read story. Allow each child opportunity to choose story.
Child enjoys looking at pictures, television programs, etc. of own choosing.	Select a book to look at during free activity time.	Provide opportunity to look at books in classroom "library" during free activity time.

Child works with arts and crafts media on an expanded scale.	
Choose favorite pictures. Mount pictures on cardboard or paste in classroom scrapbook entitled "Our Favorite Pictures."	Provide a variety of magazines, old books, etc., from which children may cut pictures.
	Limit choice to given number, i.e. "Here are four pieces of paper. Paste a picture you like best on each one." Provide scrapbook and materials for preparing and mounting pictures.
Bring favorite pictures from home to share with classmates.	
Decide on television program.	Discuss with parents the importance of allowing child opportunities to choose television programs.
Collect odds and ends of different textured paper, i.e. tin foil, sandpaper, gift wrapping, corrugated, wax, and patterned shelf paper.	*Cutting Teacing and Pasting:* Provide white glue or paste, scissors, cardboard.
Tear and cut papers, arrange and paste to a piece of cardboard.	
Close eyes; touch design with fingers.	Explain how a picture can be "seen" with fingers.
Cut or tear random shapes out of colored tissue paper and arrange on one sheet of wax paper. Place different colored tissues on top of first colors. Add crayon shavings and colored threads at random. Lay second piece of wax paper on top and cover with plain paper.	Furnish wax paper, scissors, crayon stubs, colored tissue paper, and thread. Provide each child with two pieces of wax paper approximately 13″ in length. Grate crayon stubs.
	Using warm iron, help child press papers together.
Paste "see through" picture on white paper or tape to window.	
	Crayon: Furnish newspaper or thin paper, corrugated paper, sandpaper, and crayons. Explain crayon rubbings are pictures of how things feel, i.e. wood, stone, leaves have different surfaces and feel different.

Place sheet of paper on textured surface and hold in place with hand. Rub side of crayon across paper.	Demonstrate crayon rubbing.
Make crayon rubbings of bricks, tree bark, metal grills, screens, coins, wire meshing, sandpaper, etc.	
	Utilize (B-105).
Soak tile in sink and remove paper or net backing.	*Tile:* Provide sheets of small tiles, grout, white glue, cottage cheese lids.
	Help child glue each tile in place.
Sort tiles by size and color. Select color for outside border and glue tiles to lid. Choose another color for next row, etc., working toward center. Design center to complete tiling. Apply grout between tiles.	Assist child with grouting.
Gather kitchen utensils, corks, bottle caps, screws, plugs, clothes pins, pieces of sponge, etc.	*Printing:* Prepare individual paint pads. Fold wet cloth or paper towel to fit in a saucer. Sprinkle powdered paint or brush tempera on top. Water can be added if paint pad dries while child is printing. Make separate pads for each color to be used.
	Place cushion of newspapers beneath paper to be printed.
Select one object, press on paint pad and then paper.	Encourage use of different gadgets and colors to make bright, print pictures.
	Substitute fruits and vegetables for "gadgets," i.e. orange, grapefruit, apple, lemon, carrot, celery stalk, and potato.
Press flat side of fruit or vegetable half on paint pad or brush with paint. Place painted section on paper and press firmly.	Cut fruit or vegetable in half.

Demonstrate use of different colors and how to overlap prints.

Shape clay into forms of animals. Use toothpicks to attach head, legs, tail.

Clay: Provide pliable nonhardening clay for play and manipulation (Misc-134 through Misc-137).

After children have had experience with modeling clay, introduce ceramic clay. Give each child a piece of clay the size of a lemon or small orange.

Hold ball of clay in palm of hand. Place thumb of other hand in middle of ball. Hold fingers stiffly to support clay as it is pushed by thumb. Keep sides of bowl even by pinching and turning at same time. Paint with tempera and shellac after bowl has been fired.

Help child smooth sides.

Let dry thoroughly before firing.

Child responds to rhythms.

Play song, "Children's Polka" on piano or use record of polka music (B-102).

Teach words of song and dance steps.

Face partner, taking hold of both hands. With partner, take two side steps, and stamp three times.

"Oh, slide, and slide, and stamp, stamp, stamp."

"Your knees, your hands, and one, two, three,

Slap knees, clap hands, clap partner's hands three times in patty-cake fashion.

"Oh, shake your finger, shake your finger,

One hand on hip, shake finger of other hand at partner.

"Turn around and stamp, stamp, stamp!"

Turn independently and stamp three times.

See "Recognizes rhythm change" under "Perceptual" in "Communicative Skills," "Level II" and "Walks, skips, marches, and claps to rhythm" in "Recreation and Expressive Activities," "Level I."

Child performs simple dance steps.	Demonstrate and teach basic folk dance steps, i.e. circling, bow and curtsy, do-si-do, heel and toe, etc.
	Form children into two lines. Take one child as partner, lead through dance routines. Combine steps to perform dance, e.g. Virginia Reel. Have two children do steps while others keep time by clapping. Call steps for children to follow.
	Utilize dances i.e. "Looby Lou," "Buffalo Gals," "Here We Go Around the Mulberry Bush." Use songs "Oh, Susannah," "Possum in the Cinnamon Tree" (R-119).
	Couple greets: boy bows, girl curtsies, both go down to end of lines. Boy swings girl around and both return to place in line. Do-si-do. Side steps down line. Hook arms, Skip partner back to place in line.
Child assumes roles from simple stories.	Play recordings of fables for children to listen to and dramatize (R-120, R-121).
	Make costumes from large grocery bags or obtain "Playsacks" commercially (Misc-138).
	Role-playing can also be done with children's classics, i.e. *Cinderella, Snow White, Pied Piper* and with songs "Frog Went A'Courtin'," "Animal Fair," etc.
	Listen to fables and select character to portray.
	Dress in costume and pantomime actions as record is replayed.
	Role-play parts or use puppets.
Child participates in group singing.	Introduce group singing by involving few children at a time, encouraging others to join group voluntarily.
	Teach songs of various types, i.e. Mother Goose, seasonal or holiday. Animals, work, play and folk songs.
	Include answer-back songs, i.e. "Who Has the Penny?" "Lucy Rabbit," etc.
	Accept and encourage children's original songs.
	Join in singing, enter and leave group by choice.

Objective	Activity	Method
	Make up songs about pets, school and home activities, field trips, etc.	Accompany children's songs with piano, autoharp, guitar, using familiar melodies, i.e. "This Old Man," "Twinkle-twinkle Little Star," "Pop Goes the Weasel," etc.
	Sing original songs with class.	Write down words as child sings to teach to class.
Child refines ability to use playtime equipment and apparatus.	Climb ladder placing both feet on each rung. Sit on top of slide. Place feet against sides and slide down slowly.	Assist child on slide until secure in climbing ladder and controlling speed of descent.
	Walk along line of tape on floor.	Check foot placement.
	Walk on 2 x 4 board. Walk on slightly elevated beam.	Place chair at one end to help child start properly. Stress foot placement, balancing with out-stretched arms, and keeping eyes on beam (Misc-139, Misc-140).
		Give children opportunity for free play on playground apparatus each day.
	Play ten pins. Count number of pins left standing after rolling ball twice.	Introduce bowling fundamentals by providing indoor ten pins and rubber or plastic bowling balls.
Child develops ability to use appropriate simple hand tools.	Hold hammer with one hand. Pound on circles.	*Hammer* Paint large black circle on wide block of wood. Fasten block securely. Provide lightweight hammer. Gradually reduce size of painted circles as child becomes more competent.
	Pound nails into wood.	Provide common nails.
	Imitate teacher's arm movements.	*Saw* Demonstrate use of saw.
	Push saw back and forth across wood.	Clamp block of soft wood in vise.

Broom

Demonstrate correct way of holding broom using sweeping motion with arms and sliding steps.

Sweep colored bits of paper into a pile.

Sandpaper

Obtain used bowling pins and provide sandpaper and shellac.

Sand bowling pins to remove plastic coating and rough spots. Shellac and use finished product for individual bowling trophy.

See "Identifies various tools and materials" under "Community-Help Skills" in "Economic Usefulness," "Level I," and "Discriminates between appropriate and inappropriate materials and tools for a given job" under "Community-Help Skills" in "Economic Usefulness," "Level II."

QUANTITATIVE CONCEPTS

Level II

M.A. 3 to 6 years

Measure

Behavioral Objectives	Learning Experiences to Develop Behavior	Suggested Teacher Procedures to Develop Behavior
Child distinguishes between long-short, tall-short, enough-not, enough-too much.	Point to line which is *longer* or *shorter*.	*Long-short, Tall-short* Give child pairs of dowels in contrasting lengths, Ask, "Which stick is longer?" "Which stick is shorter?"
	Compare strings of beads to see which is *longer*, towers of blocks to see which is *higher* or *taller*, yardstick and ruler, noting which is *shorter*.	Draw two lines on chalk board. Ask children to point to longer or shorter line.
		Furnish materials for simple measuring and comparing tasks. (Misc-141 through Misc-144).

Enough-too much

Use cooking experiences and projects to introduce or reinforce concepts of not enough and too much. Add salt, sugar, pepper, etc. to season food. Ask children, "Is this enough salt?" "Do we have too much sugar?"

Sample small portion and indicate whether *too much* or *not enough*.

Furnish transparent plastic cups. Mark desired level with felt pen. Pour water with food coloring up to, beyond, or below mark and ask, "Did I pour enough?" "Did I pour too much?"

Answer questions. Take turn pouring up to mark. Ask classmates, "Did I pour *enough*?" "Did I pour *too much*?"

Provide sand and graduated sizes of measuring cups. While child is pouring, ask, "Is that enough?" "Do you have too much?"

Pour smaller cups of sand into larger ones.

Big-Little

Provide flannel board objects in large and small sizes.

Child develops concept of big-little, heavy-light, full-empty.

Place all big objects on one side and little on other.

Obtain four toy cars in graduated sizes. Seat children around table. Display all four cars. Show smallest car and place in middle of table and ask, "Which cars are bigger than this one?" Continue until all four cars are in center of table. Ask one child, "Can you put the cars in a row going from smallest to largest?"

Select larger car and place next to first car.

Start with smallest car and go up to largest.

Reverse procedure.

Start with largest car and go down to smallest.

Provide items of various sizes, i.e. fruit, sea shells, toy animals, cans, etc., for additional experiences in discrimination.

Heavy-Light

Obtain bathroom, baby, or kitchen simple balance scales (Misc-145, Misc-146, Misc-147).

Place bathroom scales on table.

Place on floor and allow children to take turns standing on scale.

Explain some scales are for weighing lighter objects.

Demonstrate use of kitchen scales.

Point out weight of item printed on label and that on scale, i.e. 5 pounds sugar, 10 pounds flour, 1 pound butter, etc.

Provide simple balance scales. Show two articles of contrasting weights, i.e. rock and chalk eraser, paste jar, and pencil, etc. Ask, "Which is heavier?"

Full-Empty

Assemble wide-mouth jars and bottles, funnels, granulated sugar, sand, water, and one-quart pitchers. Pad floor with newspapers.

Fill pitcher with water.
Set containers in a row on table.

Mark several jars at varying levels with brush pen.

See Measure in "Quantitative Concepts," "Level I."

Relate previous experiences with scales and weighing.

Experiment by pressing down and observing number change.

Weigh item in classroom, i.e. blocks, books, toys, etc.

Weigh packages, cartons, and cans of food.

Point to heavier object. Place both objects on balance scale. Note which object causes scale to dip.

Place funnel in container and pour water to top.

Fill jars to level marked, using sand, sugar, etc.

Point to jars that are not full. Select jars that are full and fill to top.

Time

Behavioral Objectives	Learning Experiences to Develop Behavior	Suggested Teacher Procedures to Develop Behavior
Child relates morning, afternoon, noon, lunch, and later to specific activities.	Cut pictures from magazines of various activities and paste in appropriate section.	Furnish long sheet of butcher paper, magazines, scissors and paste. Divide paper into four sections. Print MORNING at top of one section and paste sample picture illustrating morning activity. Follow same procedure for AFTERNOON, NOON, and EVENING.
	Greet visitors saying, "Good morning" or "Good afternoon."	Reinforce concept with school activities, i.e. P.E. in morning, lunch at noon, rest in afternoon.
		Construct shadow sticks (simple sundial). Insert stick or nail into center of wooden base. Draw twelve circles on wooden base to represent hours.
	Check shadow on sundial denoting morning or afternoon.	Paint the 6 to 12 circles red to indicate morning hours. Paint 1 to 5 circles blue to indicate afternoon hours (B-106, B-107).
Child recognizes need for clocks and watches.	Note clock hands in relation to activity.	Use play clock to set hands in correct position for group activity, i.e. recess, snack time, music, lunch, dismissal (Misc-148, Misc-149).
	Look at clock for change in activity.	State, "The clock says it is time for music." "Look at the clock! It is time to clean up."

Money

Behavioral Objectives	Learning Experiences to Develop Behavior	Suggested Teacher Procedures to Develop Behavior
Child recognizes currencies.	Identify coin or repeat name after teacher.	Furnish an assortment of coins, i.e. pennies, nickels, dimes, quarters, and thin paper or newsprint and crayons. Give each child one coin.

Demonstrate crayon rubbing. Repeat for all denominations.

Rub crayon across paper over coin.

Spread coins on table. Have children stack coins, separate into piles, or sort into boxes.

"Collect" and stack all pennies. Identify sorted coins.

Prepare individual Bingo "Money" cards. Use heavy tag or cardboard, 9" x 9" and divide into 3" squares using broad felt pen. Paste a coin, i.e. penny, nickel, dime, quarter in center of each square. Cover cards with transparent plastic wrap. Make different arrangements on each card. Cut out 2" square colored markers.

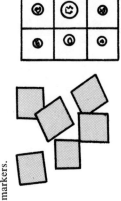

Hold up coin and identify. Say, "Cover *one* coin on your card that looks like this."

Find one matching coin. Cover with marker. First to fill all nine squares on card wins. Hold up money for next game.

Show items that can be purchased with small coins, i.e. gum, toys, candy, etc.

Find items to be purchased and take to check-out counter.

Take field trip to shopping center. Plan ahead what purchases are to be made. Pay for articles while children observe.

Child exchanges money for goods.

When preparing special cooking projects or snacks, call attention to cost of each ingredient. Give prices in terms of coins, i.e. "This package of marshmallows costs three dimes." or The jello costs twenty-five cents."

Point to coins as teacher quotes prices.

Behavioral Objectives	Learning Experiences to Develop Behavior	Suggested Teacher Procedures to Develop Behavior
Child keeps money in possession for specific use.	Carry purse with money and pay cashier.	Take class to grocery store and purchase food for party, lunch or other classroom activity. Choose one child to be "shopper" and carry money.
	Bring lunch or milk money to school. Repeat name of each coin.	Identify each coin when money is collected.
	Keep money until time to pay for ride or treat.	Occasionally arrange field trips where children may spend nickel or dime for treats, rides, souvenirs, etc. Check that each child has at least one nickel to hold and to spend.

SAFETY

M.A. 3 to 6 years

At Home

Level II

Behavioral Objectives	Learning Experiences to Develop Behavior	Suggested Teacher Procedures to Develop Behavior
Child seeks help when accidents occur.	Act as "reporter."	Present situations where help is needed, i.e. cuts, falls, upset stomach, fire, and accident.
	Role-play in home center or playhouse.	Assume role of babysitter as children must respect this authority figure.
	Tell class which neighbor to contact and how.	If there is no adult at home, discuss alternatives for obtaining help from a neighbor. Check with parents to determine which neighbor is to be contacted by child and location of the house. Discuss with children which neighbor they would contact and how. Ask, "Is your neighbor home all day?" "Is your neighbor home in the evening?" "If that person is not at home, which neighbor would you go to next?"

Child stays in his own neighborhood.	Name dangers, i.e. strangers, strange animals and pets, unfamiliar houses and streets, etc.	Discuss possible "dangers" outside child's neighborhood.
		Talk about need to be in a place where adult in charge can find child immediately.
		Stress child's importance to his home, parents, friends and pets, that they need him and he contributes to their happiness. Child must stay where these "friends" can find him.
Child learns dangers of medicine.		Discuss usefulness and purpose of medicine.
	Inspect first aid kit.	Show first aid kit and talk about contents and their use. Display prescription bottles so children can recognize "pill" bottles.
		Emphasize medicine is only for sick people. It is given by mother or other adult. Stress even mother must have a doctor tell *her* what to take.
		Show filmstrip (FS-126).
		See "Stays out of medicine cabinet" under "At Home" in "Safety," "Level I."
Child picks up toys and keeps them in proper places for safety.	Paint toy boxes to take home for storing toys.	Talk about dangers when a wheeled toy and/or other clutter is left where it can be tripped over.
		Provide large cardboard cartons, brushes and paint.
	Following clean-up time act as "room inspector."	Assign one child each day to check room for neatness and safety.
		Show filmstrips (FS-127, FS-128).

At School

Behavioral Objectives	Learning Experiences to Develop Behavior	Suggested Teacher Procedures to Develop Behavior
Child states own name when asked.		See "Develops the ability to say name" and "Develops the ability to respond to own name" under "Oral" in "Communicative Skills," "Level I."
		"Uses own last name" and "Can give name, age, birthday, . . ." under "Oral" in "Communicative Skills," "Level II."
Child participates in fire drill exercises.		See "Begins to develop ability to follow fire drill exercises" under "At School" in "Safety," "Level I."
	Participate in school fire drill exercises. March out in order, never running or pushing.	Review purpose of fire drills and proper step by step procedures to follow. Praise examples of good order and behavior.
		Show fire extinguisher and explain its purpose. Stress it is used by adults only.
	Walk around school and help locate fire alarm boxes.	Take field trip around school and point out fire alarm boxes. Explain purposes and emphasize they are used only in case of actual fire.
Child uses proper behavior on the playground.		Discuss proper behavior on playground.
	Suggest rules for good behavior, i.e. take turns, share ball, don't push others, etc.	Write rules on chart as children make suggestions.
		Show films (M-109, M-110) anf filmstrips (FS-129, FS-130).
Child uses playground equipment safely.	Discuss proper use of all playground equipment.	When an accident occurs, analyze with children what caused it and how it would have been avoided.

Objective	Activity
	Take children to playground. Show proper use of each piece of playground equipment.
	Note problem a child may have with a certain piece of equipment.
	The shy or timid child can be encouraged to use something that he otherwise may be afraid to try.
	Use designated time periods for play on certain pieces of equipment. This makes for better supervision.
	Show films (M-109, M-111) and filmstrips (FS-131, FS-132).
Take turns using equipment. Practice "buddy system." Help classmate having difficulty on the playground.	
Child recognizes his bus number.	
Match number on coat and container to number on bus.	Take children to school bus area. Introduce driver. Have driver call children to bus by name. Pin bus numbers to children's coats. Paint bus number on lunch container.
Child recognizes his bus driver.	
Match number on coat or container to number worn by driver.	Driver should wear bus number where it can be easily seen.
Put name card on flannel board under correct bus.	Make buses of construction paper matching color of school bus. Print bus number on front and glue sandpaper on back. Make name cards with sandpaper backs for each child. Place buses in a row at top of flannel board.
Child uses proper behavior on school bus.	
Play "school bus." Select chair for seat on bus and role-play part of passenger.	Place chairs in rows to simulate "school bus." Select one child to be driver. Review importance of good bus behavior.
	Explain and demonstrate reasons for bus rules: Show how a moving object is hard to stand on. Place doll in toy car. Push car along table top to demonstrate how doll falls when car stops suddenly. Review bus rules each time field trip is planned.

Behavioral Objectives	Learning Experiences to Develop Behavior	Suggested Teacher Procedures to Develop Behavior
Child obeys safety directions.	Role-play being soldier, marching with arms folded or straight down. Stop or start when directions are given. Soldiers always follow orders.	Show films (M-112, M-113, M-114). Read short stories about animals that did not obey. Discuss moral at end of story, i.e. disobedience resulted in Peter Rabbit being sent to bed. Relate safety stories to obeying fire drill directions. Show filmstrip (FS-133).

In Traffic

Behavioral Objectives	Learning Experiences to Develop Behavior	Suggested Teacher Procedures to Develop Behavior
Child learns dangers of playing in the street or alleyways.		See "Stays out of streets" under "In Traffic" in "Safety," "Level I." Show filmstrip (FS-134).
Child obeys traffic signals, i.e. red for stop, green for go.	Discriminate between green and red. Make traffic light signals from construction paper. Paste on red, yellow, and green circles for lights. Act as traffic officer and operate light. Classmates practice obeying signals while riding wheel toys.	Hold up red and green cards for relay games, i.e. red-stop, green-go. 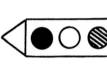 Make traffic light and mount on standard. Use flashlight batteries. Mark play area into streets.

In the Community

Behavioral Objectives	Learning Experiences to Develop Behavior	Suggested Teacher Procedures to Develop Behavior
	Listen to story. Sing safety song before dismissal each day.	Show films (M-115, M-116, M-117) and filmstrips (FS-134 through FS-138).
		Read safety story and teach safety songs (B-102, B-108).
Child keeps away from railroad tracks.	Take field trip or walk around community.	Point out danger areas, i.e. vacant lot, empty barns and houses, wrecked cars, farm machinery, or road construction equipment.
		Discuss each danger found in area.
	Construct miniature railroad using toy trains, model houses, signs, and signals.	Provide materials (Misc-150 through Misc-153).
		Display study print (SP-102).
	Make miniature freeway using model cars, trucks, bridges, signs and signals.	Show filmstrips (FS-139, FS-140).

HEALTH

M.A. 3 to 6 years

Personal Hygiene

Behavior Objectives	Learning Experiences to Develop Behavior	Suggested Teacher Procedures to Develop Behavior
Child washes hands and face.		See "Develops the ability for good grooming, eating

	Look at illustrations in books about visits to doctor.	habits, and manners in the group" under "In the School," in "Social Competencies," "Level I," and "Develops an awareness of good grooming and manners in self and others" under "In the School" in "Social Competencies," "Level II."
		"Learns to wash hands and face" under "Personal Hygiene" in "Health," "Level I."
Child learns to take bath.		See "Bathes with assistance" under "Personal Hygiene" in "Health," "Level I."
Child learns that doctor and dentist serve him.		Discuss doctors and dentists as friends. Read book about doctors (B-109 through B-113).
	Role-play doctor, nurse, and patient.	Furnish toy doctor's bag, nurse's kit and stethoscope (M-154, M-155). Direct dramatic play.
		Show filmstrips (FS-141, FS-142, FS-143).
	Discuss what happened on visit to dentist with family. Tell what dentist does and why.	Plan field trip to dentist's office or have Women's Dental Auxiliary visit room.
	Participate in dramatic play to help overcome any fear of dentist.	Direct dramatic play.
		Read books about dentists and show illustrations (B-114, B-115). Use resource kit (Misc-156). Show filmstrips (FS-144, FS-145).
Child brushes teeth after meals.		Invite Dental Auxiliary to show children proper way to care for teeth.
		Use kit (Misc-156) and coloring books.
	Draw cartoons of happy well-cared for teeth and sad uncared for teeth.	Make bulletin board display of good dental hygiene.

Behavioral Objectives	Learning Experiences to Develop Behavior	Suggested Teacher Procedures to Develop Behavior
	Have individual toothbrushes and toothpaste labeled with name.	Show films (M-118, M-119, M-120) and filmstrips (FS-146, FS-147, FS-148). Read book (B-116).
		Obtain sample kits of toothpaste and toothbrushes for each child.
	Practice brushing techniques in front of mirror in Good Grooming Corner.	Demonstrate proper brushing techniques.
	Brush teeth after meals or snacks.	Check teeth with children.
Child goes to bed when told.		Relate time to television shows. Develop idea that mother and father know best time for children to go to bed.
		Lead discussion of why one needs rest.
	Discuss appropriate time to go to bed.	Show filmstrips (FS-149, FS-150).

Physical Hygiene

Behavioral Objectives	*Learning Experiences to Develop Behavior*	*Suggested Teacher Procedures to Develop Behavior*
Child recognizes major parts of the body, i.e. head, arms, legs.		See "Develops the ability to identify main parts of body" under "Oral" in "Communicative Skills," "Level I."
	Point to major parts of body when leader gives command.	Play "Simple Simon" game.
	Draw figure and name major parts.	Do individual testing of each child by use of "Draw-a-Man" idea to note child's awareness of body parts.
	Make dolls and puppets and name parts.	Help children with paper dolls or puppets.

Behavioral Objectives	Learning Experiences to Develop Behavior	Suggested Teacher Procedures to Develop Behavior
	Balance sponge or eraser on part of body teacher has named.	Play "Balancing" game. Provide each child with chalkboard eraser or large sponge. Call out parts of body, i.e. head, shoulder, knee, palm of hand, tips of fingers, etc.
Child blows nose.	Cover nose with tissue, blow, pinch gently when wiping. Dispose of tissue in wastebasket. When using handkerchief, return to pocket or purse immediately after using. Blow nose using own handkerchief or tissue when necessary.	Always have box of paper tissue in prominent place for easy accessibility. Discuss and demonstrate correct and safe procedure for blowing nose. Check casually or by individual reminders.
Child covers mouth when coughing and sneezing.	Watch films and filmstrips. Demonstrate how to cover mouth when coughing or sneezing. Turn head away from others.	Lead discussion on why mouth should be covered. Show films (M-121, M-122) and filmstrips (FS-151, FS-152).
Child uses tissue or handkerchief.	Help to make bulletin board.	Design bulletin board using cardboard face with tissue placed over mouth. See preceding sections "Learns to blow nose" and "Learns to cover mouth when coughing and sneezing."

Food and Nutrition

Behavioral Objectives	Learning Experiences to Develop Behavior	Suggested Teacher Procedures to Develop Behavior
Child develops proper eating habits.		See "Begins to develop good eating habits, such as eats what is on his plate, learns to eat a variety of foods, to chew properly and doesn't rush" under "Food and Nutrition" in "Health," "Level I."

	Set own place at table. Help in preparation, serving, and clean-up.	Once a week, plan meal for class to prepare and eat together. Provide necessary foods, utensils, etc. Alternate breakfast, lunch, dinner.
		Verbally reinforce and call attention to examples of the following: Washing hands before eating, Sitting straight at table or desk, Eating quietly, Eating over plate, Correct use of silverware, Eating dessert last, Remaining seated until excused.
Child recognizes common foods.		Briefly explain food groups, differences between fruits and vegetables, cereals and meats, etc. Show example of each.
		Show films (M-123, M-124) and filmstrips (FS-153, FS-154).
		Provide magazines that feature articles on food and contain many full-color illustrations.
Child identifies foods that are usually eaten at breakfast, lunch, dinner.	Cut pictures of food from magazines to put under categories of breakfast, lunch, and dinner.	Mount large chart on wall and divide into the three main meal sections. Help children paste pictures under appropriate heading.
	Choose pictures of food that make a good breakfast.	Mount pictures of various foods usually associated with specific meals. Stand pictures on chalkboard tray. Remove those not chosen.
		Follow the same procedure for other meals.
	Take one picture from table and return to seat. Describe food.	Lay mounted pictures face down on table.

Behavioral Objectives	Learning Experiences to Develop Behavior	Suggested Teacher Procedures to Develop Behavior
	Use tagboard or construction paper for placement. Paste plate, cup, napkin, and utensils in proper place.	Write child's name on chalkboard. Give one mark for each fact child relates about food pictured, i.e. name, color, shape, good group, when eaten, etc.
		Provide 12″ x 18″ sheets of heavy construction paper or tagboard, scissors, paste, magazines, paper plates, napkins, cups, plastic knives, forks, and spoons.
		Help children paste materials together.
		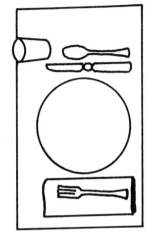
	Cut out pictures of food that would make a good breakfast and place on plate.	Follow same procedure for lunch and dinner.
Child helps wash dishes properly, i.e. hot water and soap.	Take turns washing and drying dishes.	Demonstrate correct procedure for washing and drying dishes using hot water and soap. This is more meaningful if presented after a cooking experience.

Mental Hygiene

Behavioral Objectives	Learning Experiences to Develop Behavior	Suggested Teacher Procedures to Develop Behavior
Child learns that mothers give birth.	Help make bulletin board of mothers and babies, both human and nonhuman.	Make bulletin board of mothers and their babies.
	Share experiences about baby brother or sister.	Display prints (SP-103, SP-104) and use to stimulate discussion.

Child learns that animals have babies.

Take field trip.

Observe hatching of chicks.

Make notebook of animal mothers and babies.

Arrange field trip to farm.

Provide incubator with thermostat and obtain fertilized eggs from hatchery (Misc-157).

Show films (M-125 through M-128) and filmstrips (FS-155, FS-156, FS-157).

Use nurse as resource person in addition to films.

MATERIALS AND AIDS

Level II

BOOKS (B)

101 Manners to Grow on
Lee, Tina
Doubleday and Company, Inc., 1955

102 Music Activities for Retarded Children
Gingland, David, and Winifred Stiles
Abingdon Press, 1965

103 Shhh, Bang
Brown, Margaret Wise
Harper and Row, 1943

104 New Boys and Girls Cook Book
Crocker, Betty
Golden Press, 1965

105 Creative Art Books
Whitman Publishing Company, 1966

106 My Book of Time
Hagan, Marshall
Ottenheimer Publishers, Inc., 1961

107 The True Book of Time
Ziner, Feenie, and Elizabeth Thompson
Children's Press, 1956

108 Red Light, Green Light
McDonald, Golden
Doubleday, 1944

109 Doctors' Tools
Lerner, Marguerite Rush
Medical Books for Children, 1960

110 A Visit to the Doctor
Berger, Knute, Robert A. Tidwell, and Margaret Haseltine
Grosset and Dunlap, 1960

111 Jill's Check Up
Jubelier, Ruth
Melmont Publishers, Inc., 1957

112 Doctor John
Thompson, Frances B.
Melmont Publishers, Inc., 1959

113 How Doctors Help Us
Meeker, Alice M.
Benefic Press, 1964

114 Let's Go to a Dentist
Buchheimer, Naomi
G. P. Putnam's Sons, 1959

115 A Visit to the Dentist
Garn, Bernard J.
Grosset and Dunlap, 1959

116 Your Wonderful Teeth
Schloat, G. Warren Jr.
Charles Scribner's Sons, 1954

FILMS (M)

101 Family Teamwork

102 Grandmother Makes Bread
(Stress family cooperation rather than baking process)
103 Say No to Strangers
104 Beginning Responsibility – Taking Care of Things
105 Debbie's Safety Lesson
106 Live and Learn
107 Dangerous Playground
108 Dangerous Stranger
109 Safety on the Playground
110 Let's Play Safe
111 Primary Safety – On the School Ground
112 Safety on the School Bus
113 Safety on Our School Bus
114 The School Bus and You
115 Safety on the Way to School
116 Safely to School
117 Patty Learns to Stop, Look and Listen
118 Beaver Tale
119 Save Those Teeth
120 Judy's Smile
121 How to Catch a Cold
122 The Common Cold
123 Eat Well, Grow Well
124 Big Dinner Table
125 Human and Animal Beginnings
126 Kittens – Birth and Growth
127 Animals Growing Up
128 Mother Hen's Family

FILMSTRIPS (FS)

101 New Classmate
102 Good Helpers
103 We Like to Do Things
104 We Plan Together

105 We Work Together
106 Working Together
107 Saturday
108 Janet Helps Mother
109 Family Members Work
110 Busy Timmy
111 Baby's House
112 At Home
113 On the Street
114 Visiting Friends
115 In Public Buildings
116 The Picnic
117 Shopping
118 Traveling
119 The Family Goes Shopping
120 Family Picnic
121 Lost at the Fair
122 Playing On City Streets
123 The Boy Who Went to the North Wind
124 The Cat Who Lost His Tail
125 The Little Red Hen
126 Safe and Sound at Home
127 Home Safety
128 How to Have an Accident in the Home
129 Safety in the Playground (Rev. Ed.)
130 Safety on the Playground
131 Apparatus Fun, Part I
132 Apparatus Fun, Part II
133 Safe and Sound at School
134 Street Safety
135 Safety Coming to School and in School
136 We Make Some Safety Rules
137 Mind the Sign
138 I'm No Fool as a Pedestrian
139 Summer Fun
140 I'm No Fool Having Fun

141 Doctor Examines You
142 The Doctor
143 Nurse Nancy
144 The Dentist
145 A Visit to the Dentist
146 Strong Teeth
147 The Loose Tooth
148 Billy Meets Tommy Tooth
149 Getting Ready for Bed
150 Rest and Sleep
151 Pesky the Cold Bug
152 Avoiding Infection – Treating a Cold
153 Food for Health
154 A Right Breakfast
155 Growing Up
156 Finding Out How Animal Babies Grow
157 We Grow

MISCELLANEOUS (Misc)

101 Help in the Home
Parent Check List

	cannot do	with help	by self
Puts toys away			
Hangs up own clothes			
Makes bed			
Folds clothes			
Irons flat work			
Irons garments			
Sweeps			
Mops floor			
Uses vacuum			
Operates washer			
Operates dryer			
Dusts			
Cleans sinks			

	cannot do	with help	by self
In kitchen			
In bathroom			
Washes windows			
Sets the table			
Clears the table end of meal			
Wash dishes			
Dry dishes			
Bakes cookies			
Bakes cakes			
Can open milk carton			
Can pour milk from quart carton to glass			
Can pour milk from half-gallon carton to glass			
Peels vegetables (carrots, potatoes, etc.)			
Cuts own meat, etc. at meal			
Can prepare own breakfast			
Can prepare own lunch			
Can prepare own dinner			
Can use can opener			
Sweeps walks			
Mows lawn			
Trims lawn			
Weeds flower beds			
Waters lawn			

102 Helping Hand Poster

103 Our Town
Hardwood pieces to arrange on 36" x 41" vinyl layout painted to suggest residential, recreational, and commercial areas.
Creative Playthings.

104 Tele-Trainer
Telephone equipment for class use consists of two telephones run by batteries plus booklets to teach use of telephone, manners, etc.
American Telephone and Telegraph Company

105 Private Lines
Pair of telephones joined by fifty feet of wire which operate on flashlight batteries. Press button on one phone-other rings.
Creative Playthings

106 Bendable Figures
Family set of five dolls: mother, father, brother, sister, and baby.
Creative Playthings

107 Block Play People
Free standing wooden figures colored on both sides.
Childcraft Equipment Co., Inc.

108 Peabody Language Development Kit
Preschool, Level I
American Guidance Service

109 12-Chord Autoharp
Creative Playthings

110 Chromatic Step Bells
Lakeshore Curriculum Materials

111 Resonator Pipes
Creative Playthings

112 Things Puzzles
Creative Playthings

113 First Jigsaws
Childcraft Equipment Co., Inc.

114 Independent Activities, Level I
     Liquid Duplicators
     The Continental Press, Inc.

115 What's Missing? Lotto
     Lakeshore Curriculum Materials

116 Learning Lotto
     Negative and Positive
     Geometric Pictures
     Size, Shape and Color
     Size
     Shape
     Creative Playthings

117 Materials for Matching

     Hickety Pickety
     Winnie-the-Pooh
     Candy Land
     Players move by matching colors on cards or spinning wheel.
     Lakeshore Curriculum Materials

     Shape Up
     Multiactivity game similar to lotto utilizing visual perception
     materials.
     Lakeshore Curriculum Materials

     Picture Dominoes
     Twenty-eight large heavy cardboard dominoes.
     Childcraft Equipment Co., Inc.

     Animal Puzzle Dominoes
     Each domino shows half of two different animals, match halves to
     complete animal.
     Childcraft Equipment Co., Inc.

     Object Puzzle Dominoes
     Two halves of different objects are on each domino; put together
     to complete object.
     Childcraft Equipment Co., Inc.

     Wood Lotto
     Thirty-six 2" square plywood plaques are matched to
     corresponding pictures on six 4" x 6" master boards.
     Creative Playthings

     Picture Dominoes
     Seven illustrations in four colors combined as domino set of 28
     pieces for matching game. Silk-screened on plywood.
     Creative Playthings

     Shape Dominoes
     Seven basic shapes in four colors. Twenty-eight silk-screened
     plywood pieces.
     Creative Playthings

     Ani-Match Cards
     Match bottom to tops of twenty-four animal cards. Printed in
     color.
     Creative Playthings

118 Tru-Tone No-Roll Crayons
     Kindergarten size
     Milton Bradley

119 Hand Outlines
     Teacher's Guide
     Frostig Program
     Follett Publishing Company, 1964

120 Bead Assortments
     Box of one hundred 1" beads in assorted shapes and colors.

Box of one hundred and forty-four 1/2" beads.
Creative Playthings

121 Jumbo Beads
Thirty-five 1 1.8" wooden beads in variety of shapes and colors and two laces.
Creative Playthings

122 Perception Puzzles
Series of twelve puzzles. In first set, child identifies two identical pictures from selection of three.
Creative Playthings

123 Cubical Counting Blocks
One hundred 2 1/2" square cubes in five colors.
Milton Bradley

124 Plastic Counters
Assorted 3/4" discs in red, white, blue and yellow.
Lakeshore Curriculum Materials

125 Multi-Sensory Cubes and Sphere Set
Twelve smooth and twelve rough textured spheres and cubes in six colors and four sizes. Tray is provided to prevent spheres from rolling off desk or table.
Lakeshore Curriculum Materials

126 Beaded Pegs and Peg Board
Ideal

127 Peg Activity Box
Plastic colored pegs in self-contained tray and box.
Childcraft Equipment Co., Inc.

128 Two Dimensional Block Patterns
Thirty-two 5" x 7" plastic coated block pattern cards. Numbered in order of difficulty of design.
Lakeshore Curriculum Materials

129 Colored Cubes
Twenty-seven 1" blocks that match block designs on cards from (Misc-128).
Lakeshore Curriculum Materials

130 Playplax
Rings and squares
Creative Playthings

131 Color Paddles
Creative Playthings

132 Helpmates
Set of three fasteners plus tie on hood.
R.H. Stone Products

133 Best Vests
Set of six, adjustable in size to fit preschool through teens.
Educational Teaching Aids

134 Crayola Modeling Clay
Binney and Smith, Inc.

135 Modeline Modeling Clay
Binney and Smith, Inc.

136 Play-Doh School-Pak
Childcraft Equipment Co., Inc.

137 Clayrite Modeling Clay
Milton Bradley

138 Playsacks
Strong brightly-colored paper bags with holes for face and arms. Selection of twelve animals.
Creative Playthings

139 Hardwood Walking Boards
Hardwood Saw Horses
Lakeshore Curriculum Materials

140 Balance Board
Lakeshore Curriculum Materials

141 Jumbo Pipe Stems
Lakeshore Curriculum Materials

142 Plumbing Pipe Set
Lakeshore Curriculum Materials

143 The Long Stair
Ten hardwood rods, all with same size cross-section, but varying in length.
Educational Teaching Aids

144 Unit Building Block
Creative Playthings

145 Dula Dial Scale
Educational Teaching Aids

146 Dial Produce Scale
Creative Playthings

147 Simple Balance Scale
Educational Teaching Aids

148 Clockface with Movable Gears
Movable hands controlled by visible gears to simulate movement of real clock.
Creative Playthings

149 Tactile Time Teacher
Self-correcting tactile time teacher. Discs with hour numerals fit only in correct positions. Raised beaded numerals for both hour and minute figures.
Childcraft Equipment Co., Inc.

150 Trains and Tracks
Thirty-seven sections of connecting track, including switches, five cars, two engines, crossover and underover bridge — wood.
Creative Playthings

151 Trains and Tracks Add-Ons
Signs and signals for railroading, extra cars and tracks to go with (Misc-150).
Creative Playthings

152 Highways and Byways
Thirty-one sections of roadway, including curves and intersections, six autos and trucks — wood.
Creative Playthings

153 Child Guidance Highway System
Twenty-three feet of road and eighty-five pieces consisting of overpass section, supports, cars, trucks, highway signs and signals.
Child Guidance Toys

154 Play Doctor Kit
Play Nurse Kit
GW School Supply Specialist

155 Stethoscope
Professional instrument to listen to heartbeats, pulse, internal sounds of mechanical devices.
Creative Playthings

156 Resource Kit on Dental Education
Sacramento County Office of Education

157 Thermostat 4-egg Incubator
Automatic temperature control, transparent plastic base for viewing eggs. Fertilized eggs can be secured from hatchery.
Creative Playthings

RECORDS (R)

101 Classics for Children
Bowmar Records

102 Famous Classics
Bowmar Records

103 Favorite Folk Tales
Bowmar Records

104 Carnival of Animals
Musical Sound Books
Sound Book Press Society, Inc.

105 Loud and Soft
RCA Victor

106 Sousa Marches
Bowmar Records

107 World of Marches
Bowmar Records

108 Child's Introduction to the Orchestra

109 Concerto for Toys and Orchestra
Learning Arts

110 Sounds I can Hear
Scott Foresman and Company

111 Sounds Around Us
Scott Foresman and Company

112 Melody Midget Music for Rhythm Bands
Learning Arts

113 Music for Rhythm Bands
RCA Victor

114 Songs and Stories for Children
Learning Arts

115 Songs from Walt Disney Movies
Learning Arts

116 Unicorn and Other Favorite Children's Songs
Learning Arts

117 Imagination and Insight

118 The Limelighters through Children's Eyes
RCA Victor

119 Climbing Up the Golden Stairs
Carson Robinson and his Old Timers
Columbia Records

STUDY PRINTS (SP)

101 Pedestrian Safety
102 Farm Machinery
103 Farm Animals
104 Pets

120 Fables of Aesop
Educational Materials

121 Fables
Bowmar Records

VIII

**GUIDES FOR TEACHING
THE TRAINABLE MENTALLY RETARDED
LEVEL III**

SOCIAL COMPETENCIES

M.A. 6 years and up

In the School

Behavioral Objectives	Learning Experiences to Develop Behavior	Suggested Teacher Procedures to Develop Behavior (Level III)
Child shares, takes turns, and cooperates.	Let others go first through doors, take place in lines, sit in front seat of bus, etc.	Discuss examples of courtesy, cooperation, and sharing as specific events occur, i.e. waiting in line at lunch, recess, and bus stop.
	Offer classmates last cookie, chair, cup of punch, etc.	Arrange snack time, party, social events for opportunities to share and cooperate. Occasionally have one less chair, cookie, treat, etc. than number of students. Observe reaction and give immediate reinforcement to student who gave up chair, cookie, etc.
	Do favors for others, i.e. carry lunch tray to table, hang up coat that has fallen to floor, help clean up after an activity.	Praise student who has performed favor. Call attention to opportunities to do favors for others.
		Show films (M-201, M-202) and filmstrips (FS-201, FS-202).
	Raise hand to be called upon.	Call upon student who raises hand first during activities or teacher-led discussions.
		Expose children to different arrangements of desks and chairs.
	Work out seating arrangements with classmates and accept others' suggestions and/or decisions.	Allow students to arrange seating patterns.
		See "Participates in sharing, taking turns and in cooperating" under "In the School" in "Social Competences," "Level II."

Child respects the right of others.	Work without disturbing others.	Lead discussion on "what is disturbing." Ask for specific examples. List responses on the board. Read back for students to select specific responses to illustrate or demonstrate.
	Select response and portray with stick figure cartoons, role-play, puppet play, etc.	
	Listen to tape. Note noise level within room and sounds from other rooms, i.e. laughter, shouting, chairs scraping, volume of radio, television, etc.	Turn on tape recorder before students enter room. Play back tape after all students are seated. Call attention to general noise level, not specific children.
		Show photographs of adults and children expressing a wide range of positive and negative emotions (Misc-201).
Child respects the feelings of others.	Select picture and tell about feeling portrayed, i.e. happiness, anger, sadness, etc. Imitate expression depicted in photograph.	Ask, "How does this picture make *you* feel?" "Why do you think this child is happy?" "Can you make the same face?"
	Talk about feelings, i.e. happy, sad, angry, frightened, etc., associated with experiences at school. Role-play situations.	Encourage children to verbalize feelings. Talk about how other people feel in given circumstances. Structure situations depicting events mentioned by students. Have child who described original event reenact role.
		Stress individuals react differently to same situations and feelings should be respected.
Child respects the responsibilities of others.	Assume responsibility for job assigned. Do not "take over" another sudent's assigned task.	Assign classroom responsibilities by means of Job Chart. Discuss difference between helping with and infringing upon another's assignment.
	Vote for student officers.	Explain and hold class election of officers during national or state elections.
	Respect and follow leadership of class officers.	Stress responsibilities of president, vice president, etc.

Objective	Activity	Activity
Child appreciates the value of good posture.	Play "Simon Says" imitating teacher's examples.	Demonstrate correct and incorrect posture, i.e. standing, sitting, walking, etc.
	Discuss why one stands and sits erect. Make bulletin board with yarn or pipe cleaner figures.	Remind children appropriately. Utilize nurse as resource person. Assist with bulletin board. Show filmstrips (FS-203, FS-204).
Child appreciates the value of acceptable manners.	Greet teacher by name, i.e. Miss Smith, Mrs. Jones, Mr. Adams.	Greet students by name, i.e. "Good morning, Mary." "How are you today, Peter?" "Is that a new sweater, Ruth?" Greet boys with handshake.
	Respond to question with, "Yes, Sir." "Yes, Ma'am."	Stress courtesy in not interrupting others' conversations.
	Remain silent while others are speaking.	Ask, "What would you say if I . . . gave you a piece of candy, asked how you felt, bumped into you?"
	Respond with appropriate phrase, i.e. "Thank you, Mr. Smith." "I am fine, thank you." "Excuse me."	Work toward more complete sentence combinations, i.e. "I am fine, thank you, Mr. Jones. How are you today?"
Child dresses according to the weather.	Put on outer wraps to go outside during cold weather.	Direct student's attention to weather. Ask, "What is the weather like? Do we need coats?"
	Hang up coats and sweaters in proper place in classroom.	Provide adequate space and number of hangers or coat hooks. Encourage individual responsibility for locating hanger and hanging up coat or jacket.
	Make scrapbooks of seasonal dress. Cut out pictures of men's jackets, women's skirts, men's and women's shoes, etc.	Provide mail order, seasonal catalogues, yellow and blue construction paper, scissors and paste for scrapbooks of seasonal clothing.
		Show film (M-203).

Child appreciates the need to follow the directions of those in authority.	Paste summer clothing on yellow pages (warm weather) and winter clothing on blue (cold weather).	Provide cut-outs of clothing, objects, and equipment representative of seasons (Misc-202).
	Tell story using cut-outs, i.e. walking in the rain, swimming, picnicking, etc.	Obtain various samples of clothing for different seasons from Goodwill or rummage sales. Say, "It's raining outside. What should I put on?"
	Select appropriate clothing.	
	Identify pictures of staff by name and function, i.e. Mrs. Thomas works in the cafeteria.	At beginning of school year obtain photographs of each adult staff member. Label picture with name on tagboard strip.
	Form line, follow directions, walk in orderly manner. Quietly observe work in progress.	Take tour of school and surrounding grounds. Point out personnel at work, i.e. gardener, cook, secretary, teacher, etc.
	Perform specific tasks for authority figures, i.e. assist custodian in sweeping floor; secretary folding papers; cook preparing lunch; teacher on playground.	Select students to be helpers after making arrangements with personnel involved. Prepare student for assignment by providing experience in specific task, i.e. using push broom, cutting carrots and celery tearing lettuce, etc.
	Deliver message following teacher's instructions.	Send student to library, office, or another classroom with written message.
Child fulfills obligations (time – schedules – tasks – etc.).	Follow classroom routine, i.e. hand in lunch money, hang up coat, take turn calling roll, etc.	Establish well-organized and consistent schedule. Avoid altering schedule and maintain set routine.
	Return promptly from recess, lunch, rest room, errands, etc.	
	Assemble materials to do assigned task. Carry out directions and complete task. Report completion to teacher.	

Behavioral Objectives	Learning Experiences to Develop Behavior	Suggested Teacher Procedures to Develop Behavior
	Return materials, equipment, and tools to proper place or person.	Assign individual to receive and replace tools, equipment, etc.
	Keep promises, secrets, confidences, etc.	Discuss obligations to others, i.e. respect confidences, be punctual, carry through promises, etc.

In the Home

Behavioral Objectives	Learning Experiences to Develop Behavior	Suggested Teacher Procedures to Develop Behavior
Child locates home with respect to street and number.		See "Learns to recognize and find one's home" under "In the Home" and "Knows location of home with respect to neighborhood" under "In the Neighborhood" and "Knows the location of home with respect to community" under "In the Community" in "Social Competencies," "Level II."
Child appreciates home and environment.	Plant seed in small container. Place in warm, sunny location. Water regularly. Decorate paper doily to place under plant at home. When seed has sprouted, take home as gift.	Obtain seed packets of flowers, bulbs, vines, etc. Provide egg cartons, small pots, or painted cans and commercial plant mixture. Puncture bottom of cans for drainage and prevention of mold. Mark each container with student's name. Set plants on water-proof surface. Provide doilies and crayons.
		Carrot or beet tops, sweet potato, and avocado seeds also make attractive indoor plants. (B-201).
	Bring glass or plastic bottles from home. Cover small area of bottle at a time with white glue and apply scraps of colored tissue paper, felt, rick-rack, sequins, etc. Make paper flowers to place in decorated bottles.	Obtain tissue or crepe paper, chenille pipe cleaners, florist's wire, and tape from hobby or art shops. Assist students in decorating bottles (B-202).
Child meets visitors.	Wait to be introduced. Look at visitor; smile; say, "How do you do?" Boy shakes hands with man and with woman, if she offers her hand. Girl smiles pleasantly and shakes if man offers hand.	Act as host and demonstrate introductions using students as either visitors or family members. Reverse roles, giving students experience in making introductions (B-203).

	Be a courteous, considerate listener. Answer questions promptly. Always add guest's name to "yes" or "no" responses	Emphasize conversation should not be monopolized. Conversation is when two or more people are talking together.
Child practices rules of safety in the home.		See "Safety at Home" section in "Safety," "Level III," and "Recognizes the dangers of certain household appliances and equipment" under "Home-Help Skills" in "Economic Usefulness," "Level I."
Child conforms to family schedules.	Follow family routine: Get up in morning Eat breakfast Dress Go to school Come home from school Recreation Eat dinner Family activities Bathe Go to bed.	Prepare dittoes of blank clock faces and list of typical routine family activities. Send list home for parents to fill in approximate time for each. Help child draw hands on clock to show time activity is performed.
	Make wastebasket for home. Select covering desired. Cover carton and spray with preservative.	Obtain large, round cartons from ice cream parlors. Have variety of materials available, i.e. wallpaper samples, contact paper, finger paintings, etc.
	Keep bedroom attractive by making bed, hanging up clothes, putting away toys.	
	Have personal area to display craft items and art projects made at school.	
	Help to keep yard and driveway uncluttered.	Discuss returning bicycles, balls, and other belongings to proper storage area.

	Take walk in school neighborhood to look at houses and yards.	Point out attractiveness of some homes and what might be done to make other homes more attractive.
Child assists with tasks and chores around the home.		See "Assists in the routine of daily living in the home" under "In the Home" in "Social Competencies," "Level II."
Child accepts social responsibilities within the home.	Share television time and cooperate in selection of program and accept decision.	Permit students to select and watch television programs during rainy day recess. Check program selection and reinforce cooperative behavior.
	Practice proper use of telephone, i.e. answering, dialing, replacing receiver, etc.	Stress telephone is not a *toy*, but is used to give or receive information.
	When requested, answer door and relay message from caller to parent or adult in charge.	At parent conference determine parents' attitude toward child answering door or telephone.
	Open door, greet caller. Say "One minute please, I'll get my mother. Close door and immediately inform parent or adult in charge.	Discuss precautions when answering door, i.e. look out window, leave door chained, don't invite strangers in, and close door before leaving to get adult.
	Role-play answering door and informing parent of caller.	
	Use acceptable manners, i.e. keep elbows off table, hands in lap, wait for everyone to be seated and served before eating.	Set table with dishes and silverware. Have students eat together with teacher and guest.
	Knock on door before entering. Close door when using bathroom.	Reinforce at school.
	On left side of scrapbook, paste picture or drawing of activity. Paste clock on opposite page.	Assist child in assembling "My Family Schedule" scrapbook.

In the Neighborhood

Behavioral Objectives	Learning Experiences to Develop Behavior	Suggested Teacher Procedures to Develop Behavior
Child finds help within the neighborhood in time of emergency.		See "Learns of helpful people within the neighborhood" under "In the Neighborhood" in "Social Competencies," "Level II."
Child locates service resources within the neighborhood.	Draw or cut out pictures of resources found in neighborhood. Include fire station, post office, church, service station, bowling alley.	Design bulletin board of neighborhood service resources using students' drawings and pictures.
	Point to appropriate picture or drawing on bulletin board.	Label pictures with familiar trade names, i.e. Safeway, Rexall Drug, Shell, etc.
	Suggest items to be purchased.	Hold up objects commonly found in service facilities. Ask, "Where would you go to obtain this?"
		Make shopping list of snack, lunch, or special occasion items.
	Respond by raising hand.	Before going to store, ask, "Who knows what a bag of sugar looks like?" "Who knows what salt looks like?" "Who knows where the frozen peas are?"
	Participate in shopping trip. Take assigned item to teacher for purchase.	Assign two students from those who raised hands to find each product.
		Contact local park and recreation district to obtain information on programs for exceptional children.
		Obtain brochures describing activities and send home to parents.

	Show film of young people using recreation facilities (M-204).
	Have recreation director visit class to meet students and talk about available programs.
	Make prior arrangements with director of sheltered workshop for visitation.
	See "Learns of 'dangers' of neighborhood" under "In the Neighborhood" and "Knows of 'dangers' in the community" under "In the Community" in "Social Competencies," "Level II."
	See "Knows location of home with respect to neighborhood" and "Learns key points within the neighborhood" under "In the Neighborhood" in "Social Competencies," "Level II."
	"Knows how to travel from home to important points in the community" under "In the Community" in "Social Competencies," "Level III."
	Visit nearest park and recreation center to home. Participate in activities, i.e. swimming, bowling, tumbling, etc.
	Take field trip using public transportation to theaters, restaurants, sheltered workshops.
Child avoids the "dangers" of the neighborhood.	
Child recognizes principle streets and landmarks in the neighborhood.	

Behavioral Objectives	Learning Experiences to Develop Behavior	Suggested Teacher Procedures to Develop Behavior
Child respects rights and property of others.	*DO* I keep my things in my yard. I only go in other yards when invited. I stay out of neighbors' trees. I stay out of neighbors' garages. I keep my hands to myself. *DON'T* I don't run on lawns. I don't throw rocks or sticks. I don't run through flower beds and hedges. I don't take things that aren't mine.	Design bulletin board with happy and sad faces. Print *DO* under happy face and *DON'T* under sad face. Print rules on strips of tagboard and place under appropriate heading. 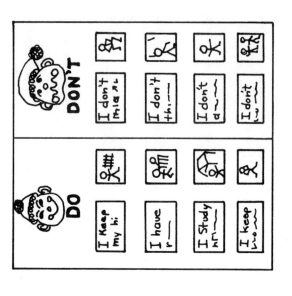 Make illustrations for rules using cut-outs, stick figures, yarn outlines, etc., and mount on cards.
	Place illustration under appropriate face and match with rule.	

In the Community

Behavioral Objectives	Learning Experiences to Develop Behavior	Suggested Teacher Procedures to Develop Behavior
Child travels from home to important points in the community.	Ask permission before leaving home. Give specific destination and route.	Stress not changing plans without informing parents.

Look at map.
Name the four landmarks.

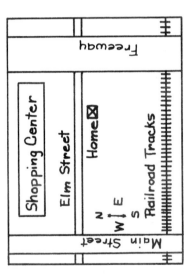

Point to own house on map and name street.

Locate neighborhood mailbox.

Child locates recreational facilities in community – church, post office, parks, pools.

Deposit letter in mailbox.

Use school bus driver as resource for knowledge of key points and landmarks within child's immediate environment.

With bus driver's help, design a map for each student, drawing four main landmarks to form boundaries and serve as directional clues.

Keep map boundaries within walking distance.

Ask bus driver to call out names of major arteries, landmarks, and general directions, north, south, east, west, when driving students to and from school.

Say, "Show me where your house is."

Explain there is usually one large post office in each community and mailboxes in each neighborhood.

Obtain picture or facsimile of mail box (Misc-203).

Arrange to have several letters for students to deposit in mailbox within walking distance of school.

For additional activities, see "Knows proper behavior in public places" under "In the Community," "Social Competencies," "Level II," and "Knows the location of service resources within the neighborhood" under "In the Neighborhood" in "Social Competencies," "Level III."

Objective		
Child shows pride in the community and its activities.	Share experiences with class about events attended. Tell about activities that took place and which were most enjoyable.	Contact local Chamber of Commerce for listing of major community activities and special attractions, i.e. fairs, parades, festivals, etc.
		Precede each event with a study unit containing brief description of background and reason for observance. Utilize advance publicity, i.e. posters, newspapers, brochures, television, etc.
		Invite planning committee member to make presentation to class describing special activities or events.
	Print name at bottom of note.	Write thank-you note to committee member.
		Notify parents of community activity. Include location, time and cost.
	Draw pictures related to community event. Bring souvenirs for "Show and Tell."	Have students who attend share experience with classmates.
Child contributes to services within the community – sheltered workshop.	Tour facilities with parents and teacher.	Locate and tour Sheltered Workshops, Activity Centers, Day Camps, etc. to inform students and their parents of facilities available after graduation.
		Check with Park and Recreation Department for community activities designed for the handicapped.
		Make arrangements with Sheltered Workshop for on-the-job experience and work training for group of older students ready to graduate.
	Learn and perform task assigned, use proper tools, remain in designated work area, etc.	Carry through with training skills in classroom, i.e. punctuality, responsibility, cooperation, etc.

COMMUNICATIVE SKILLS

M.A. 6 years and up

Oral

Behavioral Objectives	*Learning Experiences to Develop Behavior*	Level III *Suggested Teacher Procedures to Develop Behavior*
Child converses to exchange information or convey desires.		Place words "who," "what," "where," "when," "why," and "how" on chalkboard as examples of words that begin questions.
	Answer questions.	Use words to begin questions, "Who has their lunch money?" "What is your name?" Explain this is how information is exchanged between people.
	Respond to question and ask next student, "*How* are you, Mary?"	Initiate question and answer period. Ask one student, "How are you, Terry?" Continue until each student asks and answers a question.
		Take advantage of spontaneous questions, i.e. "When do we eat?" "What's on television?" "Where are you going?"
	Answer question when called upon.	Call attention to question and refer to another student to answer, i.e. "Mike, can you answer Johnny's question?"
	Ask question and place X or O in vacant square.	Divide class into two teams, boys versus girls. Play tic-tac-toe; boys are O's, girls are X's. X's and O's are earned when students ask questions.

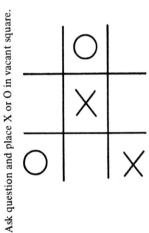

Child uses telephone.	Sit in pairs and exchange questions and answers, i.e. "Where do you live?" "I live near here."	When necessary assist student to restate response in form of question. Give positive reinforcement for all attempts at participation.
		Work with pairs to encourage verbalization.
		Tape record conversations. Emphasize care in speaking versus speed and quantity. Use kits (Misc-204).
	Elect Council officers, President, Vice-president, Secretary-treasurer.	Establish Student Council. Explain each office and function, i.e. "President 'runs' Council meeting. He sits here and uses the gavel to keep order in the meeting. . . ." Ask for nominations.
	President conducts Council meeting. Classmates speak when recognized by the President.	Tell students, "This is your time to tell what you want to do."
	Communicate ideas to class, i.e. spend class money for picnic, invite principal to snack time, plan ping pong tournament.	Schedule bi-monthly meetings. Use meetings to give each student a voice in planning class activities.
	Place finger firmly in "0." Pull dial around to finger stop. Remove finger and allow dial to spin back.	Obtain large black dial from telephone company.
	Dial numbers as directed by teacher.	Provide Tele-Trainer or battery operated telephones from telephone company (Misc-205).
	Practice dialing home telephone number from printed card.	Print each student's home phone number on large card. Assist student in memorizing number.
	Lift receiver, listen for dial tone, and dial home number. Greet parent and give reason for calling from school.	Transfer from practice phone to school phone. Permit students knowing home phone number to call parents. Have entire class observe as motivation.

Objective	Activity
Identify self, give location, and reason why help is needed.	Explain telephone is a source of help in emergency.
	Determine parents' rules and limitations concerning child's use of telephone.
Child tells a story in correct sequence.	Demonstrate use of story cards. Place cards in random order.
Listen to and observe teacher. Arrange picture story cards in correct sequence.	Provide a variety of commercial or teacher-made sequence cards (Misc-206 through Misc-209).
Select set of pictures. Arrange in sequence and tell story.	See "Can retell familiar stories in correct sequence" under "Oral" in "Communicative Skills," "Level II."
Child gives Pledge of Allegiance.	Show film (M-205) and filmstrip (SFS-201). Utilize (B-204-206).
Listen as teacher tells about flag.	Explain briefly what a flag is, why the United States has a flag, and why it is saluted.
Stand very straight, heels together, head up. Place right hand over heart, look at flag and give Pledge.	Demonstrate proper procedures for saluting flag while repeating Pledge of Allegiance, i.e. place right hand over heart, stand erect, look at flag.
Take turns leading class in daily salute.	Schedule each student to lead Pledge.
Sing patriotic songs.	Follow Pledge with patriotic songs, i.e. "God Bless America," "America the Beautiful," "My Country 'Tis of Thee."
Stand when National Anthem is played.	Play recording of "Star-Spangled Banner." Explain standing while National Anthem is played shows respect.

Behavioral Objectives	Learning Experiences to Develop Behavior	Suggested Teacher Procedures to Develop Behavior
Child conveys ideas after listening to group or demonstration, radio program, etc.	Choose character to portray. Rehearse play with two participants.	Divide students in groups of three. Suggest plot and characters for play. Give brief outline and direction to each group.
	Perform play before classmates.	Have groups take turns presenting plays.
	Describe main idea or action depicted by play.	Leading discussion on interpretation by asking key questions.
	Show completed item to class. Classmates tell what they think item is, how it was made and what it is for.	Provide materials, i.e. Lincoln Logs, Tinker Toys, or craft supplies for two or three students to construct a project.
	Listen to weather report on radio. Tell appropriate clothing to wear based on forecast.	List terms used by newscaster, i.e. windy, cloudy, precipitation, velocity, etc. and define.

Word Recognition

Behavioral Objectives	Learning Experiences to Develop Behavior	Suggested Teacher Procedures to Develop Behavior
Child recognizes own street name, phone number, etc.		See "Can give name, age, birthday, address and telephone number" under "Oral" and "Recognizes own name in print" under "Word Recognition" in "Communicative Skills," "Level II," and "Uses telephone to give or get information or for pleasure" under "Oral," "Communicative Skills," "Level III."
Child reacts appropriately to signs and labels within environment.	Recognize word or letter, i.e. small (S), medium (M), large (L), extra large (XL).	Introduce general terms and provide facsimiles of labels on clothing.
		Estimate size of student's clothing in terms of small, medium, large, etc.

Behavioral Objectives	Learning Experiences to Develop Behavior	Suggested Teacher Procedures to Develop Behavior
	Check labels and select correct size.	Obtain cardigan sweaters from Goodwill, rummage sales, parents, etc., ranging in size from small to extra large. Clean or wash before using. Fold and arrange on table.
		On field trips look for vending machines, pay telephones, and admission turnstiles.
	Practice procedure with candy, soft drink, and gum ball machines.	Point out "INSERT" and "COIN RETURN" and demonstrate by placing coin in slot of pay telephone. Hang up phone to demonstrate coin return process.
		For protective signs and labels within environment see "Recognizes simple words or cues of safety" under "Word Recognition" in "Communicative Skills," "Level I," and "Recognizes danger words such as danger, poison, etc." and "Recognizes restricting signs and labels . . ." under "Word Recognition" in "Communicative Skills," "Level II."

Listening

Behavioral Objectives	Learning Experiences to Develop Behavior	Suggested Teacher Procedures to Develop Behavior
Child identifies sounds by source and cause.	Close eyes while clock is being hidden. Walk quietly around room listening for ticking sound to find clock.	Provide loud ticking alarm clock. Hide clock in classroom. Limit groups to five or six children.
	Finder hides clock for next game.	See "Distinguishes specific sound within group of sounds (whistle with drums)" and "Responds to everyday sounds" under "Listening" in "Communicative Skills," "Level II."

Child listens to and and carries out more detailed instructions.	See "Can follow directions" under "Listening" in "Communicative Skills," "Level II."
Listen to instructions and make appropriate marks with crayon.	Paste six large colored pictures on sheet of chipboard. Cover with acetate.
	Start with simple instructions: "Put mark on wagon." "Put mark on pony." "Put mark on ball."
	Increase level of difficulty: "Draw circle around ball and pony." "Draw line from wagon to pony."
Follow verbal instructions.	Provide a 12″ x 12″ sheet of newsprint for each child. Say, "Pick up one edge of paper and bring it over to the other edge. Hold it there and press the paper flat with your other hand." "Take another edge that you haven't used and bring it over to the other edge and press flat." Now unfold the paper. You can see four squares."
Paste one shape in each square of newsprint.	Provide selection of various colors and shapes of paper.
Child enjoys a variety of auditory stimulation	
Participate in music program.	Schedule routine time for listening to records, tapes, radio, etc. Expose student to a variety of music from country-western to classical.
	Present brief background on each type of music.
Express feelings music arouses. Role-play emotions stimulated by music.	Ask, "Does music make you want to dance, march, sway, rest; Is it sad, happy, lonely?"

Behavioral Objectives	Learning Experiences to Develop Behavior	Suggested Teacher Procedures to Develop Behavior
Child reacts appropriately to auditory stimuli.	Listen to poems. Talk about funniest, favorite, happiest, etc.	Read poems: "Bursting" (B-207), "Lines and Squares" (B-208), and "Ten Little Indian Boys" (B-209).
	Take walk; listen to poem. Point out clouds that resemble animals and describe.	Read "Clouds" (Misc-210). Discuss poem to help children understand and enjoy idea of clouds as sheep, etc. Additional poems (B-210).
	Identify feeling protrayed by the sound, tone, volume, control of voice.	Demonstrate various voice qualities, i.e. anger, fear, happiness, sadness, etc.
	Role-play.	Introduce idea that some sounds require action.
	Identify sounds from tape.	Tape sounds of sirens.
	Give corresponding actions to emergency sounds.	Demonstrate proper response, i.e. stay on sidewalk, etc.
		Show films (M-206, M-207).
	Imitate sounds of fire truck, ambulance, etc.	Read stories about fire trucks, ambulances (B-211).
		See "Responds to everyday sounds" under "Listening" in "Communicative Skills," "Level II."

Perceptual

Behavioral Objectives	Learning Experiences to Develop Behavior	Suggested Teacher Procedures to Develop Behavior
Child prints numbers, letters, and simple words, and own name.	Roll clay into coils. Form letters of name with clay and place between lines on toweling.	Draw lines two inches apart on paper toweling with felt pen. Demonstrate forming letters from clay and placing within lines. Prepare large name card for each student with letters carefully printed.

Make up and down marks, circles, etc.

After letter forms are mastered in clay, demonstrate proper way to hold pencil.

Provide Primary pencils and 9″ x 12″ ruled newsprint with dotted interlines.

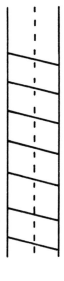

Practice printing name using pencil and paper.

Assist student with printing. Print letter first. Give directions, "Say letter as I print it."

Print name on place card.

Furnish individual place cards made from tagboard, heavy construction paper, or cardboard. Draw lines to guide printing. Distribute place cards at random on table.

Sit in chair in front of name card.

Explain, "Look at the names and see if you can find yours."

"See "Prints single numbers and letters" under "Perceptual" in "Communicative Skills," "Level II."

ECONOMIC USEFULNESS

M.A. 6 years and up

Self-help Skills

Behavioral Objectives	*Learning Experiences to Develop Behavior*	**Level III** *Suggested Teacher Procedures to Develop Behavior*
Child chooses appropriate dress for various occasions.		*Weather* Use flannel board set of boy and girl figures and various types of clothing, i.e. dresses, shirts, skirts, shoes, hats, jackets, coats, trousers, etc. (Misc-202).
	Place rain coat, umbrella, boots, rain hat, etc. on flannel board figure. 	Utilize existing weather conditions to introduce appropriate dress, i.e. on rainy days provide matching weather symbol and corresponding outer garments. Follow same procedure for other types of weather.
	Select and put on appropriate clothing for a rainy day, i.e. umbrella, rain hat, boots, scarf, etc. Open and close umbrella.	Add actual clothing and accessories needed for different types of weather to the "Dress-Up Box." Demonstrate use of umbrella.

	Activities
Select appropriate clothing to match activities.	Show and discuss pictures of various types of activities, i.e. picnic, swimming, dancing, skiing, dining out, church, etc. Call attention to clothing being worn. Provide an assortment of pictures of clothing obtained from catalogues, advertisements, etc.
Child cares for personal belongings.	See "Recognizes and cares for personal belongings . . ." under "Self-Help Skills," "Economic Usefulness," "Level I."
	Develops an appreciation for personal belongings" under "Self-help Skills" in "Economic Usefulness," "Level II."
Child grooms self property.	In addition to individual Tote Trays, have available electric shaver, spray deodorant, after shave, and hand lotion, etc.
	Set up grooming area containing necessary equipment and supplies, i.e. shampoo, creme rinse, hair dressing, curlers, drier, wash basin with spray hose, shampoo tray, shampoo cape, etc.
Shampoo, set, and comb classmate's hair. With a classmate's help, do own hair.	Demonstrate shampooing hair or invite beautician to instruct class in hair care.
	Show film (M-208).
Use soap, nail brush, clippers, etc., when necessary. Show clean hands at inspection time.	For hands and nails provide nail clippers, emery board, orange sticks, cotton, nail brushes, heavy duty hand cleaners for boys, soap, etc.
	See "Appreciates good grooming, toileting, and feeding habits" under "Self-help Skills" in "Economic Usefulness," "Level II."

Behavioral Objectives	Learning Experiencies to Develop Behavior	Suggested Teacher Procedures to Develop Behavior
Child controls emotions and personal feelings.	Role-play incident as it happened. Redramatize how participants should have behaved.	Encourage free discussion of problems which arise during day. Point out both sides of issue.
		Set up dramatic play situations utilizing a typical classroom or playground incident, i.e. sharing playground equipment, being first in line, etc.
		Differentiate between reporting (to help) and tattling (to get someone in trouble). Give verbal reinforcement for desired behavior.
		Devise constructive ways for children to "let off steam."
		Recognize signs of emotional problems. Let child know you understand he is upset. Help child to find more adequate ways to deal with upsets and problems.
		Always praise successes.
		Be available to parents for any guidance they might seek.
		See "Respects the right, feelings and responsibilities of others" under "In the School" in "Social Competencies," "Level III."

Home-help Skills

Behavioral Objectives		Suggested Teacher Procedures to Develop Behavior
Child willingly performs household chores: makes beds, sweeps, vacuums, etc.		See "Assists in routine of daily living in the home" under "In the Home" in "Social Competencies," "Level II."

Child cares for family property and possessions.		"Appreciates completed task: feeling of pride in achievement" under "Community-help Skills" in "Economic Usefulness," "Level II."
		See "Appreciates use of family property and possessions" under "Home-help Skills," in "Economic Usefulness," "Level II."
		"Takes pride in home and environment" under "In the Home" in "Social Competencies," "Level III."
		For proper usage of telephone, television, radio, see "Accepts social responsibilities within the home" under "In the Home" in "Social Competencies," "Level III."
Child takes care of pets.	Look at pictures and state preference for class pet. Discuss kinds of food and shelter necessary for various animals.	Collect pictures of animals suitable for pets. Make final decision as to appropriate pet. Provide adequate enclosure and provisions for care during week-ends and vacations.
	Draw pictures to illustrate each need.	Make chart of "Things to Remember," i.e. right kind of food, fresh water, place to rest or sleep, beds and cages kept clean, and kindness.
	Visit zoo, aquarium, pet shop. Observe ways in which animals' needs are met.	Arrange field trips and have attendants or shop owners conduct tours. Children's zoos are ideal.
	Bring pet to school.	Set aside one day for class "Pet Parade." Notify parents, bus drivers, and school personnel.
		Make colored tags for awards denoting classification for prizes, i.e. biggest, smallest, shaggiest, skinniest, shortest, etc. Award every pet a ribbon.

	Learning Experiences to Develop Behavior	Suggested Teacher Procedures to Develop Behavior
	Lead or carry pet along parade route. Stop before judge's stand, identify pet, and tell name. Receive award to take home.	Make arrangements for parade route. Choose judges and present awards.
	Select class pet or pets. Take turn caring for pet, i.e. feeding, watering cleaning facilities, etc.	Assign area for storage of food and supplies. (B-212, B-213).

Community-help Skills

Behavioral Objectives	Learning Experiences to Develop Behavior	Suggested Teacher Procedures to Develop Behavior
Child utilizes community resources.		See "Knows the location of service resources within the neighborhood" under "In the Neighborhood" and entire section, "In the Community" in "Social Competencies," "Level III."
Child completes simple assignments.	Pick up office memo; circulate among teachers. Wait for each teacher to read and initial. Return memo to office.	Assign routine "clerical" tasks, i.e. collecting attendance slips, lunch count, milk and picture money, distributing materials to be sent home to parents, etc.
		Select "experienced" child to work with "inexperienced" child until task is understood and can be carried out alone.
		Rotate assignments weekly.
Child enjoys working as a team member on common task.		Canvass community nonprofit service organizations, i.e. Hearing Society, Easter Seal, P.T.A., Hospital Auxiliaries, Chamber of Commerce, etc.

Objective	Child Activities	Teacher Activities
		Volunteer class help in mailing, i.e. fund raising, meeting notices, special events, conferences, etc.
	Pick up pages in sequence. Carry to student who is stapling. Staple pages. Hand to another to fold. Fold pages. Put in envelopes.	Place pages on table in sequence to be picked up by student. Provide stapler and folding box. Set aside separate working areas for each step of task.
		Rotate assignments to provide students opportunity to perform each step.
Child selects and utilizes appropriate materials in completion of a task.	Offer suggestions for possible projects. Describe similar project carried on at home.	Plan a garden project, i.e. plant ground cover, reseed or plant new lawn, plant flower bed and/or vegetable garden.
		Furnish seeds and plants either individually or in flats.
	Identify tool and describe or demonstrate function.	Provide soil conditioner, fertilizer, and garden tools, i.e. hose, rake, hoe, wheelbarrow, trowel, gloves, spade, etc.
	Select proper tool for task.	Design chart listing necessary steps, including clean-up and storing of tools. Discuss each step with students. Assign a task to each student and ask what tools or materials are needed.
	Participate in project by carrying out assigned task.	Take class to garden area. Supervise project, i.e. safety factors, doing task correctly and in area assigned, total class participation, etc.
	Check bulletin board for daily assignment. Choose correct tool and return to storage area when task is completed.	Make an on-going check list for maintenance, i.e. watering, hoeing, weeding, thinning and pruning, etc.

RECREATION AND EXPRESSIVE ACTIVITIES

M.A. 6 years and up

		Level III
Behavioral Objectives	*Learning Experiences to Develop Behavior*	*Suggested Teacher Procedures to Develop Behavior*
Child selects programs for leisure time enjoyment.	Name favorite television programs and describe best-liked characters.	Discuss various television programs for children. Suggest good programs that children have not mentioned. Call attention to specials that will be shown. Send note home alerting parents to time and channel. After viewing program, discuss with children.
	Share television time, cooperate in selection of programs, and accept class decision.	Allow students to select and watch television program during rainy day recess.
		Observe program selection and reinforce cooperative behavior.
		Follow same procedure with radio programs and films.
Child selects pleasing objects to view.	Take field trip and observe: Trees Shrubs Leaves and blossoms Birds Clouds Gardens Houses Yards Flowers	Ascertain when local flower shows, blossom festivals, art shows, county fairs, etc., are being held. Plan field trips. Inform parents of activities occurring on weekends.
	Look at other children's art work and reproductions in magazines and books.	Select well-illustrated books (B-214, B-215, B-216) and show to class.

Child produces art and craft objects.

Bring collections to share with class, i.e. shell, stamp, rock, doll, dried flower, etc.

Use simple tools and equipment to produce art and craft objects.

Provide opportunity for children to share and display collections.

Pictures:
Paint
Crayon
Chalk
Pen
Mosaic
Straw and string painting
Dried leaves and flowers

Media:
Paint   — Tempera, water color, oil, finger, spray
Crayon   — Chunk-O Crayon, Broad Line
Chalk   — Pastel, poster, colored
Brush pen — Felt-tip, Flo-master

Equipment and Additional Materials:
Brushes
Easel
Scissors
Glue and paste
Newsprint, corrugated, construction, waxed, butcher, wrapping paper
Colored sand, egg shells, seeds, gravel, rocks, tiles, macaroni, paper

Stencils and Prints:
Paper

Cloth

Media:
Paper   — Newsprint, cardboard, newspaper, paper toweling, Handiwipes
Powdered or liquid tempera, chalk, crayon, Textile paint
Cloth   — unbleached muslin, canvas, burlap

Equipment and Additional Materials:
Brushes   — flat, round, fine, in wide and narrow widths

X-acto knives and Blades

Sponge   – natural, synthetic

Vegetable – potato, carrot, cabbage, celery stalk

Fruit   – lemon, orange, grapefruit, apple

Media:

Paper   – construction, tagboard, tissue

Raffia   – bleached, Madagascar, natural

Lacing   – Pyro, plastic, leather

Looper   – Jersey, nylon, cotton

Yarn   – rug warp, school jute, roving

Straw   – paper, plastic

Reed   – plastic, natural dried grasses

Equipment and Additional Materials:

Square loom frames, weaving hooks and/or needles, crochet hooks, nails.

Cardboard forms for raffia mats.

Heavy wrapping string.

Wooden frames or boxes outlined with nails at regular intervals

Tongue depressor shuttle

Commercial or cardboard looms

Pipe cleaners

Empty thread spools with four nails in top

Plywood bases for reed baskets, commercial or teacher-made

Wrought iron frames (Misc-211)

Shellac

Sewing machine

Leather punch

Media and Additional Equipment:

Background – burlap, muslin, linen, fruit or vegetable mesh bags, dishcloth

Weaving:

Finger and frame

Shuttle and heddle

Spider Web

Circle

Novel

Spool

Waffle

Reed

Stitchery:

Stitch and create

Mesh bags

Screen wire

Applique

		Trimming — beads, buttons, rope, rick-rack Applique — felt, leather, netting, paper, terry cloth Threads — cotton, yarns, embroidery floss, string raffia, ribbons Utilize (B-217).
Child responds to rhythm by dancing and playing simple musical instruments.		See "Experiments with appropriate arts and crafts media" in "Recreation and Expressive Activities," "Level I," and "Practices working with arts and crafts media on an expanded scale" in "Recreation and Expressive Activities," "Level II." See "Recognizes rhythm change" under "Perceptual" in "Communicative Skills," "Level II." Responds to rhythms with rhythm instruments, dancing, clapping, and body rhythm" and "Learns simple dance steps and assumes roles from simple stories" in "Recreation and Expressive Activities," "Level II."
Child performs more intricate dance steps.	Choose partner and practice following steps demonstrated by teacher.	Review dance terms and positions, i.e. left, right, head couple, side couple, partner position.
	Select a new partner and repeat procedure.	Pair experienced with inexperienced dancers when possible.
	Dance alone to music moving freely.	Play music that lends itself to free interpretative dancing. Utilize (B-218, B-219).
	Take turn joining teacher in demonstrating new steps. Classmates tap out rhythm while observing. Take part in folk dances.	Play record of folk songs. Demonstrate new steps to music. Encourage one or more out-going students to join in demonstrations.

	Master art of tapping rhythms, performing dance steps. Create steps to favorite music.	Introduce dances with more complicated steps as students master each set.
		Provide records stressing rhythms of many cultures (R-201, R-202, R-203).
Child enjoys individual and group singing.	Sing and play instruments: bongo drum, triangle, tambourine, wood blocks, melody tone bells, glockenspiel, organ, and tonette.	Encourage students to sing, listen to records, and experiment with instruments.
	Assume role of "acting teacher." Turn chart until another child says, "Stop!" indicating choice of song.	Make up charts of songs with corresponding pictures for each song. Select songs with wide ranging subjects, i.e. cowboys, Indians, space, community workers, animals of farm, circus and zoo. Choose one child to be "acting teacher."
	Sit on floor in circle, feet pointed toward center, clap to rhythm, and sing: "Who is wearing red shoes, red shoes, Who is wearing red shoes all day long? Skip around the outside, outside, outside, Skip around the outside, then sit down."	Sing "Who is Wearing Red Shoes?" to tune of "Mary Has a Red Dress."
		Suggested songs: "I've Been Working on the Railroad," "Yankee Doodle," "Go Tell Aunt Rhody," "Jimmie Crack Corn," "Little White Duck," "Over the River and Through the Woods," "Rain Drops Keep Falling on My Head" (B-220, B-221).
Child enjoys sports.	Relate experiences.	Discuss sporting events children attend or watch on television.
		Prepare displays depicting various sports: Football – field, player ball Baseball – diamond, bat, player Basketball – court, hoops, player (Misc-212).

Child enjoys sports.	Handle equipment and answer questions.	Provide equipment and ask, "Which game is played with this?" Hold up football, etc.
		Provide opportunity to watch short segments of World Series on television in classroom.
	Collect cards of famous sports figures from bubble gum, candy wrappers, cereals, etc.	Encourage parents to allow children to watch sporting events at home, i.e. bowling, basketball, football, baseball, etc., and to explain basic elements of each game.
		Develop simple adaptions of each sport, i.e. flag football, half-court basketball, single team baseball.
		Make arrangements with bowling alley to schedule time for class to bowl.
	Form teams and play game.	Arrange for class swimming instruction, i.e. YMCA, swimming and tennis clubs, parks and recreation, etc.
Child uses appropriate tools.		See "Discriminates between appropriate and inappropriate materials and tools for a given job" under "Community-help Skills" in "Economic Usefulness," "Level II."
		"Develops abilities to use appropriate simple hand tools" in "Recreation and Expressive Activities," "Level II."
		"Selects and utilizes appropriate materials in completion of a task" under "Community-help Skills" in "Economic Usefulness," "Level III."
Child selects leisure time activities.	Ride bicycle, scooter, and skate board. Roller skate, fly kite, play tetherball, jump rope. Shoot baskets, bat and throw ball, kick soccer or football.	*Large muscle activities:* Provide as much equipment as possible to develop skills.

Small muscle activities:
Provide wide variety of games, puzzles, construction sets, hobby items, etc.

Assemble puzzles, model airplanes, cars. Build with Tinker Toys, Erector Set, Lincoln Logs, Toggles. Play card games, i.e. Fish, Hearts, Steal the Pack, Old Maid.

Outdoor activities:
Survey camps, outdoor education programs, day camps, etc. for exceptional children.

Camp, fish, hike, swim.

Quiet activities:
Provide quiet corner or "library."

Look at books and magazines. Listen to records and radio. Watch television.

Hobbies and crafts:
Encourage and assist children to select hobbies.

Sew, garden, cook, paint, color, collect stamps, rocks, shells, etc.

QUANTITATIVE CONCEPTS

M.A. 6 years and up

Measure

Behavioral Objectives	*Learning Experiences to Develop Behavior*	**Level III** *Suggested Teacher Procedures to Develop Behavior*
Child continues to develop concepts of long-short, tall-short, enough-not enough.		See "Develops discrimination . . ." under "Measure" in "Quantitative Concepts," "Level II."
Child discriminates between other comparative concepts.		Show films (M-209, M-210) and utilize (B-222, B-223).
		Color: Obtain sets of color samples from paint companies or stores.

Behavioral Objectives	Learning Experiences to Develop Behavior	Suggested Teacher Procedures to Develop Behavior
	Point to lightest or darkest. Place chips in row, progressing from lightest to darkest, or vice versa.	Use five shades of chips for each color set, i.e. green, olive, Kelly, light, chartreuse, and lime. Introduce extremes first, light and dark.
	Place a variety of crackers on a large platter and serve classmates. Ask, "What shape cracker would you like?" Respond, "I would like a square," etc., when served.	*Geometric shapes:* During snack time, provide crackers in a variety of shapes, i.e. Ritz, soda, Sociables, Triscuit, etc.
	Point to objects that are open and those that are closed.	*Position:* Display pictures of objects which can be opened or shut, i.e. refrigerator, stove, box, window, etc. Ask, "Which are open, which are shut?"
		Vary procedures with up and down, in or out, front or back, over or under, etc.

Time

Behavioral Objectives	Learning Experiences to Develop Behavior	Suggested Teacher Procedures to Develop Behavior
Child relates clock or watch face positions with scheduled activities.	Assemble puzzles. Manipulate hands on individual dials.	Provide clock puzzles and individual dials with movable hands (Misc-213 through Misc-217).
		Place large clock face on table or chalkboard tray (Misc-218).
	Match hands on individual clocks.	Move hands into time positions denoting scheduled activities, i.e. ten o'clock for recess, eleven-thirty for lunch, two o'clock for dismissal.
	Repeat time after teacher.	Say, "At recess time the hands say ten o'clock." "When the hands say two o'clock, we go home."

Behavioral Objectives	Learning Experiences to Develop Behavior	Suggested Teacher Procedures to Develop Behavior
Child uses concepts: tomorrow, yesterday, with understanding.	Place card with name of day in appropriate slot.	See "Recognizes purpose for clocks and watches" under "Time" in "Quantitative Concepts," "Level II."
		Make large chart for children to read and change each day. Yesterday was _____. Today is _____. Tomorrow will be _____.
	Tell about events that have happened or will happen, i.e., "I helped set the table *yesterday*." *"Tomorrow* we are going to see my uncle." *"Today* my mother is going to the dentist."	Arrange time for children to share home experiences.
		At end of day review school activities or discuss plans for future, i.e. *"Today* we made cookies." "What did we have for snacks *yesterday?"* "Where are we going *tomorrow?"*
Child uses calendar: day, week, year.	Take turn pointing to date on calendar and repeat name of day, month, and year.	Display calendar in classroom. Refer to daily, calling attention to day, month, and date (Misc-219, Misc-220, Misc-221).
	Associate favorite activity with each day.	Make chart for days of week showing schedule: Monday – Back to school day Tuesday – Film day Wednesday– Make plans day Thursday – Swim day Friday – Square dance day Teach song "Days of the Week" (B-221).

Money

Behavioral Objectives	Learning Experiences to Develop Behavior	Suggested Teacher Procedures to Develop Behavior
Child recognizes relative values of money.		See "Money" section in "Quantitative Concepts," "Level II."

Behavioral Objective	Learning Experiences to Develop Behavior	Suggested Teacher Procedures to Develop Behavior
Child makes small purchases.		
Child counts money to a limited degree.	Count pennies in stacks of one, five, and ten. Indicate which is more or less.	Before students can learn to count, concept of "more" or "less" must be established.
		Beginning lessons in counting money should be limited to pennies, i.e. five pennies are more than one, ten are more than five, etc.
	Exchange two nickels for dime.	Substitute nickel and dime for corresponding stacks of pennies.
	Collect milk money. Determine coins to give for change, i.e. dime for milk, nickel – change.	

SAFETY

Level III

M.A. 6 years and up

At Home

Behavioral Objective	Learning Experiences to Develop Behavior	Suggested Teacher Procedures to Develop Behavior
Child learns causes of home accidents.	Name articles and give location in home, i.e. kitchen, garage, bathroom, etc.	Discuss safe use of tools in kitchen and workshop, i.e. knives, cleansers, cleaning equipment, appliances, etc.
	Demonstrate proper use of knives and other sharp instruments.	Display items, demonstrate use and explain restrictions.
	Present tools to others with handle first.	

Child recognizes importance of personal orderliness.	Keep desk free of waste paper, candy wrappers, litter, etc.	Show films (M-211, M-212) and filmstrip (FS-205).
		Discuss care of self, desk, and personal belongings.
	Pick up crayons, pencils, papers from floor.	Display "litterbug" signs and posters. Explain meaning.
		Show film (M-213).
	Display badge or award on desk.	Reward children for neat, orderly desks with special badges or awards.
	Hang up all articles with handles, i.e. mops, brooms, rakes, hoes, etc.	Reinforce correct storage of tools after use.
	Dispose of cracked, chipped, or partly broken objects.	Explain danger of sharp edges and unsound furniture.
Child properly stores toys and personal effects.	Return toys and games to proper place after use. Close cupboard doors and drawers.	Provide specific areas to store toys and games.
	Make individual safety booklets using magazine pictures. Circle safe and unsafe areas for storage of personal possessions with crayon or felt pen.	Guide children in finding suitable pictures, i.e. driveway, yard, kitchen, bedroom, garage, etc. Provide magazines, scissors, crayons, felt pens, paste, etc.
		Show film (M-214).
		See "Develops ability to pick up toys and keep them in proper places for safety" under "At Home" in "Safety," "Level II."
Child recognizes dangers of medicine.		See "Stays out of medicine cabinet" under "At Home" in "Safety," "Level I" and "Understands dangers of medicine" under "At Home" in "Safety," "Level II."

Child reports fire or accidents to person in authority.	Role-play telephone call to report car and home accidents, fire, etc.	See "Uses telephone to give or get information or for pleasure" under "Oral" in "Communicative Skills," "Level III." Display study print (SP-201). Show filmstrip (FS-206) and films (M-215, M-216).
Child recognizes dangers of gas and other inflammables.	Discuss dangers and how to prevent accidents. Look at products and point to warning. *DON'T* Play with matches or cigarette lighters Play near open fire Use inflammable materials, i.e. gasoline, kerosene, white gas, etc. without supervision. *DO* Turn handles of cooking utensils inward on stove Use potholders Store paint, spot remover cleaning cloths in metal container. Draw stick figure pictures to illustrate rules.	Obtain booklet from National Safety Council. Read to children. Provide samples of inflammable products and point out warning on containers. Review rules of safety with matches, fire, stove, etc. State in form of "Do's" and "Don't's" and design chart with students' drawings as illustrations.
Child observes simple safety rules for electricity.	*NEVER* Touch an electric wire which is broken, loose or hanging down Put foreign objects into electrical outlets or sockets Touch a piece of metal that electricity might be going through.	Stress safety rules when dealing with electricity. Point out electrical outlets in classroom. Demonstrate correct method of placing plug in outlet.

Behavioral Objectives	Learning Experiences to Develop Behavior	Suggested Teacher Procedures to Develop Behavior
	Before using appliance: Dry hands Be sure feet are dry Do not stand in or near water Check that plug and cord are in good condition Use correct method for turning on and off.	Use actual appliances to demonstrate safety rules. Show film (M-217). Review rules before student uses electric appliances.
Child recognizes the dangers of power tools.	Cut out pictures of power tools to paste in scrapbook. Identify by name.	Provide magazines, scissors, paste, and construction paper. Assist with booklets.
	Use jigsaw, rock polisher, sander. Wear goggles, safety visor, protective mask, shield, etc.	Furnish tools and equipment (Misc-222). Provide one-to-one adult supervision.
	Observe gardener working with power lawnmower, trimmers, edgers, etc.	Take small group of students to watch gardener working on school grounds. Arrange for demonstration and ask gardener to point out dangers of power equipment.

At School

Behavioral Objectives	Learning Experiences to Develop Behavior	Suggested Teacher Procedures to Develop Behavior
Child uses proper behavior on playground, i.e. does not throw rocks.	Discuss school rules with emphasis on playground behavior.	See "Begins to understand proper behavior on the playground" under "At School" in "Safety," "Level II." Show films (M-218, M-219). Review safety rules.

Behavioral Objectives	Learning Experiences to Develop Behavior	Suggested Teacher Procedures to Develop Behavior
Child participates in fire drills.	Talk over rules before and after drills. Walk through specific drills.	See "Begins to develop ability to follow fire drill exercises" under "At School" in "Safety," "Level I," and "Participates in fire drill exercises" under "At School" in "Safety," "Level II."
		Stress importance of knowing rules for emergency.
		Change times of fire drills to give students experience in emergencies in a variety of activities and locations.
Child reports fire or accidents to teacher.	Role-play reporting accident or fire.	Stress urgency and necessity of reporting fire or accident to adult in charge as quickly as possible.
		Set up situations depicting a fall on playground, fire in janitor's supply room, accident in restroom, etc.
		See "Understands how to get help when accidents occur" under "At Home" in "Safety," "Level II."
Child observes safety rules when using playground equipment.		See "Develops ability to play on playground equipment safely" under "At School" in "Safety," "Level II."

In Traffic

Behavioral Objectives	Learning Experiences to Develop Behavior	Suggested Teacher Procedures to Develop Behavior
Child respects law and authority.	Discuss films.	Show films (M-207, M-220).
	Ask questions.	Invite policeman, deputy sheriff, highway patrolman to speak to class.
		See "Recognizes and accepts the authority of school personnel" under "In the School" in "Social Competencies," "Level II."

Behavioral Objectives	Learning Experiences to Develop Behavior	Suggested Teacher Procedures to Develop Behavior
Child obeys vehicle traffic signs and signals.		"Appreciates the need to follow the directions of those in authority" under "In the School" in "Social Competencies," "Level III."
		"Obeys authority in safety directions" under "At School" in "Safety," "Level II."
		See "Begins to understand and obey traffic signals, i.e. red for stop, green for go" under "In Traffic" in "Safety," "Level II."
	Identify signs and demonstrate correct behavior.	Design bulletin board using traffic safety aids (Misc-223).
	Role-play traffic situations and manipulate flannel board figures and objects.	Use flannel board figures (Misc-224) to present typical traffic situations and patterns, i.e. pedestrian crosswalks, electric signals, parked and moving cars, four street corners, etc.
		Emphasize traffic signs and signals are designed for pedestrians as well as vehicles and must be obeyed.
		Show films (M-221, M-222).

In the Community

Behavioral Objectives	*Learning Experiences to Develop Behavior*	*Suggested Teacher Procedures to Develop Behavior*
Child observes safety precautions when getting on or off vehicles.		Show films (M-223, M-224).
		See "Learns how to behave on the school bus" under "At School" in "Safety," "Level II."
		Adapt school bus rules to passenger cars and public transportation.

Behavioral Objectives	Learning Experiences to Develop Behavior	Suggested Teacher Procedures to Develop Behavior
	DO Remain in designated area until time to enter vehicle. Walk to vehicle. Wait turn to enter. Sit quietly. Remain seated. Look both ways for traffic before stepping out. *DON'T* Get on or off moving vehicle. Push or shove other passengers. Distract driver. Jump out.	List "Do" and "Don't" rules for children to learn and follow.
Child learns danger of playing on railroad tracks.		See "Stays away from railroad tracks and other danger areas" under "In the Community" in "Safety," "Level II."

HEALTH

Level III

Behavioral Objectives	Learning Experiences to Develop Behavior	Suggested Teacher Procedures to Develop Behavior

M.A. 6 years and up

Personal Hygiene

Behavioral Objectives		Suggested Teacher Procedures to Develop Behavior
Child practices good oral hygiene.		Discuss reasons for good dental care: Help prevent decay. Promote healthy gum tissue. Aid to pleasant breath. Enhance appearance. Healthy teeth contribute to over-all good health. See "Brushes teeth after meals" under "Personal Hygiene" in "Health," "Level II."

Child recognizes the importance of proper grooming.	Mark chart after brushing teeth.	Post "Class Toothbrushing Record" (Misc-225) to check student's brushing habits.
	Take kit home and practice dental health rules.	Distribute "Dental Instruction Kits" to each student (Misc-226).
		Send for "Free Dental Hygiene Education Materials" (Misc-227).
		Show filmstrip (FS-207).
		See "Keeps self properly groomed" under "Self-help Skills" in "Economic Usefulness," "Level III."
Child washes hands before eating and after toileting.		Explain briefly relationship between disease and germs, how germs are carried by dirty hands.
		Show filmstrip (FS-208).
		Describe many objects hands touch and reasons for not putting hands or fingers in mouth.
		Emphasize necessity for washing hands after going to bathroom.
	Make up story on "When We Wash Our Hands."	Write story as students talk. Read back to class.
	Wash hands before handling or eating food.	See "Learns to wash hands and face" under "Personal Hygiene" in "Health," "Level I."
		"Develops the ability for good grooming, eating habits and manners in the group" under "In the School" in "Social Competencies," "Level I."

Child practices good grooming habits.	"Develops an awareness of good grooming and manners in self and others" under "In the School" in "Social Competencies," "Level II."	
	See "Develops and awareness of good grooming and manners in self and others" under "In the School" in "Social Competencies," "Level II."	
	"Appreciates good grooming, toileting, and feeding habits," under "Self-help Skills" in "Economic Usefulness," "Level II."	
	"Keeps self properly groomed" under "Self-help Skills" in "Economic Usefulness," "Level III."	
Child dresses according to weather conditions.	See "Recognizes clothing which is appropriate and dresses accordingly" under "In the School" in "Social Competencies," "Level III."	
	"Chooses appropriate dress for various occasions" under "Self-help Skills" in "Economic Usefulness," "Level III."	
Child bathes regularly.	Stress need for bathing regularly. Explain briefly concept of pores and sweat glands and that oil, perspiration and dirt accumulate on skin. Point out unpleasant odors come from unclean bodies.	Mount sample of each item on large sheet of tagboard titled "I Bathe With." Describe effects of bath or shower, i.e. stimulating, refreshing, relaxing, cleansing.
	Feel forehead and arms after running on playground. Describe how people react toward persons with unpleasant body odors.	
	Tell essentials to use when taking a bath or shower: wash cloth / soap / bath mat / bath towel / deodorant / powder or lotion (if desired)	

Child selects clothes that fit properly.	Bring an old misshapen pair of shoes to classroom. Discuss how uncomfortable feet would be wearing these shoes.
Tell how tight-fitting clothing feels when running, jumping, square-dancing, etc.	Stress importance of selecting clothing that is neither too big nor too small.
	Compliment students who come to school looking especially nice. Make certain each student receives a compliment on his clothing.
Child prepares for menstrual periods.	Have school nurse show film (M-225) to girls and mothers.
View film with mother.	Utilize (B-224, B-225).
	Relate menstrual process to other changes occuring in body, i.e. tenderness and enlargement of breasts, growth of hair under arms and in pubic area.
Use appropriate vocabulary when discussing menstruation, i.e. "perineum; "vagina," "uterus," "ovaries."	Provide small calendar for each girl. Encourage mother to assist child in keeping calendar.
Use calendar to keep track of anticipated beginning day of each period.	Utilize (Misc-228).
Identify and describe devices used for protection, how to wear, how to change and dispose of when soiled.	Describe the increased importance of cleanliness and use of deodorants during menstrual period. Explain the importance of sponging or bathing.
Be aware that menstruation is a personal matter and discuss only with parent, teacher, nurse, or doctor.	

Physical Hygiene

Behavioral Objectives	Learning Experience to Develop Behavior	Suggested Teacher Procedures to Develop Behavior
Child discusses the importance of visiting the doctor and dentist.	Share experience of visit to doctor and dentist with classmates.	Describe doctor and dentist as community helpers.
	Tell about examination, dental, check-up, shots, etc.	Emphasize visiting doctor and dentist regularly to maintain good health, i.e. check-ups, dental examination and cleaning, immunizations, etc.
		Show film (M-226) and filmstrip (FS-209).
		Arrange for class to visit a medical or dental clinic.
		See "Knows the doctor and the dentist" under "Personal Hygiene" in "Health," "Level II."
Child learns about vital organs: heart, lungs, etc.	Examine models of heart, eye and torso. Repeat name of parts.	Use Models (Misc-229, Misc-230, Misc-231). Display models and name main parts.
	Take deep breath of air and blow through tube, letting air from lungs displace water in jar.	Set up experiment to show function of lungs: Fill large jar with water. Turn upside down in pan or sink partially filled with water. Insert small tube into jar.
		Call attention to amount of air in lungs that displaced water.
	Feel pulse when sitting quietly. Run around playground and feel pulse again.	Explain briefly function of heart. Show students how to place fingers on pulse or use (Misc-232).
	Participate regularly in physical education activities.	Discuss necessity of exercise for developing strong bodies.

Food and Nutrition

Behavioral Objectives	Learning Experiences to Develop Behavior	Suggested Teacher Procedures to Develop Behavior
Child learns that proper nutrition is essential to good health.		See "Can recognize common foods . . ." under "Food and Nutrition" in "Health," "Level II."
	Name food and tell what group it represents.	Design bulletin board of foods containing samples from each of the four food groups.
		Discuss place of sweets, soft drinks, etc., in daily diet.
	Become familiar with wide variety of foods.	Encourage children to taste all food put on plate. Review "One-Bite Rule."
		Plan new and different foods to serve in classroom, i.e. broccoli, artichokes, asparagus. Serve in small portions, allow for second helpings. Provide variety by serving same foods preserved in different ways, i.e. frozen, canned, or cooked.
Child practices cleanliness in food preparation.	Talk about what farmers do to protect crops from destruction from insects.	Inform children of dangers of insecticides and need for properly cleaning fruits and vegetables before eating.
	Wash hands. Wash produce thoroughly, i.e. lettuce, tomatoes, cauliflower, apples, strawberries, etc.	Demonstrate method of washing and draining fruits and vegetables. Provide colander, paper towels, brush, etc.
		Inform children of dangers of handling foods when there are sores on hands.
	Make charts displaying utensils used to handle food in place of hands.	Furnish utensils and assist children with chart.

Behavioral Objectives	Learning Experiences to Develop Behavior	Suggested Teacher Procedures to Develop Behavior
Child practices cleanliness with utensils used when eating or cooking.	Tell about other insects that might get into food.	Discuss spread of disease by flies. Perform experiment: Put small piece of ground meat in open container in classroom. Keep moist and allow flies access to it. Call attention to what happens to meat.
	Wash and dry dishes in classroom after cooking activity.	Demonstrate proper techniques of washing dishes, stressing use of clean dishcloth or sponge, towel, etc.
	Observe how rinsing glasses with hot clean water helps to make them cleaner.	Wash glasses with soap and hot water, do not rinse. Point out film on glasses when dry. Wash another set of glasses and rinse. Compare.
	Wash greasy pot or pan in cold water without soap. Use soap and hot water. Note difference.	
	Check dishes and utensils to see if they are properly stored in classroom.	Discuss the necessity of storing dishes and cooking utensils away from dust and insects.
Child observes refrigeration practices for certain foods.	Observe difference in food after two days.	Provide carrots, lettuce, tomatoes, etc. to conduct experiment. Place one of each food in refrigerator and one of each in open container on windowsill.
	Put milk, eggs, butter, meat, etc., in refrigerator. Put TV dinners, frozen vegetables, juices, etc., in freezing compartment. Wash fruits and vegetables and place in refrigerator. Store canned goods on shelves.	Demonstrate proper handling and storage of dairy products. Emphasize need for immediate refrigeration to prevent souring or spoiling. After shopping trip place groceries on table and ask, "Where should you put each of these?"

Mental Hygiene

Behavioral Objectives	Learning Experiences to Develop Behavior	Suggested Teacher Procedures to Develop Behavior
Child seeks help when faced with a problem.		See "Controls emotions and personal feelings" under "Self-help Skills" in "Economic Usefulness," "Level III."

Role-play approaching teacher or parent with specific problems.

Encourage and participate in role-playing with children. Be a good listener at all times. Be available and willing to be a counselor. Have a sharing time that is not too restrictive.

Show films (M-227, M-228, M-229).

Child gets adequate rest.

Describe body processes that occur while sleeping, i.e. breathing, heartbeat slows, muscles relax, etc.

Tell about difference in how one feels in morning and at night.

Clear with parents before sending chart home.

Keep "Sleep Chart" for one week. Have parent enter number of hours of sleep each night. Return chart to school.

Impress children with need for adequate sleep to help bodies grow and develop properly.

Show film (M-230) and filmstrips (FS-210, FS-211).

MATERIALS AND AIDS

Level III

BOOKS (B)

201 Fun Time Window Garden
Cooke, Emogene
Children's Press, 1957

202 You Can
Pflug, Betsy
Van Nostrand Reinhold Co., 1969

203 Manners to Grow On
Lee, Tins
Doubleday, 1955

204 About Our Flag
Rees, Elinor
Melmont Publishers, Inc., 1963

205 A Book to Begin on Our Flag
Waller, Leslie
Holt, Rinehart and Winston, 1960

206 The Star Spangled Banner
D'Aulaire, Ingri and Edgar
Doubleday and Company, 1942

207 All Together
     Addis, Dorothy
     G. P. Putnam's Sons, 1952

208 Poems for Children
     Farjeion Eleanor
     J. B. Lippincott Co., 1958

209 Let's Enjoy Poetry (2 vol.)
     Hughes, Rosalind
     Houghton Mifflin Co., 1958

210 Singing on Our Way
     Pitts, Lilla, Maybelle Glenn, and Lorraine Walters
     Ginn and Company, 1949

211 I Want To Be a Policeman
     Greene, Carla
     Children's Press, 1964

212 My Book of Pets
     Capian, Lydia
     Ottenheimer Publishers, Inc., 1961

213 The True Book of Pets
     Podendorf, Illa
     Children's Press, 1954

214 Where the Wild Things Are
     Sendak, Maurice
     Harper and Row, 1965

215 May I Bring a Friend?
     De Regniers, Beatrice S.
     Atheneum, 1964

216 Once A Mouse
     Brown, Marcia Jean
     Charles Scribner's Sons, 1961

217 Creative Crafts
     Cresse, Else Bartlett
     F. A. Owen Publishing Company, 1963

218 Dance in Elementary Education
     Murray, R. L.
     Harper and Row, 1963

219 Games, Rhythms and Dances
     George Stanley Company, 1950

220 American Folk Songs for Children
     Seeger, Ruth
     Doubleday, 1948

221 Musical Activities for Retarded Children
     Ginglend, David R., and Winifred E. Stiles
     Abingdon Press, 1965

222 Realm of Measure
     Asimov, Isaac
     Houghton Mifflin, 1960

223 New Boys and Girls Cook Book
     Crocker, Betty
     Golden Press, 1965

224 How to Tell the Retarded Girl About Menstruation
     Jones, Marion, R. N.
     Kimberly-Clark Corporation, 1964

225 American Journal of Nursing
Pattullo, Ann W., and Kathryn E. Barnard
December, 1968

FILMS (M)

201 Courtesy for Beginners
202 The Golden Rule – Lesson for Beginners
203 Dress for Health
204 Fun on the Playground
205 American Flag
206 The Fireman (2nd Ed.)
207 The Policeman (2nd Ed.)
208 Measurement in the Food Store
209 Care of Hair and Nails
210 Measuring in Cooking
211 Safety Begins at Home
212 Safety in the Home
213 Litterbug
214 Let's Be Safe at Home
215 Fire Prevention – In the Home
216 Fire Safety is Your Problem
217 Electricity: How to Make a Circuit
218 Playground Safety
219 Safety on the Playground
220 Why Take Chances
221 Safe Living in Your Community
222 Be Your Own Traffic Policeman
223 School Bus and You
224 City Bus Driver
225 Story of Menstruation
226 The Magic Touch
227 Appreciating Our Parents
228 Beginning Responsibilities
Series of four films
229 Your Family
230 Sleep for Help

FILMSTRIPS (FS)

201 At Home
202 Visiting Friends
203 Let's Stand Tall
204 Straight and Tall
205 Safety at Christmas
206 Fire – Friend or Foe
207 Your Hair
208 Controlling Germs
209 We Have You Covered
210 Getting Ready for Bed
211 Rest and Sleep

MISCELLANEOUS (Misc)

201 Understanding Our Feelings
Twenty-eight 8 1/2" x 11" photgraphic reproductions of adults and children expressing wide range of emotions.
Lakeshore Curriculum Materials.

202 We Dress for the Weather
Fifty-eight felt pieces: boy and girl, clothing for all kinds of weather, thermometer, weather symbols, word cards for weather conditions, and days of the week.
Instructo

203 Postal Station
Red and blue city mailbox. Slots for blocks to fit through and bottom drawer.
Lakeshore Curriculum Materials.

204 Peabody Language Development Kit
Level I, Level II
American Guidance Service

205 Tele-Trainer
Telephone equipment for class use. Two telephones run by batteries, plus booklets to teach use, manners, etc.
American Telephone and Telegraph Company

206 Picture Sequence Cards
Cards are combined in groups of four depicting actions in sequence.
Milton Bradley

207 Sequence Charts
With manual
Ideal Reading Materials

208 Let's Learn Sequence
Illustrations of favorite stories nursery rhymes, everyday experiences. Children build stories placing either three or six pictures in sequence.
Instructo

209 See-Quees
Complete stories cut into separate episodes. Different levels of difficulty from four to eight years. 3" squares fit into heavy board inlay backgrounds.
Judy

210 Frances the Fourth Little Fox
The Three Bears
The Three Billy Goats Gruff
Language Arts for Beginners
Heath Kit, Heath and Company

211 Reedcraft
Wrought iron frames from weaving with reed. Kits consist of letter or napkin holder, pencil caddy, sleigh bowl.
S and S Arts and Crafts
Colchester, Connecticut

212 Visual Aids – Community Helpers, Family, Sports
Eureka Decorative Cutouts
Palfrey's Educational Aids

213 Timmy Time Clock
Thirteen pieces form face of clock. Can be assembled in only one way so child cannot make mistake. Movable hands.
Sifo

214 Peg Time Clock
Set includes thirty pegs in red, blue and green to mark minutes. Clock face is divided into quarter-hour periods by four colors.
Sifo

215 Schola Student's Clock
All metal with hand-operated sealed gears. Individual-sized so each student has own clock to manipulate.

216 Individual Clock Dials
Printed on heavy cardboard with metal hands and plastic stand. 5 3/8" in size.
Milton Bradley

217 Judy Mini-Clocks
Four-inch miniatures of large Judy clock with movable hands.
GW School Supply Specialist

218 Touch to Learn Clock
Face is printed with raised beaded surface. Metal hands. 13 3/4" square.
GW School Supply Specialist.

219 Calendar Chart
Ideal

220 Day by Day Calendar
Full color with changeable date cards. Picture cards for holidays,

special events, changes of seasons.
Milton Bradley

221 Calendar Board
Perpetual Calendar of steel with days of the week, days of the month and months.

222 Rock Polishing Kit
Double tumbler, starter set of one pound of agate and jasper, various grits.
F. A. O. Schwartz

223 Traffic Safety
Eleven full color prints of traffic signs, policeman, and safety slogans.
Dennison

224 Safety on Streets and Sidewalks
Flannel board aids for construction situations involving pedestrian safety. Four street corners, traffic light and signs, cars, policeman, crossing guards, children.
Instructo

225 Class Toothbrushing Record
Colorful chart to post in classroom to keep two week record of students' brushing habits.
Crest Professional Services Division

226 Dental Instruction Kit
Contains toothbrush, toothpaste, two checkup (disclosing) tablets to see if toothbrush techniques are effective.
Proctor and Gamble
Cincinnati, Ohio, 45202

227 Free Dental Health Education Materials
Posters, booklets, guides, filmstrip, parent folders, take-home letters geared to second and third grade level.
Professional Services Division

Proctor and Gamble
Cincinnati, Ohio, 45202

228 Kimberly-Clark Introductory Kit
Designed for mothers to help daughters. Priced at $2.00 each.
Kimberly-Clark Corporation
Box 551, Department MK-R
Neenah, Wisconsin 54956

229 Model of Torso

230 Model of Heart

231 Model of Eye

232 Stethoscope
Professional instrument to listen to heartbeats, pulse, internal sounds of mechanical devices.
Creative Playthings

RECORDS (R)

201 Folksongs of Many People
Bowmar Records

202 Folksongs of Canada
Bowmar Records

203 Folksongs of the U.S.A.
Bowmar Records

SOUND FILMSTRIPS (SFS)

201 Our Flag and Our Country

STUDY PRINTS (SP)

201 Fire Prevention

BIBLIOGRAPHY

1. A teacher's guide to classroom management. Nat Educ Ass J, October 1962.
2. Allen, R. J., and Gibson, R. M.: Phenylketonuria with normal intelligence, Amer J Dis Child, 102:115-123, 1961.
3. American Association for Health, Physical Education and Recreation: Recreation and Physical Activity For the Mentally Retarded. Washington, D. C., National Education Association, 1966.
4. Association for Supervision and Curriculum Development: Human Variability and Learning. Washington, D. C., National Education Association, 1961.
5. Association for Supervision and Curriculum Development: Learning More About Learning. Washington, D. C., National Education Association, 1959.
6. Ausubel, David P.: Theory and Problems of Child Development. New York, Grune and Stratton, 1958.
7. Axline, Virginia: Play Therapy. New York, Ballantine Books, 1969.
8. Barnett, C. D., and Cantor, G. N.: Discrimination set in defectives. Amer J Ment Defic, 62:334-337, 1957.
9. Baroff, G.: Current theories on the etiology of mongolism. Eugen Quart, 5:212-215, 1958.
10. Baumeister, I. A. (Ed.): Mental retardation. Selected Problems in Appraisal and Treatment. Chicago, Aldine, 1967.
11. Baumgartner, Bernice: Guiding the Retarded Child. New York, The John Day Co., 1965.
12. Baumgartner, Bernice: Helping the Trainable Mentally Retarded Child. New York, Bureau of Publications, Teachers College, Columbia University, 1960.
13. Benda, C. E.: The Child With Mongolism. New York, Grune and Stratton, 1960.
14. Benda, C. E.: Mongolism. In Carter, C. H.: Medical Aspects of Mental Retardation. Springfield, Charles C Thomas, 1965.
15. Bensberg, Gerard J.: Teaching the Mentally Retarded. Southern Regional Education Board, Atlanta, Georgia, 1965, p. 23.
16. Bensberg, G. J.: Teaching the profoundly retarded self-help activities by behavior shaping techniques. Amer J Ment Defic, LXIX:674-679, 1965.
17. Berkson, Gershon, and Baumeister, Alfred: Reaction time variability of mental defectives and normals. Amer J Ment Defic, 72(2):262-266, 1967.
18. Berman, P. F. et al: Psychologic and neurologic status of diet-treated phenylketonuric children and their siblings. J Pediat, 28:924-934, 1961.
19. Bernhardt, Karl S.: Discipline and Child Guidance. New York, McGraw-Hill, Inc., 1964.
20. Berry, Helen K. et al.: Treatment of phenylketnouria. Amer J Dis Child, 113:2-5, 1967.
21. Bigge, Morris L.: Learning Theories For Teachers, New York, Harper and Row, 1964.

22. Bjornson, J.: Behavior in phenylketonuria. Arch Gen Psychiat, 10:65-69, 1964.
23. Blackham, Garth J.: The Deviant Child in the Classroom. Belmont California, Wadsworth Publishing Co., Inc., 1967.
24. Blessing, Leo B.: But judge what is proper discipline? Reader's Digest, September, 1967.
25. Blodgett, H., and Warfield, G. J.: Understanding Mentally Retarded Children. New York, Appleton-Century-Crofts, 1959.
26. Bossone, Richard M.: What is discipline? Clearing House, December, 1964.
27. Brainard, Edward: Classroom control. Clearing House. May, 1964.
28. Brown, Edwin J., and Phelps, Arthur T.: Managing the Classroom. New York, The Roland Press, 1961.
29. Cain, L. F., and Levine, S.: A Study of the Effects of Community and Institutional School Classes for Trainable Retarded Children. United States Office of Education, Cooperative Research Branch, Contract 589; SAE 8257, Washington, D. C., Government Printing Office, 1961.
30. California State Department of Education: Programs for the Trainable Mentally Retarded. Sacramento, California, 1967.
31. Carlson, B. W., and Ginglend, D. R.: Play Activities for the Retarded Child. New York, Abingdon Press, 1961.
32. Carpenter, G. G. and *et al.,* Phenylalaninemia, Pediatric Clinics of North America, 15:313-323, 1968.
33. Carter, C. O. *et al..:* Chromosome translocation as a cause of familial mongolism. Lancet, II:678-680, 1960.
34. Carter, M. L.: Parents' attitudes and school discipline. Education, October, 1964.
35. Cassidy, J. M., and Stanton, J. E.: An Investigation of Factors Involved in the Educational Placement of Mentally' Retarded Children. Columbus, Ohio State University, 1959.
36. Chamberlin, L. J.: Discipline and the Public School. Education, January, 1967.
37. Chamberlin, L. J.: Group Behavior and Discipline. Clearing House, October, 1966.
38. Chess, Stella, and Thomas, Alexander: A Modern View of Discipline, Parents' Magazine, February, 1966.
39. Clarke, C. A.: Genetics for the Clinician. Oxford, Blackwell Scientific Publications, Ltd., 1962.
40. Coleman, James, C.: Abnormal Psychology and Modern Life, New York, Scott, Foresman and Co., 1964. pp. 523-535.
41. Conner, Francis P., and Talbot, Mabel E.: An Experimental Curriculum for Young Mentally Retarded Children. New York, Bureau of Publications, Teachers College, Columbia University, 1964.
42. Cowley, John F., and Chase, Donna V.: Productive thinking in retarded and non-retarded. Brit J Educ Psychol, 37(3):356-360, 1967.
43. Cox, James J.: Help your child to self-esteem. Today's Health, February, 1968.
44. Craig, Robert C.: The Psychology of Learning in the Classroom. New York, The Macmillan Co., 1966.
45. Cranefield, P.: Historical perspectives. In Philips, I. (Ed.): Prevention and Treatment of Mental Retardation. New York, Basic Books, 1966.
46. Crispin, David: Discipline behaviors of different teachers. Contemporary Education,

January, 1968.

47. Crossman, Russ: Humor in the Classroom. Clearing House, May, 1964.

48. Crothers, B., and Paine, R. S.: The Natural History of Cerebral Palsy. Cambridge, Massachusetts, Harvard University Press, 1959.

49. Cruickshank, William M., and Blake, K. A.: A Comparative Study of the Mentally Handicapped and Intellectually Normal Boys on Selected Tasks Including Learning and Transfer, Project No. 127. United States Office of Education, Cooperative Research Studies, Syracuse, New York, Syracuse University, 1957, p. 146.

50. Cruickshank, William, and Johnson, G. D.: Education of Exceptional Children and Youth, 2nd ed., Englewood Cliffs, New Jersey, Prentice-Hall, 1967, p. 196.

51. Dauer, Victor P.: Fitness For Elementary School Children. Minneapolis, Burgess Publishing Co., 1962.

52. Davenport, Frank T.: Discipline by Contract. The Science Teacher, January, 1965.

53. Dayan, M.: Toilet training children in a state residential institution. Mental Retardation, II:116-117, 1964.

54. Dollard, J., and Miller, N. E.: Personality and Psychotherapy. New York, McGraw-Hill, 1950.

55. Doris, J., and Solnit, A. J.: Treatment of Children With Brain Damage and Associated School Problems. J Child Psychiat, 2:618-635, 1963.

56. Dreikurs, Rudolph, and Soltz, Vickie: Your Child and Discipline. Nat Educ Ass J, January, 1965.

57. Driscoll, Gertrude P.: How to Study the Behavior of Children. New York, Bureau of Publications, Teachers College, Columbia University, 1941.

58. Dunn, L. C.: A Short History of Genetics. New York, McGraw-Hill, 1965.

59. Dunn, Lloyd M. (Ed.): Exceptional Children in the Schools. New York, Holt, Rinehart and Winston, Inc., 1963.

60. Edgren, H. D., and Gruber, J. J.: Teacher's Handbook of Indoor and Outdoor Games. Englewood Cliffs, New Jersey, Prentice-Hall, 1963.

61. Ellis, N. R.: Amount of reward and operant behavior in mental defectives. Amer J Ment Defic, LXVI:595-599, 1962.

62. Ellis, N. R.: Handbook of Mental Deficiency. New York, McGraw-Hill, 1963.

63. Ellis, N. R.(Ed.): International Review of Research in Mental Retardation. New York, Academic Press, 1966, vol. I-II.

64. Ellis, Norman R. *et al.:* Short-term memory in the retarded: Ability level and stimulus meaningfulness. Amer J Ment Defic, 75(1):72-80, 1970.

65. Ellis, N. R.: Toilet training the severely defective patient: An S-R reinforcement analysis. Amer J Ment Defic, LXVIII:98-103, 1963.

66. Erickson, Marion J.: The Mentally Retarded Child in the Classroom. New York, Macmillan Co., 1965.

67. Faber, Nancy: The Retarded Child. New York, Crown Publishers, Inc., 1968.

68. Fantani, Mario D.: Reward and punishment. Clearing-House, February, 1966.

69. Farber, B.: Effects of a severely mentally retarded child on family integration. Monogr the Soc Res Child Develop, XXIV:210, 1959.

70. Farber, B. S. and Ryckman, D. B.: Effects of severely mentally retarded children on family relationships. Mental Retardation Abstracts, 2:1-17, 1965.

71. Farina, A. M. *et al.:* Growth Through Play. Englewood Cliffs, New Jersey,

Prentice-Hall, 1960.

72. Fifteen County Project Curriculum Development Committee: Guides For Teaching Trainable Mentally Retarded Children. Sacramento, California, Sacramento County Office of Education, 1970.

73. Flavell: The Developmental Psychology of Jean Piaget. Princeton, New Jersey, D. Van Nostrand Co., Inc., 1963.

74. Fox, Edna J.: The diagnostic value of group test as determined by the quantative differences between normal and feeble-minded children. J Appl Psychol, 11:127-134, 1927.

75. Francis, Sister Marian: Discipline is _____. Nat Educ Ass J, September, 1965.

76. Francis, R. J., and Rarick, G. L.: Motor Characteristics of the Mentally Retarded. Cooperative Research Bulletin, No. I, USOE 35005, Washington, D. C., Government Printing Office, 1960.

77. Frankel, Max *et al.*: Functional Teaching of the Mentally Retarded, Springfield, Charles C Thomas, 1966.

78. Freeman, Frank N.: How Children Learn. Boston, Houghton Mifflin, 1917.

79. Frostig, Marianne, and Horn, David: Frostig Program for the Development of Visual Perception. Chicago, Follett Publishing Co., 1964.

80. Garcia, Joseph: Movement Exploration in "TMR" Curriculum. Sacramento, California, Grant Union High School District, 1969.

81. Gardner, John W.: Excellence. New York, Harper and Brothers, 1961, chapter IX.

82. Garfunkel, F.: Probabilities and possibilities for modifying behavior of mentally retarded children: Tactics for research. Boston University, Journal of Research, 64:907-915, 1960.

83. Gesell, Arnold, and Ilg., Frances: Infant and Child in the Culture of Today. New York, Harper Brothers, 1943, p. 224.

84. Gesell, Arnold, and Ilg, Frances: The Child From Five to Ten. New York, Harper Brothers, 1946.

85. Gladwin, T.: Poverty USA, New York, Little, Brown, 1967.

86. Gleitman, H.: Place learning. Sci Amer, 209(4):116-122, 1963.

87. Gnagey, William J.: Controlling Classroom Misbehavior. Department of Classroom Teachers, American Educational Research Association of the NEA, Washington, D.C., 1965.

88. Goldstein, Edward: Selective Audio-Visual Instruction For Mentally Retarded Pupils. Springfield, Charles C Thomas, 1964.

89. Goldstein, H.: Treatment of congenital acromicria syndrome in children, Archi Pedagogy, 73:153-167, 1956.

90. Gordon, S., O'Connor, N. and Tizard J.: Some effects of incentives on the performance of imbeciles on a repetitive task. Amer J Ment Defic, 63:236-240, 1955.

91. Gotkin, L. G.: A calendar curriculum for disadvantaged kindergarten children. Teachers College Record, 68:406-417, 1967.

92. Gottesman, I. I.: Genetic aspects of intelligent behavior. In Ellis, N. R. (Ed.): Handbook of Mental Deficiency. New York, McGraw-Hill Book Co., 1963.

93. Gross, Nancy E.: Living With Stress. New York, McGraw-Hill Book Co., 1958.

94. Guess, D.: The influence of visual and ambulation restrictions on stereotyped

behavior. Amer J Ment Defic, 70:542-547, 1966.

95. Guilford, J. P.: The structure of intellect. Psychol Bull, 53:267-293, 1956.
96. Hackett, L. C., and Jenson, R. G.: A Guide to Movement Exploration. Palo Alto, California, Peek Publications, 1967.
97. Hamilton, Lucy: Basic Lessons for Retarded Children. New York, John Day Co., 1965.
98. Hanson, F., Daly, F. and Campbell, L. W.: Programs for the Trainable Mentally Retarded in California Public Schools, Sacramento, California, California State Department of Education, 1966.
99. Havinghurst, Robert: Human Development and Education. New York, Longmans, Green and Co., Inc., 1953.
100. Hebb, D. O.: Intelligence, Brain Function and the Theory of Mind. Brain, 82:260-275, 1959.
101. Hebb, D. O.: The Organization of Behavior. New York, Wiley, 1949.
102. Herrick, Virgil E.: Perception of Symbols in Skill Learning by Mentally Retarded Children, Project No. 151. United States Office of Education Cooperative Research Studies, Madison, Wisconsin, University of Madison, 1957, p. 61.
103. Hickman, L. C.: Corporal punishment: Still used, Still needed. Nation's Schools, December, 1965.
104. Highet, Gilbert: The Art of Teaching. New York, Vintage Books, Inc., 1958, part 2, pp. 8-65.
105. Hilgard, E. R.: Theories of Learning. 2nd ed., New York, Appleton-Century-Crofts, Inc., 1956.
106. Himelstein, Philip: The use of behavior modification procedures in MR classes. The Journal For Special Educators of the Mentally Retarded, vol. VI. (no. I), 1969.
107. Hindman, D. A.: Handbook of Indoor Games and Stunts. Englewood Cliffs, New Jersey, Prentice-Hall, 1955.
108. Hodgson, F. M.: Special education: Facts and attitudes. Exceptional Children, XXX:196-201, 1964.
109. Hollingsworth, Leta: Psychology of Subnormal Children. New York, MacMillan Co., 1920. p. 285.
110. Hollis, J. H.: The effects of social and non-social stimuli on the behavior of profoundly retarded children, I and II. Amer J Ment Defic, 69:755-789, 1965.
111. Howard, Alvin W.: Discipline: Three F's for the Teacher. Clearing House, May 1965.
112. Howett, Lilhan C.: Creative Techniques for Teaching the Slow Learner. New York, Teachers Practical Press, Inc., 1964.
113. Hudson, Margaret: Procedures for Teaching Trainable Children. Washington D. C., Council for Exceptional Children, NEA Research Monographs, Series A, No. 2, 1960.
114. Hunt, J. McV.: Intelligence and Experience, Roland Press, 1961.
115. Hutt, M. L., and Gibby, R. G.: The Mentally Retarded Child, 2nd. ed. Boston, Allyn and Bacon, Inc., 1965.
116. Hymes, James L., Jr.: Behavior and Misbehavior. Englewood Cliffs, New Jersey, Prentice-Hall, Inc., 1957, pp. 3-4.
117. Hymes, James L., Jr.: Discipline. New York, Bureau of Publications, Teachers

College, Columbia University, 1962.

118. Hysia, D.: Phenylketonuria: A study of human biochemical genetics. Pediatrics. 38:173-184, 1966.

119. Ilg, Frances L., and Ames, Louise B.: Child Behavior. New York, Dell Publishing Co., 1964.

120. Inhelder, Bärbel: The Diagnosis of Reasoning in the Mentally Retarded. New York, John Day Co., 1968.

121. Ingraham, C. P.: Education of the Slow-Learning Child. New York, The Roland Press, 1953.

122. Jencks, Christopher: Is it all Dr. Spock's fault? New York Times Magazine, March 3, 1968.

123. Jensen, A. R.: Social class and verbal learning. In Dececco, J. P. (Ed.): The Psychology of Language, Thought, and Instruction. New York, Holt, Rhinehart and Winston, 1967.

124. Jersild, Arthur T.: When Teachers Face Themselves. Bureau of Publications, Teachers College, Columbia University, 1955.

125. Johnson, G. O., and Blake, K.: Learning Performance of Retarded and Normal Children. Syracuse, New York, Syracuse University Press, 1960.

126. Johnson, R. C., and Medinnus, G. R.: Child Psychology: Behavior and Development. New York, John Wiley and Sons, 1964.

127. Jones, David, and Benton, Arthur: Reaction time and mental age in normal and retarded children. Amer J Ment Defic 73(1):143-147, 1968.

128. Jubenville, C. P.: A state program of day-care centers for severely retarded. Amer J Ment Defic, vol. LXVI, 1962, 829-837.

129. Kaufman, M. E., and Levitt H.: A study of three stereotyped behaviors in institutionalized mental defectives. Amer J Ment Defic, 69:467-673, 1965.

130. Kennedy, J. L. et al.: The early treatment of phenylketonuria. Amer J Dis Child, 113:16-21, 1967.

131. Kephart, N. C.: The Slow Learner in the Classroom. Columbus, Ohio, Charles E. Merrill, 1960.

132. Kessler, J. W.: Learning disorders in school age children. In Psychopathology of Childhood. Englewood Cliffs, New Jersey, Prentice-Hall, 1966.

133. Kirk, Samuel A.: Educating Exceptional Children. Boston, Houghton Mifflin Co., 1962.

134. Kirman, B. H.: The patient with Down's syndrome in the community. Lancet, 2:705-714, 1964.

135. Klapper, Z. S., and Birch, H. G.: A fourteen-year follow-up study of cerebral palsy: Intellectual change and stability. Amer J Orthopsychiat, 37:540-547, 1967.

136. Knobloch, H., and Pasamanick, B.: Complications of pregnancy and mental deficiency. In Bowman, P. W., and Mautner, H. V. (Eds.): Mental Retardation. New York, Grune and Stratton, 1960, pp. 182-193.

137. Knobloch, H., and Pasamanick, B.: Environmental factors affecting human development, before and after birth. Pediatrics, 26:210-218, 1960.

138. Kolburne, L. L.: Effective Education for the Mentally Retarded. New York, Vantage Press, 1965.

139. Kugel, R. B. et al.: An analysis of reasons for institutionalizing children with

mongolism. J Pediat, 64:68-74, 1964.

140. Krug, Othilda, M. D.: A Guide to Better Discipline. Englewood Cliffs, New Jersey, Prentice-Hall, Inc., 1962.

141. La Grand, Louis E.: Discipline in the Secondary School. West Nyack, New York, Parker Publishing Co., 1969, pp. 4-5.

142. Larson, Knute, and Karpas, Melvin: Effective Secondary School Discipline. Englewood Cliffs, New Jersey, Prentice Hall, 1966.

143. Lejeune, J., and Turpin, R.: Chronomosomal aberrations in man. Amer J Hum Genet, XIII, 175-184, 1961.

144. Leland, H.: Some psychological characteristics of phenyleketonuria. Psychol Rep, 3:373-376, 1957.

145. Lesser, G. S. *et al.:* Mental abilities of children from different social-class and cultural groups. Monogr Soc Res Child Develop, 30:4 (Serial no. 102), 1965.

146. Levinson, Abraham: The Mentally Retarded Child, New York, John Day Co., 1965.

147. Lunzer, E. A., and Hulme, I.: Discrimination learning and discrimination learning sets in subnormal children. Brit J Educ Psychol, 37(2):75-187, 1967.

148. Mager, Robert: Preparing Instructional Objectives, Palo Alto, California, Fearon Publishers, Inc., 1962.

149. Maslow, Abraham H.: Motivation and Personality. New York, Harper and Row, Inc., 1954.

150. McPherson, Marian W.: Learning and mental deficiency. Amer J Ment Defic, 62:870-877, 1958.

151. Menolascino, F. J.: Psychiatric aspects of mongolism. Amer J Ment Defic, 69:653-660, 1965.

152. Michaels, R. H. and Mellin, G. W.: Prospective Experience With Maternal Rubella and Associated Congenital Malformations. Pediatrics, XXVI:200-209, l960.

153. Milgram, Norman A. and Furth, Hans G.: Factors Affecting Conceptual Control in Normal and Retarded Children, Child Development, 38(2):531-545, 1967.

154. Morrison, I. E. and Perry, I. F.: Kindergarten-Primary Education: Teaching Procedures, New York, The Roland Press, 1961.

155. Mullen F. A. and Itkin, W.: The value of special classes for the mentally handicapped. Chicago Sch J, May 1961, pp. 353-363.

156. Muster, Karl W.: These techniques work for me. Nat Educ Ass J, September 1967.

157. Neisser, Edith G.: The goals of discipline. Parents' Magazine, October, 1967.

158. Pascal, G. R. *et al.:* The delayed reaction in mental defectives. Amer J Ment Defic, 56:152-160, 1951.

159. Patterson, Gerald R., and Guillion, M. E.: Living With Children. Champaign, Illinois, Research Press, 1968.

160. Pavlov, I. P.: Conditioned Reflexes. New York, Oxford University Press, 1927 (Translated by G. Vanup).

161. Peale, Norman V.: Enthusiasm Makes the Difference. Englewood Cliffs, New Jersey, Prentice-Hall Inc., 1967.

162. Penrose, L. S.: The Biology of Mental Defect, 3rd ed. New York, Grune and Stratton, Inc., 1963.

163. Perry, N.: Teaching the Mentally Retarded Child. New York, Columbia University Press, 1960.

164. Phillips, E. Lakin *et al..:* Discipline, Achievement and Mental Health. Englewood Cliffs, New Jersey, Prentice-Hall, Inc., 1960.
165. Pollack, Jack H.: Five frequent mistakes of parents. Today's Health. May, 1968.
166. Poser, Charles M.: Mental Retardation: Diagnosis and Treatment. New York, Harper-Row, 1969.
167. Prescott, A. J.: Classroom control. Clearing House, January, 1964.
168. Pullen, M. V.: Classroom guidance: Human relations comes first. The Instructor, March, 1965.
169. Radler, D. H., and Kephart, N. C.: Success Through Play. New York, Harper and Row, 1960.
170. Reed, E. W., and Reed, S. C.: Mental Retardation: A Family Study. Philadelphia, Saunders, 1965.
171. Richard, Wayne C., and Rosenburg, Sheldon: Searching behavior in the retardate as a function of exposure time and matrix size. Amer J Ment Defic, 75(1):53-59, 1967.
172. Robinson, H. B., and Robinson, N. M.: The Mentally Retarded Child. New York, McGraw-Hill Book Co., 1965.
173. Roos, P.: Development of an intensive habit-training unit at Austin State School. Ment Retard, III:12-15, 1965.
174. Rosenberg, Shirley: Should teachers wield the rod. Parents' Magazine, February, 1964.
175. Rosenblith, Judy, and Allinsmith, W.: The Causes of Behavior, 2nd ed., Boston, Allyn and Bacon, 1968.
176. Rosenzweig, Louis E.: Understanding and Teaching the Dependent Retarded Child, Darien, Connecticut, The Educational Publishing Co., 1960.
177. Rundle, A. T.: Etiological factors in mental retardation: I. Biochemical, II. Endocrinological. Amer J Ment Defic, LXVII:61-78, 1962.
178. Russell, D.: Cue out discipline problems. The Instructor. June, 1965.
179. Schain, Robert L.: Discipline: How to Establish and Maintain It. Englewood Cliffs, New Jersey, Prentice-Hall, Inc., 1961 (Teachers Practical Press, Inc.).
180. Scheerer, M. E. *et al.:* A case of "idiot savant:" An experimental study of personality organization. Psycho Monogr, 58:4, 1945.
181. Schulz, Jeanette: Chromosome disorders in mental retardation. Pediat Clin N Amer, 15(4):871-883, 1968.
182. Sheviakov, George V., and Redl, Fritz: Discipline for Today's Children and Youth (rev. ed.). Department of Supervision and Curriculum, NEA, Washington D. C., 1961.
183. Simon, Henry: Preface to Teaching. New York, Oxford University Press. 1938, Chapter 3.
184. Skinner, B. F.: The Behavior of Organisms. New York, Appleton-Century-Crofts, 1938; and Mowrer, O. H.: On the dual nature of living — A re-interpretation of "conditioning" and "problem-solving." Harvard Educational Review, 17:120-148, 1947.
185. Smith, J. M., and Smith, Donald: Child Management. Ann Arbor, Michigan, Ann Arbor Publishers, 1969.
186. Smith, J. O.: Group language development for educable mental retardates.

Exceptional Child, 58:111-123, 1962.

187. Sparkes, R. S., Beutler, E., and Wright, S. W.: Galactosemia in a 24-year old man: Detection by enzyme studies: Amer J Ment Defic, 72(4):590-593, 1968.

188. Spradlin, J. E., and Girardeau, F. L.: The behavior of moderately and severely retarded persons. Ellis, N. R. (Ed.): International Review of Research in Mental Retardation. New York, Academic Press, 1966.

189. Stanburg, J. B.: The Metabolic Basis of Inherited Disease. New York, McGraw-Hill Book Co., 1960.

190. Stern, C.: Principles of Human Genetics, 2nd ed. San Francisco, California, Freeman, 1960.

191. Stevens, H. A., and Heber, R.: Mental Retardation: A Review of Research. Chicago, Illinois, The University of Chicago Press, 1964.

192. Stinnett, Ray D., and Prehm, Herbert J.: Retention in retarded and non-retarded children as a function of learning method. Amer J Ment Defic, 75(1):39-46, 1970.

193. Strang, Ruth: Child Study. New York, The Macmillan Co., 1959.

194. Strauss, A. A., and Kephart, N. C.: Psychopathology and Education of the Brain-Injured Child. New York, Grune and Stratton, 1955, vol. II.

195. Tartakow, I. J.: The teratogenicity of maternal rubella. J Pediat, 66:380-391, 1965.

196. Taylor, H., and Olsen, K.: Team teaching with trainable mentally retarded children. Exceptional Child, XXX:304-309, 1964.

197. Thomas, Rachel: A new approach to discipline. Parents' Magazine, May, 1967.

198. Thormahlen, P. W.: A study of on-the-ward training of trainable mentally retarded children in a state institution. Calif Ment Health Res Monogr, no. 4, 1965.

199. Thorne, Gareth D.: Understanding the Mentally Retarded. McGraw-Hill, 1965.

200. Tobias, J., and Gorelick, J.: Work characteristics of adults at trainable level. Ment Retard, I:338-344, 1963.

201. Tredgold, R. F., and Soddy, K.: Tredgold's Text-Book of Mental Deficiency. Baltimore, Wilkins and Wilkins, 1963.

202. Trow, William C.: Psychology in Teaching and Learning. Cambridge, Massachusetts, 1960.

203. Telford, C. W., and Sawrey, J. M.: The Exceptional Individual. Englewood Cliffs, New Jersey, Prentice-Hall, 1967.

204. Unknown: Heaven's Special Child.

205. Vannier, Maryhelen, and Foster, Mildred: Teaching Physical Education in Elementary Schools. Philadelphia, Pennsylvania, W. B. Saunders Co., 1963.

206. Vergason, Glenn A.: Facilitation of memory in the retardate. Exceptional Child, 34(8):589-594.

207. Vroom, V. H.: Work and Motivation. New York, Wiley, 1964.

208. Waldrip, Donald R.: Get tough in the beginning and then relax-nonsense! Phi Delta Kappan, February, 1966.

209. Weatherwax, J., and Benoit, E. P.: Concrete and abstract thinking in organic and non-organic mentally retarded children. Amer J Ment Defic, 62:548-553, 1957.

210. Weber, Elmer W.: Educable and Trainable Mentally Retarded Children. Springfield, Illinois, Charles C Thomas Publishers, 1962.

211. Wilhelms, Fred T.: Discipline in a quicksand world. The Education Digest. Vol. XXXIII, April 1968.

212. Willey, R. D., and Waite, K. B.: The Mentally Retarded Child, Springfield, Illinois, Charles C Thomas Publishers, 1964, p. 150.

213. Williams, Harold M.: Education of the Severely Retarded Child. Bulletin No. 20., Washington D. C., United States Printing Office, 1961.

214. Wilson, John A. R., and Spinning, James M.: Corporal punishment. Nat Educ Ass J, September 1963.

215. Winkler, James E.: Reflections on Discipline. Clearing House, October, 1963.

216. Woodrow, Herbert: Practice and transference in normal and feeble minded children. J Educ Psychol, 8:85-96, 151-165, March 1917.

217. Wright, John C.: Those who can't teach, shouldn't. Clearing House, October, 1963.

218. Wright, S. W. *et al.:* The frequency of trisomy and translocation in Down's Syndrome. Pediatrics, 70:420-424, 1967.

219. Wunch, W. L.: Some characteristics of mongoloids evaluated at a clinic for children with retarded mental developement. Amer J Ment Defic, 62:122-130, 1957.

220. Yarrow, L. J.: Maternal deprivation: Toward an empirical and conceptual reevaluation. Psychol Bull, 58:459-490, 1961.

221. Young, Milton: Teaching Children With Special Learning Needs: A Problem Solving Approach. New York, John Day Co., 1967.

222. Zeaman, D., and House, B. J.: An attention theory of retardate discrimination learning. In Ellis, N. R. (Ed.): Handbook of Mental Deficiency, 1963.

223. Zeaman, D., and House B. J.: The relation of I. Q. and learning. In Gagne, R. M. (Ed.): Learning and Individual Differences. Columbis, Ohio, Merrill Books, 1966.

224. Zigler, E.: Research in personality structure in the retardate. In Ellis, N. R. (Ed.): International Review of Research in Mental Retardation, New York, Academic Press, 1966.

225. Zigler, E.: Social deprivation and rigidity in the performance of feebleminded children. J Abnorm Soc Psychol, 62:413-421, 1961.

226. Zigler, E.: Social reinforcement, environment and the child. Amer J Orthopsychiat, 33:614-623, 1963.

227. Zigler, E.: The effect of social reinforcement on normal and socially deprived children. J Genet Psychol, vol. 104, 235-242, 1964.

228. Zueler, W. W.: Mental retardation and neonatal jaundice. In Bowman, P. W., and Mautner, H. V. (Eds.): Mental Retardation. New York, Grune and Stratton, 1960, pp. 375-384.

NAME INDEX

SUBJECT INDEX

T

Thinking disorders, 12
Trainable, 6
  child, 73
  retardate, 6

W

Withdrawal, 63
Woodwork, 107